Essential Monastic Wisdom

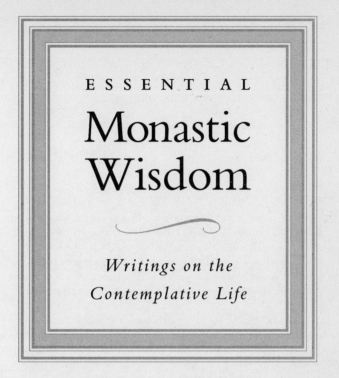

ESSENTIAL

Monastic Wisdom

Writings on the
Contemplative Life

Edited, Translated, and Introduced by

Hugh Feiss, O.S.B.

FOREWORD BY

Kathleen Norris

HarperSanFrancisco
A Division of HarperCollinsPublishers

ESSENTIAL MONASTIC WISDOM: *Writings on the Contemplative Life.*
Copyright © 1999 by Hugh Feiss, O.S.B. All rights reserved. Printed in the
United States of America. No part of this book may be used or reproduced in
any manner whatsoever without written permission except in the case of brief
quotations embodied in critical articles and reviews. For information address
HarperCollins Publishers, 10 East 53rd Street, New York, NY 10022.

HarperCollins books may be purchased for educational, business,
or sales promotional use. For information please write: Special Markets Department,
HarperCollins Publishers, 10 East 53rd Street, New York, NY 10022.

HarperCollins Web Site: http://www.harpercollins.com
HarperCollins®, ▇®, and HarperSanFrancisco™
are trademarks of HarperCollins Publishers Inc.

FIRST EDITION

Library of Congress Cataloging-in-Publication Data
Essential monastic wisdom : writings on the contemplative life / edited,
translated, and introduced by Hugh Feiss. —1st ed.
p.   cm.
Includes bibliographical references.
ISBN 0–06–062483–3 (cloth)
ISBN 0–06–062482–5 (pbk.)
1. Benedictines—Spiritual life. 2. Monastic and religious life.
3. Christian life-Catholic authors. I. Feiss, Hugh.
BX3003.E88 1999
255'.01—dc21   98–49369

99 00 01 02 03 ❖RRD(H) 10 9 8 7 6 5 4 3 2 1

Contents

Acknowledgments

Some of the key ideas in this book originated in a conversation with Abbot Celestine Cullen, O.S.B., president of the Annunciation Congregation of Benedictines. He probably doesn't remember the conversation, but talking to him helped me sort out my ideas. I have Kathleen Norris to thank for suggesting that I might be the one to write a book such as this. Kathleen and I first met when we both went to the wrong place for a concert. She has been doing kindnesses to me ever since, not the least of which is her foreword to this book. I owe thanks also to the late Ambrose Zenner for material I used from his dissertation on Benedictine peace. Tom Grady kindly acted as my agent and guide in the unfamiliar world of publishing. Marilyn Hall was theological consultant, friend, and proofreader; I needed all three. I am grateful to my editors, John Loudon, Karen Levine, Terri Leonard, and Carl Walesa, at Harper San Francisco for their patience with an aging novice. The book is dedicated in gratitude to my parents and to Father Bernard Sander, O.S.B., all of whom have by my calculations spent collectively 165 years teaching me by word and example. In particular, I owe to Fr. Bernard my strong conviction that the cloister of the monastery is not primarily a barrier but a meeting place where monks and others can encourage one another on the journey to God and to human wholeness.

Foreword

by Kathleen Norris

This book constitutes an excellent guidebook to the literature of monasticism, a guide I searched for in vain when I first encountered the Benedictines some fifteen years ago. Now the general reader, as well as the one who is seeking to enrich an understanding of monasticism, can benefit from Fr. Hugh Feiss's prodigious reading in the monastic tradition, as well as his many years of experience as a Benedictine monk. Fr. Hugh is one of those rare scholars who have a gift for assimilating obscure material in such a way as to make it accessible and relevant to the contemporary reader. In this book he has more than fulfilled his desire to spark "a conversation between some interesting monastic authors and contemporary people who might like to meet them."

Among the lively characters whose words enliven this book are Amma Syncletica, a wise and fierce fifth-century nun, who sounds quite up-to-date when she observes that "towards women generally there is great hostility in the world." Writing with great poignancy about the suffering of women in childbirth—it was a major cause of death for women in the ancient world—she reminds monastics not to become puffed up with piety, nor to look down on people outside the monastery walls. We meet Benedict, author of the monastic rule that has served Benedictines well for over fifteen hundred years, and find him bested by his sister in an argument. We encounter the twelfth-century monk and biblical commentator Peter of Celle stating that a room without reading is "a hell without consolation . . . a tomb without ventilation." The wisdom of Hildegard of Bingen rings through these pages along with that of the thirteenth-century nun Gertrude the Great, who was but one of the remarkable nuns of the monastery of Helfta. Among the twentieth-century writers we find not only the well-known American monk Thomas Merton but Esther de Waal, a British Anglican who has generated an interest in monastic spirituality and practice among many Protestants.

Spirituality is a well-known buzzword, but I think it is safe to say that this book will help people to understand better the seventeen-hundred-year-old branch of Christian spirituality known as monasticism. Originally a lay movement, it has flowed through those many centuries as an underground stream, at times running counter to the fancy trappings of Christendom, at times corrupted by them, at times surfacing like a pure, cold drink to refresh the faith of ordinary Christians. It has always allowed for contradiction, leaving plenty of room for the imaginative and the mystical, even as it remains solidly grounded in orthodox theology and a disciplined way of life.

One of the intriguing things about this book is that Fr. Hugh does not offer a dry chronology, but has organized his citations around the nonnegotiables of Benedictine life, such as prayer, work, and hospitality. He also examines lesser-known practices and values, including reading, communication, mutual support, and leadership, peppering his commentary with asides that reveal a great deal about contemporary monastic life. Monasteries are not immune to the ills of society, and Feiss comments that for today's American Benedictines, work and workaholism are threatening the traditional balance of monastic life. It is a spiritual issue, he insists, a matter of character, as "in the end we are judged by who we have become, rather than what we have accomplished."

The trust that is essential for human life has taken a beating in our time, and Fr. Hugh returns us to a basic understanding that "we are life and death for each other." The mutual support that a monastery (or a family, for that matter) requires is a rare commodity, but as Feiss reminds us, it is an essential part of Christian faith. "If a person is not properly related to one's neighbors," he writes, "that person is not properly related to Christ." Over the centuries, the trials of community life have inspired Benedictines to much impassioned commentary, and some marvelously sound advice. When another person angers you, writes the sixteenth-century monk Louis de Blois, "regret that your heart is bitter and ask for God's help."

The stereotypical monk is given to silence, but Fr. Hugh makes it clear that in a monastery, even silence is made to serve the value of peaceable interpersonal relations. In one of the most striking passages in the book, he sums up the monastic life as "a training in the art of listening, which begins in silence, develops in attentiveness, and is perfected in communication." People who visit monasteries often comment on how well they are listened to. That stands out, because for most of us the art of careful listening is drowned out by the sheer noisiness of our everyday lives: television, faxes, Muzak, busy freeways, and airwaves. But with characteristic Benedictine insight and humility, Feiss remarks that "the principal enemy of interior and exterior silence for most of us is our own tongue."

Fr. Hugh and the writers he has cited in this book make it clear that monastic spirituality is not a romantic venture, but a demanding, daily practice, and that its wisdom is based on a practical and humane understanding of human beings. The monastic men and women quoted here can offer anyone, no matter what his or her religious beliefs—or lack thereof—sensible, useful, and sometimes even beautiful insights into what it means to live and love more deeply, striving for peace with oneself and one's neighbor. The twentieth-century Benedictine Joan Chittister, writing on the subject of humility, really sums up one of the central goals of monastic life, and a goal accessible to anyone, when she speaks of the importance of retaining "a proper sense of self in a universe of wonders."

Introduction

This book aims to tap into the practical wisdom of the seventeen-century-old monastic tradition. A selection of short texts from Christian monastic authors arranged by topic and prefaced by introductory essays invites readers to ponder what the men and women of this tradition have learned about how to be integral human beings who live peacefully and reverently in their place and time with their comrades and their God. The book is written primarily for those who are not monks, but in the hope that even monks might learn something from the texts and ideas presented here.

The reader will find these pages divided into three parts: ordering time and place; character; and the good desired and possessed. The first section studies how Benedict arranged the day, dividing it into three regularly scheduled activities—work, prayer, and reading—but making provision for interruptions arising from the needs of colleagues or guests. In the second part of the book, the longest, the chapters present eleven character traits that the Benedictine monastery tries to inculcate in its members. The third section looks beyond order and character to two passions that give them life and purpose: longing and love.

Although this book is not addressed specifically to Catholics or Christians, no effort has been made to hide the Christian matrix of Benedictine monasticism. My conviction is that a rich and reasonable human life will have certain characteristics, whatever the religious convictions of the reader. This book queries an ancient tradition for guidance about how to live sanely. For this reason, one should look here not for a complete picture of Benedictine life, but for an exposition of those features of Benedictinism that seem likely to be of interest and inspiration to people living in the world of today. Hence, the reader will look in vain for a discussion of topics peculiar to monks or Catholicism—for example, the Eucharist or celibacy.

Christian monasticism emerged in the third century in various parts of the Mediterranean world. Although monks of later centuries would look to Antony (ca. A.D. 251–356) and Pachomius (ca. A.D. 292–346) as founders, they were not the first monks. The deeds and sayings of many desert fathers *(abbas)* and mothers *(ammas)* were gathered in oral and written collections. The rules and traditions governing many Christians experimenting with a solitary life (hermits or anchorites) and celibate community (cenobites) were also handed on. Most of these early monks were not members of the clergy, and, then as now, most of the clergy (deacons, priests, and bishops) were not monks.

In the sixth century, the *Rule of Benedict* synthesized the teachings of these pioneer traditions. It drew particularly on the writings of Cassian and a strange document called the *Rule of the Master.* The *Rule of Benedict* gradually became the dominant monastic rule in the West. It enjoyed something close to a monopoly from the time of Charlemagne until the twelfth century.

In 909–910 the monastery of Cluny was founded in Burgundy. Subject only to the papal authority and free to elect their own abbot, the monks of Cluny developed customs that were adopted by many others monasteries. Cluny stressed private and liturgical prayer. Under Hugh, who served as abbot from 1049 to 1109, the influence of Cluny was at its zenith; hundreds of monasteries emulated its way of life. Some of those monasteries were subject to the abbot of Cluny, while others retained their own abbots. Monks of Cluny were mainstays in the renewal efforts that swept the church in the latter half of the eleventh century; some of them were elected pope. There were also other monastic reform centers, such as Hirsau and Gorze, and only a minority of Benedictine monasteries ever affiliated with Cluny.

In the twelfth century there were many new experiments in eremitical and cenobitic Christianity. Some of the resulting innovative orders, such as the Cistercians, followed the *Rule of Benedict.* Spreading out from the abbey of Cîteaux, founded in 1098 near

Dijon, the Cistercians had by the end of the century founded hundreds of monasteries. As an instrument of uniform observance and mutual assistance, the Cistercian founders produced the Charter of Charity. Their monasteries were connected to each other by filiation, so that the abbot had the right and duty to visit those monasteries founded by his monastery to make sure that observance in the daughter houses was up to standard. Moreover, the abbots of all the houses were supposed to meet annually in general chapter at Cîteaux. The statutes of the general chapters became the law of the order. Thus there emerged the first full-blown religious order in the church, even though the abbots of individual houses retained some autonomy and monks joined individual houses and not the order as a whole. The Cistercian Order had an immense flourishing in the twelfth century, as did the traditional Benedictines and the new canons regular, who followed the *Rule of Saint Augustine* but for the most part adapted the customs of Cluny or Cîteaux.

Throughout the monastic age, from Charlemagne until the end of the twelfth century, there were monasteries of women also. Sometimes these shared a superior with a house of men; sometimes they were established near a house of men or incorporated into an association of monasteries (like the Cistercians or Cluniacs) that included men's and women's houses; sometimes the women's communities were independent of juridical bonds with men's houses. In that case, an abbess might arrange to have a chaplain sent from a men's community or might hire the services of a priest or small community of priests. However, it was more difficult for women's communities to support themselves, so they were not as numerous as men's communities.

Tentatively in the twelfth century and explosively in the thirteenth, Christians went beyond the *Rule of Benedict* and the practices spelled out in the monastic customaries (detailed guides to observance) to explore new forms of religious life. Orders emerged that abandoned the Benedictine emphasis on the local community. Instead of joining a single monastery, a candidate joined a province, within which he could be moved about at will by his superiors. The provinces of these religious orders had several layers of government and connected the individual communities to the entire order and its superior general. Of these new orders, two of the most numerous and durable are the Dominicans and Franciscans. The Franciscans emphasized voluntary poverty; the Dominicans were especially dedicated to preaching. The male members of both orders are called *mendicants* or *friars;* there were also Augustinian, Carmelite, and Servite friars. For several centuries the female members of these orders lived much like the Benedictine nuns of earlier ages; in fact, enclosure was gradually made stricter during the later Middle Ages. Women who did not want to be enclosed nuns or were unable to find a place in a monastery developed the alternative of becoming Beguines, less strictly organized semireligious women who lived in towns, supported themselves by working, and lived and prayed together.

Meanwhile, during the thirteenth and fourteenth centuries the older monastic tradition represented by the Benedictines foundered. At the urging of the papacy, Benedictine monasteries were organized into congregations, which provided for mutual visitation and support. However, in most cases monks continued to join a single monastery, and the general chapters and visitors had only limited powers to interfere in the life of individual monasteries. There were various efforts at renewal within the Benedictine and Cistercian families, some of which were quite successful. Ludovico Barbo (1381–1443), John Trithemius (1462–1516), and Louis de Blois (1506–1566) were among the leaders of those reform movements.

About half the monasteries in Europe were closed at the time of the Reformation. Meanwhile, many new orders arose in the church, many of them dedicated to particular apostolic tasks, such as the education of the poor, the care of the sick, and missionary outreach. Their members usually did not live in large communities, but rather in small groups who worked together at a particular apostolic endeavor. Many did not say the traditional liturgy of the hours, which was a primary concern of the *Rule of Benedict*. The most important of these new orders was the Society of Jesus. Some women tried to develop similarly mobile and ministry-directed orders, but met with resistance from churchmen who insisted on enclosure for women's communities.

In seventeenth-century France, Benedictine life revived in the Congregations of Saint-Vanne and Saint-Maur. The Maurist Congregation had a superior general who resided in Paris. The priors of the individual houses were appointed to one-year terms. The houses were divided into six provinces, each of which had its own visitator and council, its own novitiate and house of studies, but members could be moved anywhere in the congregation. New members benefited from a solid seven-year program of studies. The scholars of the congregation published editions of the writers of the early church, monastic authors, and a literary history of France. The Maurists were a very diverse group, which varied from monastery to monastery and province to province. They produced many forceful personalities, of whom Jean Mabillon (1632–1707) was perhaps the greatest. Their theological outlook was nourished by Cartesian currents as well as by Thomism, but its main inspiration was the early Christian writers.

Armand-Jean le Bouthillier de Rancé (1626–1700), who became an adversary of Mabillon, a Benedictine, over the question of which studies were suitable for monks, initiated a reform movement among the Cistercians. By the time he was ten years old, de Rancé held several religious houses *in commendam,* including the Cistercian Abbey of La Trappe. From these houses he was entitled to a certain income. Theoretically, in return he was to be their protector. de Rancé went on to become a distinguished classical scholar, a graduate of the Sorbonne, and a priest. He led a worldly life, but the death of an older woman whom he had known since childhood led to his conversion. He gave away all his ecclesiastical holdings except La Trappe. He invited the Strict Observance of the Cistercian Order to take over the abbey in 1662. He made a year's novitiate at another abbey and then was appointed abbot of La Trappe in 1664. There he enforced a very strict discipline. Almost miraculously, the community of La Trappe survived the French Revolution under the leadership of Abbot Augustin de Lestrange (elected abbot in 1794). In 1893 the Trappists were recognized as a new, separate order called the Cistercians of the Strict Observance, or Reformed Cistercians. The order inherited a strongly penitential bent from de Rancé and Lestrange, as well as an emphasis on uniform observance.

Most of the Benedictine and Cistercian monasteries that survived the Reformation were closed during the French Revolution and its aftermath. By 1840 or so, there were very few monasteries, and in many areas of Europe all religious orders were outlawed. The revival of religious life after 1840 was almost miraculous. Many new orders were founded, especially for women, and for the next 150 years members of these women's orders, some of which adopted the *Rule of Benedict,* rendered enormous service to the church as teachers, nurses, intercessors, and models of dedication to God. Monastic communities following the *Rule of Benedict* flourished as well, and by 1990 there were more than thirty thousand Benedictine and Cistercian monks and nuns. However, their number had been falling since around 1965. The reasons for the decline are many, and may have more to do with the plan of God than human choice.

As the number of men and women in monasteries declines, the number of people interested in the monastic tradition seems to be increasing rapidly. As a result, the family of most monasteries consists of a core of vowed men and women inside the cloister and a larger number of associates who live outside the cloister but look to the Benedictine tradition for guidance in leading their Christian lives in the secular world. They find that this ancient and resilient tradition has something to teach men and women of all walks of life about how to live wisely and joyfully, how to budget time, how to get along together, how to walk gently on the earth. This book presents to a wider audience some of the values these associates (some of who are formally connected to a monastery as lay oblates) find in the Benedictine tradition.

The writings chosen to represent the Benedictine monastic tradition are eclectic. The quotations in each chapter are arranged in chronological order. Four pre-Benedictine sources are cited: Antony and Pachomius, the titular founders of anchoritic and cenobitic monasticism; the desert fathers and mothers; and Syncletica, a woman monastic who lived around A.D. 400. Next, the *Rule of Benedict* is cited extensively; I have also included several selections from Gregory the Great's account of Benedict's life. The first representative of the tradition after Benedict is Bede, a renowned Anglo-Saxon monk and scholar, whose sermons are quoted a number of times. He is followed by Wulfstan of Worcester, a monk and bishop from eleventh-century England; again, it his from his life that I quote. The great monastic movement led by Cluny is represented by Abbot Hugh, a French contemporary of Wulfstan.

The twelfth century was probably the golden age of Christian monasticism. It is represented here by Anselm of Canterbury, Bernard of Clairvaux, Peter of Celle, and Hildegard of Bingen. From the late thirteenth century comes Gertrude the Great, a nun who is claimed by both Benedictines and Cistercians. The next three centuries are represented by didactic and legislative works by three Benedictine abbots: Ludovico Barbo, John Trithemius, and Louis de Blois (Blosius), each of whom was touched by the reform impulses that enlivened Christendom in the period 1350–1600. From the seventeenth century, I have quoted from Jean Mabillon, a great Benedictine scholar.

The twentieth century is represented by the Trappist Thomas Merton and by two women each of whom has cast fresh light on the *Rule of Benedict* both for Benedictines and for men and women who are not monks but who are interested in monastic spirituality. Esther de Waal and Sr. Joan Chittister have both written commentaries on the *Rule of Benedict,* and it is from those that I quote; de Waal, a married woman and member of the Church of England, speaks for all those in married life and in other Christian traditions who have discovered Benedictine spirituality.

Those who would like to know more about the writers whose works are drawn from here should consult the biographical sketches at the back of the book. Also included there is a short bibliographical essay detailing the sources I have used and indicating some related reading.

There are certain subjects I have deliberately avoided. Celibacy is one. I am writing primarily for people who have no intention of being lifelong celibates, and monastic writers have not been very much interested in the theology of marriage. In fact, the authors I have studied do not seem to have been particularly preoccupied with celibacy either. There are also aspects of the Benedictine rule and tradition that seem outdated or of little relevance to non-monastics: the arrangement of the office, the penalties inflicted for coming late to services, and so forth. I have tried to select themes that are both prominent in the tradition and meaningful to me, in the hopes that these same topics will be helpful to others today as well.

I have never been an abbot or any other kind of monastic official in or out of my monastery. Moreover, by measures of the *Rule of Benedict,* I am a beginner. I have no desire and no right to tell people how to live. In fact, I have a deep suspicion of people who are confident that they know what is good for other individuals, because so often they seem to cross the line between telling and controlling. All I wish to do is facilitate a conversation between some interesting monastic authors and contemporary people who might like to meet them. My qualifications are a broad and long and occasionally deep acquaintance with the writings of the monastic tradition; forty years of struggling to live in that tradition; familiarity with many different monasteries, male and female; and a sympathy for my fellow inhabitants of late twentieth-century America.

I have tried to use inclusive language, both in my translations and in my own writing. Occasionally, it seemed best to alternate between masculine and feminine pronouns.

In writing this book, I was primarily concerned with the goals of monastic practices, what sort of persons Benedict wanted the people in his monastery to become. It is very difficult to properly evaluate practices, customs, and observances. Looking at them, as this book does, from the three angles I described earlier—the primary uses of time, the construction of character, and desire and love for the good—might help monastics appreciate the meaning and purpose of some of the things they customarily do. It might also suggest that the same purposes could be better achieved by doing things differently than in the past. As the book says, discernment is hard-won, and only after trial and error.

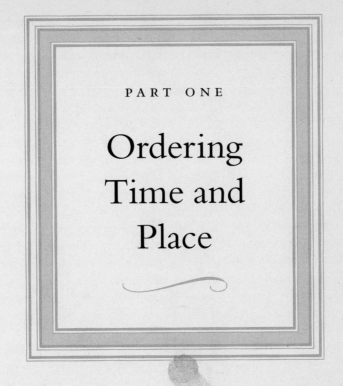

PART ONE

Ordering Time and Place

VISITORS ARE ALMOST ALWAYS impressed by the order that characterizes monastic life. The monks and nuns walk quietly through the cloister precincts. They walk two by two to solemn liturgies. Each member of the community has an assigned place and assigned duties. It all seems to run like clockwork.

Some of this order appears to be a fairly modern invention as far as Christian monastic history goes. Benedict said nothing about marching two by two into church, though he certainly did value decorum. One can theorize—justifiably, I think—that orderly communities tend to attract personalities for whom order is a high priority, so that order almost becomes a religious norm, if not a religion, to which freer spirits are forced to conform. This irritated Thomas Merton. There is, he commented in *Contemplation in a World of Action,*

> a fatal tendency to dramatize the monastic life. A special costume and decor. A unique behavior, . . . a ritual solemnity and obsequiousness. In the end this amounts to attachment to feudal anachronism, and the monk who pretends to justify himself by these masks is only convincing people that he is an object for the museum.

Nevertheless, some kind of order is clearly necessary and important. Community life requires ordering. It is important to know who is doing the cooking today, what time we say morning prayer, who will get the mail, and so on. It is even important that we observe certain standards of polite behavior, just to avoid irritating those closest to us.

Even in one's individual life there needs to be order. It may not be necessary that I make my meditation every day at the same time or that I read Scripture a half hour a day instead of three and a half hours a week, but it is necessary that there be some sort of plan whereby I set aside time to do the activities to which I am committed. Left to chance, some of those activities will not get done.

How structured life should be depends in part on personality and circumstance, but structured it must be.

Benedict was legislating for a community of people who evidently were ethnically and educationally diverse. There were children and old men, monks who had transferred from elsewhere, priests and laymen. He needed to integrate this diverse cross section of humanity into a kindly, well-organized community so that everything would be done at the proper time. He achieved this integration through several mechanisms, the most important of which were seniority and the daily order, or horarium. Seniority meant that each member of the community was assigned a place that depended on the time of his or her arrival. All the members of the community had a place of their own. They knew where they belonged. Some tasks were assigned in rotation on the basis of seniority; others were assigned according to talent and skill.

More important for us was the horarium. Benedict divided the day into three principal activities: work, prayer, and reading. The details varied according to the season of the year, but the division left four to five hours for work, about three hours for prayer, and slightly less than three hours for private reading (there was also public reading in the dining room during meals and elsewhere in the interval between supper and compline). Benedict specified when the members of the community should be occupied with these activities. He also made provision for two other activities: hospitality toward guests and mutual help and support. These two activities could be required at any time and were unpredictable. In order to be hospitable and helpful to each other, the monks had to have some flexibility in their schedules. If their schedules were completely full and unalterable, and thus no time was available to be hospitable and helpful, those schedules needed to be changed.

Saint Benedict did not like idleness, but he does not seem to have assigned any of these activities simply as a remedy for idleness. Work, prayer, and reading were activities to which his monks were obligated by their calling, talents, and humanity, and if they devoted themselves to those activities zealously, they would not be idle. But the value of work, prayer, and reading far exceeded their contribution to keeping the monks from idleness.

In fact, in the prologue and elsewhere, the *Rule of Benedict* conveys a sense of urgency: one must hasten and run toward the goal of everlasting life. The goal is precious; there is no time to waste getting there.

Each of these five activities of the horarium will be discussed later. What is important here is the fact that there had to be time for hospitality and for mutual help and support. Saint Benedict teaches a very important truth here, a truth most of us know but often neglect to act upon: after God, other persons are the most important realities in our lives. If we are too busy to make time for people who need us, whether they are strangers or neighbors, there is something wrong with our priorities. Worse yet, we may be using our obligations to work and prayer (and perhaps reading) as an excuse to try to evade our obligation to be helpful and hospitable.

These five activities not only divided up the hours of the monks' day; they also correlate to the defined space of the monastery. Prayer was done in church, reading in the cloister (and later in the library or the cell), work in the workshops; hospitality was provided in the guest house; and mutual support was given wherever it was needed.

Beyond these five activities, other, basic human needs—for sleep, food, personal hygiene, and so forth—had to be accommodated. For sleeping there was a dormitory (and later private rooms); for eating, the dining room or refectory with a lectern for the reader; for hygiene, toilets and a place to wash; for the sick, an infirmary; for beginners or novice monks not yet fully integrated into the community, a novitiate. As time went on, monasteries added other rooms not specified in the *Rule,* but needed for conversing (parlor), for meeting (chapter room), and, once monasticism moved to northern Europe, for warming people (calefactory).

Thus time and space were divided and ordered, so that members of the community could live together in harmony, welcome guests, meet unexpected needs within the community, and individually fulfill those daily activities that were the basis of the monks' life, a life whose goal was to lead each member of the community to life everlasting.

The schedules for days and weeks varied somewhat with the seasons and the availability of sunlight. For monastics the most important temporal cycle was the annual liturgical cycle centered on Easter. This cycle fitted the story of Christ to the annual cycle of the seasons. It put the stamp of the mystery of birth and death, the paschal mystery, on the praying and reading, on the eating and fasting, on the consciousness of each monk. For each bit of dying to self there was the promise of resurrection; for each surrender, the promise of freedom.

Underlying all this concern for order, one senses a deep respect for the order of the universe, the harmony of the spheres, the beauty of the heavenly Jerusalem. Medieval monks spoke of the cloister using metaphors of heaven, of paradise, of the garden enclosed in the *Song of Songs.* In this they echoed the longing Benedict had for order and predictability in a world that was constantly threatened by chaos. His own career was evidence enough of the tumultuous times in which he lived. Monte Cassino, his last, best attempt at founding a monastery, was destroyed in 581 and several times afterward, but each time it arose from the rubble, and there monks once again sought to order their lives and their world for and with God.

Everything will be done at the proper time.

RULE OF BENEDICT

Idleness is the enemy of the soul, and so monks should be occupied at some times with manual labor, and at certain times with holy reading.

RULE OF BENEDICT

If you are hastening toward the heavenly homeland, with Christ's help carry out this minimal rule for beginners, and then with God's protection you will arrive finally at the greater heights of doctrine.

RULE OF BENEDICT

See to it that your private exercises are organized to be performed regularly. Prescribe for yourself what you will do and when, and what things you want to be doing, but in such a way that if sometimes obedience or some other reasonable cause or emergency requires it, you may abbreviate any of your exercises, or even omit them, without inordinate worry.

LOUIS DE BLOIS,
MIRROR FOR MONKS

The monk renounces a life of agitation and confusion for one of order and clarity. But the order and clarity are not his own making; nor are they, so to speak, an institutional product, an effect of exterior regularity. They are the fruit of the Spirit.

THOMAS MERTON,
CONTEMPLATION IN A WORLD OF ACTION

After a few days of newspapers and reflection on their contents [the author had been in the hospital], I am convinced that what we need above all, and seem to have lost, are the following: First we need to recover the belief that order is possible, and that it rests with us to preserve it. Then we need to desire to do this. . . . If, today, genuine order has become incredible it is because people are not fully capable of experiencing themselves as persons with sufficient dignity and responsibility to contribute to an order in which all are fully and personally concerned.

THOMAS MERTON,
CONJECTURES OF A GUILTY BYSTANDER

To have a place to stand is a basic human need in order that I know where I belong, and it is necessary both in relation to the places and to the people in my life. It means, above all, that I have time and space for listening to the Word of God in all the many ways that God is reaching out to me. That will be totally impossible if I am always running, late, distracted, feeling ajar and torn apart. Benedict is helping me to find my own center. . . . Respecting boundaries, not letting things drift, means that I am totally present to whatever I am doing, present with awareness, and therefore with energy for whatever that place, that moment may bring me.

ESTHER DE WAAL, *A LIFE-GIVING WAY*

The Benedictine is clean, simple, and proper to the time and place because the stewardship of the universe demands a commitment to order, harmony, and rightness if it is to survive.

SR. JOAN CHITTISTER, *THE RULE OF BENEDICT*

CHAPTER I

Prayer

Saint Benedict was not a theorist about prayer, its nature, forms, and stages. On the other hand, he valued prayer very highly. He organized the liturgy of the hours or divine office very minutely, assigning psalms and other prayers to each of the seven daytime offices—lauds, prime, terce, sext, none, vespers, and compline—and the night office that his monks chanted or recited each day. He legislated that his monks spend more than three hours a day reading or listening to reading. He expected this reading to be prayerful and to lead to spontaneous or wordless prayer. Finally, he assumed that various monks would be moved to solitary prayer during the day, and he sought to make sure the oratory would be quiet and so suitable for such prayer. Benedict wanted reverent and frequent prayer, but he did not legislate any particular postures or breathing techniques. To those preoccupied with techniques, Benedict's teaching is something of a disappointment. Of course, he did recommend Cassian highly, and Cassian's *Institutes* contains a good deal of guidance about prayer, even suggesting a version of the Jesus Prayer.

Benedictine prayer is less about technique than it is about perseverance and attentiveness. Anyone who reads the Bible in a reverent, faith-filled manner or who attends carefully to the words of the liturgy of the hours will think about the application of what she reads and hears to her own life. Her reflection (meditation) will suggest changes in her behavior or cast new light on the teachings of the faith. Such reflection will then lead her to prayer: praise to God for his wondrous truth, thanks for his gifts, sorrow for her failures, and requests for forgiveness and help. If a person perseveres in such reading, reflection, and prayer, she will eventually find words less necessary, or even a hindrance, and she will simply rest in the presence and love of God. This, at least, is the way medieval monastic authors describe the development of prayer, from reading and recitation *(lectio divina),* through reflection *(meditatio)* and prayer *(oratio),* to contemplation *(contemplatio).* In fact, this fourfold schema appears several times in the readings selected here.

Benedictine authors show a predilection for this kind of prayer, rooted in the communal or private reading of the Bible and related works. However, monastic authors never felt a need to confine their discussion of prayer to this traditional schema. In each age, monks learned new ways to structure prayer from the wider church. This is especially obvious in the writings of the Ludovico Barbo, John Trithemius, and Louis de Blois, all of whom lived between 1380 and 1560, and so were heavily influenced by the *Devotio moderna,* and especially Thomas à Kempis (1390–1471). This movement, which was centered in the Netherlands but was echoed elsewhere in Europe, emphasized methodical meditation techniques that served to guide reflection. These methods helped focus the mind on the topic of meditation.

Nevertheless, for the Benedictine, prayer is never primarily a matter of technique. It is the natural outflow from the heart of a believer nourished by the Word of God in the Scriptures and the liturgy. God has spoken; the Benedictine listens and answers with words, with actions, with silence.

During Benedictine history, there have been times when there were exaggerations about prayer. In many places, liturgical prayer was expanded beyond the generous limits allotted it by Saint Benedict as masses and additional offices and prayers were added to the daily horarium. This was somewhat self-defeating, since private reading, one of the two essential fonts of Benedictine prayer, was curtailed. Work was also curtailed, and so the monks became liturgical specialists, expected to pray on behalf of others. Insofar as this was thought to relieve others of the duty to pray, it was a manifest error. For the monks, it was also the destruction of the delicate balance and order that Benedict envisioned. One can imagine that this overemphasis on liturgical prayer ultimately led to a distaste for that very liturgical prayer, a rather specific sort of *akedia* or spirit of tedium regarding the things of God.

Another difficulty, more subtle perhaps, is that the concentration on ornate liturgical prayer tended to attract onlookers. Monastic prayer was no longer a model and encouragement for others to prayer, not an invitation to enter into prayer themselves, but a spectacle they watched. Saint Bernard thought he detected in the ornate churches of Benedictine monasteries a sort of come-on to pilgrims and benefactors who were attracted more by glitter than by grace. Insofar as people come to watch monks do splendid liturgies today, there is still a danger that performance for onlookers will contaminate the purity of monastic prayer. The way to avoid the problem is to encourage visitors to join in the prayer, not watch it. This danger of praying before others can also stain private prayer. Wulfstan solved that problem by having a hidden prayer room in each of his manor houses.

Prayer becomes difficult when we are preoccupied. If lack of time for surprise guests is a sign that our schedule is too full, then lack of concentration at prayer is a sign that our minds are too cluttered. Either we have too many distracting concerns or we need to learn how to loosen the grip that legitimate concerns have on our minds and imaginations. At times, however, distractions and difficulties in concentration are beyond our control. Then, Blosius says, we should patiently and cheerfully pray as best we can, trusting that God is pleased with our effort.

When there is just no time to set aside to pray because one's children require constant attention (a friend said that her one attempt to pray lauds after her son was born took four hours, with interruptions for nursing, changing, burping, etc.), or deadlines have to be met, or a family member is sick, Benedict's idea of spacing prayer times throughout the day (liturgy of the hours) needs adapting. The prayers will be rushed and silent, no more than an offering or a request for strength, but they can still be woven into the fabric of the day. The goal of regular prayers at appointed intervals is to "pray always," to draw the mind explicitly to God at regular intervals so that the rest of the time one can attend prayerfully to work, reading, brothers and sisters, spouses and children, guests and strangers. Short, hurried prayer like this will do for a while, but over the long haul abiding in the presence of God requires more time and concentration than we can give it at our busiest moments.

Saint Gertrude suggests that occasionally each nun should set aside a day for prayer, when she simply praises and thanks God. In the circumstances of modern life, when there are so many demands on our time and attention, such quiet days are all the more necessary. Everybody should have some noise-free, news-free place where she can spend a day or an hour in quiet, with God and with herself. There are many retreat centers and religious houses and parks where one can go for some quiet hours.

Ultimately, prayer is a means to and an expression of self-offering to God, a surrender of one's life and activities into God's hands. One can offer God splendid liturgy, daily meditation, competence in esoteric contemplative techniques, but none of this means anything unless one can surrender oneself. Second, prayer is meant to be a part of life. One brings one's activities and concerns to times of prayer; one slips short prayers into the intervals that occur in working and walking and weeding. In the end, prayer is about awareness of the divine presence, and that presence is everywhere.

⟋⟍

A brother said to Abba Antony, "Pray for me." The old man answered him, "I will not have mercy on you, and neither will God if you yourself do not make an effort and if you do not entreat God."

ANTONY, *SAYINGS*

But if Pachomius prayed about someone's health and was not granted his request by the Lord, he was not surprised or afflicted at not being heard, for he knew the purpose toward which the saints tended. And he said in his prayer, "May your will be done, not mine" [Lk 22.42]. For he who is one with the Father in all things taught us that it ought to be so.

LIFE OF PACHOMIUS

There is a sadness that is helpful and a sadness that is destructive. It is a function of the useful sorrow, then, to lament about one's own sins as well as the ignorance of one's neighbors, but also to avoid falling away from one's purpose and to achieve the goal of goodness. These concerns, therefore, are the signs of a sorrow that is legitimate and good. There is also another kind of sorrow, prompted by the Enemy, which knows how to merge with the first kind. For he himself imposes a sorrow, completely irrational, which by some has also been called *akedia*. This spirit, therefore, must be driven off especially by prayer and psalmody.

LIFE OF SYNCLETICA

First, whenever you undertake to do something good, pray insistently to the Lord that he bring it to completion.

RULE OF BENEDICT

Give yourself frequently to prayer.

RULE OF BENEDICT

Pray for your enemies out of the love of Christ.

RULE OF BENEDICT

Let us ask God in prayer that his will be done in us.

RULE OF BENEDICT

In the winter, from November 1 till Easter, reasonable consideration suggests monks should rise at the eighth hour of the night—that is, so that they can rest until a little after the midpoint of the night, and so rise with digestion completed. Whatever time remains after the night office can be used by those brothers who need to learn the Psalter or the readings. From Easter till November 1, the times shall be arranged that vigils are followed very closely by lauds at daybreak. This provision for a short interval allows the brothers to go out for the needs of nature.

RULE OF BENEDICT

From Holy Easter until Pentecost, Alleluia is sung without exception in both the psalms and the responsories.

RULE OF BENEDICT

Let us therefore render praises to our creator for his just judgments at these times: lauds, prime, terce, sext, none, vespers, compline; and let us rise at night to praise him.

RULE OF BENEDICT

We want to emphasize this: if this arrangement of the psalms displeases anyone, let him arrange them differently if he judges it better.

RULE OF BENEDICT

Those monks who sing less than the Psalter with the customary canticles in the space of a week show themselves indolent in their devout service, since we read that our holy fathers strenuously fulfilled in one day what we lukewarm people take a whole week to complete.

RULE OF BENEDICT

Let us keep in mind how one should act in the sight of God and his angels, and let us so conduct our psalmody that our mind is in tune with our voice.

RULE OF BENEDICT

We should petition the Lord God of all things with all humility and pure devotion.

RULE OF BENEDICT

We should realize that we are heard not by multiplying words, but because of purity of heart and tears of compunction.

RULE OF BENEDICT

Hence, prayer should be brief and pure, unless it happen to be lengthened by an impulse or inspiration of divine grace.

RULE OF BENEDICT

In community [silent] prayer should always be kept short.

RULE OF BENEDICT

Those who wish to pray quietly by themselves at times when there is no community prayer should simply enter [the chapel] and pray, not in a loud voice, but in tears and with full attention of heart.

RULE OF BENEDICT

While the other brothers were asleep, Benedict, the man of God, was at his vigils, for he had advanced the time of his night prayers. He was standing at the window praying to almighty God. Suddenly in the deep of the night he looked up and saw a light spreading from above. This light drove back all the darkness of the night. This light shining in the darkness shone with such brightness that it was brighter than the day. A very wonderful thing occurred during this contemplation, for as Benedict himself told afterward, he saw the whole world as though it had been gathered under a single ray of the sun. . . . The whole of creation seems narrow to the person gazing at the Creator.

GREGORY THE GREAT, DIALOGUES

Whenever on his travels Wulfstan came to a chapel, neither haste nor urgent need could move him to pass by without a visit. He would go in and offer to God and the patron saint of the church the incense of his prayers with those tears that someone reported were always ready to flow.

LIFE OF WULFSTAN

When Wulfstan was traveling by horseback, he began the Psalter as soon as he was mounted on the animal. He didn't stop until he reached the end. He added litanies with many collect prayers, as well as vigils and vespers for the souls of the dead. . . . If he was free of business he always prayed or preached. If not, with his mind fixed on heaven he longed for God. When he was lying down, standing, walking, sitting, there was always a psalm in his mouth and Christ ever in his heart.

LIFE OF WULFSTAN

In each of his manors, Wulfstan had a little room in which he shut himself in the morning after mass and locked the doors. There he found solitude as great as in the desert in which he meditated on the "contempt of the world" and on contemplation of God. There was no one to interrupt him except a cleric who warned him by a knock on the door that it was time for dinner or the hours.

LIFE OF WULFSTAN

The prayers and meditations that are written down here were composed in order to arouse the mind of the reader to love or fear of God or to self-examination. They should not be read in a rush, but quietly, not cursorily or quickly, but section by section with intent and leisurely meditation. The reader should not feel obliged to read any one of them completely, but only to the point that he feels God helping him to enkindle an impulse to pray, or as much as he likes. Nor is it necessary that he always begin each one at the beginning; he can start wherever he wants. The parts are divided up into paragraphs to make it easier to begin or end at will. This should prevent the length of the prayers or frequent repetition from causing boredom; instead, the reader can gather from them that impulse toward prayer for which they were composed.

ANSELM OF CANTERBURY, PRAYERS

When you pray, pray in spirit and mind; enter into your room, close the door, and pray to your father, more with heart than voice, more with faith than singing.

PETER OF CELLE, THE SCHOOL OF THE CLOISTER

When grace comes first and touches the mind, prayer is enjoyable and devout. It is like a morning rain shower. Prayer is laborious when your heart is far away from your prayer, and God is far away from your heart. Your heart is faraway from you if it is preoccupied with unimportant concerns, lukewarm in religious fervor, or immersed in carnal desires. God is away from your heart when he withdraws grace, postpones his presence, or exercises the patience of the petitioner.

PETER OF CELLE, *THE SCHOOL OF THE CLOISTER*

Wordiness in the divine office counts for almost nothing before God.

HILDEGARD OF BINGEN,
EXPLANATION OF THE RULE OF BENEDICT

Now and then, set aside for yourself a day on which, without hindrance, you can be at leisure to praise God and to make amends for all the praise and thanksgiving you have neglected all the days of your life to render to God for all the good he has done. This will be a day of praising and thanksgiving and a day of jubilation, and you will celebrate the memory of that radiant praise with which you will be jubilant to the Lord for eternity, when you will be satisfied fully by the presence of God, and the glory of the Lord will fill your soul.

GERTRUDE THE GREAT, *SPIRITUAL EXERCISES*

Without mental prayer, it would be virtually impossible for frail humanity to bear the fierce struggles of religious life. You can inebriate with sweetness your dryness of heart, making use of the water of prayer drawn from the fountains of the Savior. As a tree experiencing drought sheds its unripened fruit and leaves, so the soul that is deprived of the dew of prayer brings forth incomplete works infected with distaste.

LUDOVICO BARBO, *FORM OF PRAYER*

First, beloved brothers and sisters, you should know that according to the teaching of all the saints who have written

about prayer, there are three ways of praying. The first is
vocal, when one says the Lord's Prayer or a psalm, or reads
some other part of sacred Scripture with devotion, or when
one invokes some devout saint who asks the Lord God for
various graces. . . . This is the common form of prayer,
which is easily understood and is suitable especially for beginners. Great contemplative saints make it their custom to
always start from this form of prayer before ascending to the
other, higher ways of prayer.

LUDOVICO BARBO, *FORM OF PRAYER*

Next, you will ascend to the second stage of prayer—
namely, meditation. When you have been warmed by
vocal prayer, go up to the table of the Lord, to the place
of pasture, to the stage of meditation. Meditation happens
this way: it prays not with words, but in the heart, understanding, and affectivity. For when the works of God and
the order and beauty of creation are represented before the
understanding, the understanding inquires, rejoices, and is
rapt into the love of God, and the affectivity of the soul is
totally suffused with the sweetness in God, moved with love
and zeal in the service and honor of God and the love of
neighbor in God, and attains many other good things at
the same time.

LUDOVICO BARBO, *FORM OF PRAYER*

There is no teaching about the third stage of contemplation,
because ears have not heard nor has it entered into the human heart what things God prepares for the soul, which
God makes ready for divine contemplation. However, I tell
you the truth, beloved brothers: that if you are faithful to the
aforesaid meditations in purity of heart and humility . . .
finally you will arrive at such sweetness, to such love of the
Lord Jesus, that your soul will be totally liquefied as it experiences divine and supertranscendent illuminations.
Your intellect will be faint from stupor since it does not
have the power to examine the depths of this ineffable

enlightenment, whereas your affectivity will be totally en-
flamed and will ascend with elevated heart, tasting God's
beauty.

LUDOVICO BARBO, *FORM OF PRAYER*

We should pray without ceasing because we cannot complete anything without God's help.

JOHN TRITHEMIUS, *RULE*

The divine office is to be prayed by the brethren with the
greatest reverence and faithful intention.

LOUIS DE BLOIS, *MONASTIC STATUTES*

Prayer and meditation have an important part to play in
opening up new ways and new horizons. If our prayer is the
expression of a deep and grace-inspired desire for newness
of life—and not the mere blind attachment to what has
always been familiar and "safe"—God will act in us and
through us to renew the Church by preparing, in prayer,
what we cannot yet imagine or understand. In this way our
prayer and faith today will be oriented toward the future
which we ourselves may never see fully realized on earth.

THOMAS MERTON,
CONTEMPLATION IN A WORLD OF ACTION

Better just to smell a flower in the garden . . . than to have
an unauthentic experience of a much higher value. Better to
honestly enjoy the sunshine or some light reading than to
claim to be in contact with something that one is not in
contact with at all.

THOMAS MERTON,
CONTEMPLATION IN A WORLD OF ACTION

Benedict says that the Lord's Prayer is to be recited aloud
[twice] daily. . . . To fail to forgive is to be trapped in the
past, caught up in resentment and bitterness, staying with
wounds that remain open and raw—everything that will

prevent new life and new growth. It is not only damaging to
the individual, but destructive of community as well. When
I choose not to forgive, I am choosing death rather than life,
and Benedict, who is trying to lead us all the time forward
into freedom and fullness of life, wants to rescue me.

ESTHER DE WAAL, *A LIFE-GIVING WAY*

The opening verse [at most of the hours of the liturgy or
divine office], "God come to my assistance," is a small
phrase commonly used by monastics as a means of recalling
themselves to the presence of God in their mind and heart.
It prompted Cassian to write some of his most inspiring
teaching in which he said that if these words were repeated
throughout the day—at work, in reading, in physical weakness, in moments of temptation—they would lead to a
continuous state of prayer and so to contemplation.

ESTHER DE WAAL, *A LIFE-GIVING WAY*

It is important not to see *lectio divina* as one more technique
or method to be grasped or acquired. It is essentially a
process, and a gentle one. Yet it does have its rhythm and
framework, and it is useful to see this as four steps or rungs.
The first is *lectio* by which we read some short passage from
the Bible. . . . Then comes *meditatio,* which is the seeking,
finding a word or phrase that strikes us, touches us. We repeat it, reflect on it, come to grips with what it is saying to
us personally. . . . The vital thing is that it is to and fro, to
and fro, time and again, until it becomes like a heartbeat inside of [our] own self. For then the word touches the heart
and we reach the third step, *oratio.* . . . It is now that we allow ourselves to be drawn to God as though with a magnet,
and all the false self, with its games and facades, falls away
and instead we surrender totally to God. This brings us to
the final step, *contemplatio,* in which we learn a new language, silence. We are content simply to be, standing in the
presence of God. We let God take us beyond ourselves. . . .
As Abbot Marmion puts it: we read *(lectio)* under the eye of

God *(meditatio)* until the heart is touched *(oratio)* and leaps into flame *(contemplatio)*.

ESTHER DE WAAL, *A LIFE-GIVING WAY*

The function of prayer is not to establish a routine; it is to establish a relationship with God who is in relationship with us always. . . . The function of prayer is to bring us into touch with ourselves, as well. To the ancients, "tears of compunction" were the sign of a soul that knew its limits, faced its sins, accepted its needs and lived in hope.

SR. JOAN CHITTISTER, *THE RULE OF BENEDICT*

"Let the oratory be what it is called," Benedict said. Have a place where you can go in order to be about nothing but the business of being in the presence of God so that every other place in your life can become more conscious of that Presence as well. More than that, Benedict asks us to be there in a special way—with quiet and with awareness, not laughing or talking or lounging or distracting but alert and immersed and enshrouded in the arms of God.

SR. JOAN CHITTISTER, *THE RULE OF BENEDICT*

CHAPTER 2

Reading

The most striking thing about reading in Christian monasticism is that, from the founders of the movement through Benedict to the monastic reformers of the Renaissance, literacy and reading were highly esteemed among monastic theorists, even at times and places when levels of literacy in the surrounding culture were quite low. Such reading was hard work before the invention of printing: the books were often cumbersome, the script difficult to decipher. Perhaps for that reason, but for others that deserve more attention than they have received, monks seem to have regularly failed to read as much as Benedict and Benedictine reformers required of them. They are still failing regularly. In spite of that, the reading of monks—and the production of books that this required—has made a tremendous contribution to Western civilization.

Reading was closely connected with eating; it was food for the soul. As food nourished physical life, reading nourished prayer. Hence, public reading during meals is a very ancient monastic custom. The reading that the members of a community heard in common, at meals and at other times, helped give them their unique culture. Hence, reformers like Louis de Blois urged that on a regular basis members of their congregation listen to certain specific works read out loud. The same realization of the importance of reading in shaping one's mind led monastic teachers to urge that monks not read haphazardly or simply for entertainment. As Saint Benedict said regarding Lenten reading, each monk should be assigned a book and should read it straight through from beginning to end. Many authors urged that important passages be committed to memory and so made one's own in a particularly intimate way.

The primary reading material of the monastic tradition was the Bible. The monks were immersed in a biblical culture, which also defined the flow of the seasons from Advent to Christmas to Lent to Pentecost, to the "little Lent," which began on the Feast of the Holy Cross (September 14). To the Bible were added the works of Christian writers, especially those that commented on the Bible. Beyond that, monks read what background material was necessary for understanding the Bible—everything from grammar books to love poetry.

Medieval readers, monastic and otherwise, were very flexible in their interpretation of texts. In particular, the Bible was thought to have several layers of meaning—literal or historical, doctrinal, and moral—so that readers found moral and spiritual guidance in the strangest places. Each helpful interpretation was thought to be inspired by the Holy Spirit. Hence, the interpretation of texts was a very creative process in which the reader was personally involved.

Jean Mabillon and others warn that unless reading and study are encouraged in the monastery there will not be a suitable pool of educated and intelligent persons from which to choose leaders for the monastic community. It is a monastic commonplace, derived from the *Rule of Benedict* itself, that abbots must teach by word and example. This requires that abbots be well read, both before and after their election.

Mabillon makes a particularly important point when he cautions that at first one should read not to teach others, but simply to form oneself. Later, when one is involved in helping others, one can direct some of one's reading toward their instruction. However, he observes, the latter sort of reading tends not to touch one's own mind and heart so deeply. There also seems to be a law that things read and studied for their own intrinsic worth turn out to be more practical and pastoral than books that aim to offer practical and utilitarian guidance.

Reading habits changed gradually over the centuries. Reading became less devotional, more impersonal. Spiritual reading became distinguished from other sorts of reading: study, recreational reading, informational reading, professional reading, and so forth. It is probably not possible to go back to a steady diet of *lectio divina,* if for no other reason than that reading the Bible today requires the study of technical works of scholarship and commentaries that are not suitable for *lectio divina.* However, monks' reading should continue to be self-reflective and prayerful whenever possible. Just as dedication to prayer should lead to a continuous awareness of the presence of God, so *lectio divina* should lead us to an awareness of God in all the words one reads and hears.

The application of this monastic tradition outside the cloister— and even inside it—becomes steadily more difficult as audio-visual entertainments fill the hours once dedicated to reading. No longer can a monastery assume that its recruits will be regular readers. Perhaps the days of print-based monastic culture are coming to an end. Even if that should be the case, many of the monastic guidelines for reading are applicable to watching videos and television or using the Internet, both in terms of what one should watch and how one should watch it.

Another problem is the growing separation between secular culture and the biblical tradition. Generally, a person who wants to stay current with contemporary culture while at the same time deepening his immersion in the Christian tradition must read two quite separate lists of books. Because contemporary culture is changing so rapidly, there is less time to read the classic and contemporary works of Christian culture, which immerse one in the vision of the church and the rhythms of the liturgy.

This means that religious people, whether in monasteries or out of them, have some difficult choices to make about what and how much to read and watch. The most fundamental choice of all is whether to devote oneself to reading and learning regularly and attentively. The next question is what to read or watch. The monastic tradition would suggest that one should favor the classics, the Bible, and the great writers of the early church, as well as the best biblical scholars, theologians, and creative writers of more recent times. The primary criterion is the formation of the individual in the tradition of which he wants to be a part. Helping others comes next. Impressing them doesn't count for anything.

Something should be said in favor of recreational reading. Eugene

Burke, C.S.P., a distinguished historian of theology, used to tell his classes that he learned the methods of historical research by reading murder mysteries. He might have added that from the best of that genre one can learn style and grace as well. However, the monk or Christian does not need to resort to such half-serious arguments in order to read a murder mystery, a novel, or a book of poetry, or watch a movie or TV program. Reading good literature, which can be described as well-written fiction or poetry that probes the human heart, is a way to connect with the human race, to meet people who think or live differently from us, or to meet people like us coping with the same problems. More than that, literature provides us with a relaxing escape from the pressures of everyday life in a small community. However, too much time devoted to literature or history or thoughtful films, too much time devoted to diversions like murder mysteries or entertaining films, any time devoted to books that prey upon the worst instincts of their readers, is time wasted. Each community and each person has to discern what particular mix of religious and secular reading and viewing is right for them. A criterion of judgment might be whether this reading or viewing helps develop in the person the qualities of character presented in the second part of this book.

[The newly converted Antony] was so attentive at the reading of the Scripture lessons that nothing escaped him: he retained everything and so his memory served him in place of books.

LIFE OF ANTONY

Love to hear holy readings.

RULE OF BENEDICT

The books read at vigils should have divine authority: the Old and New Testaments and explanations of them given by recognized and orthodox catholic fathers.

RULE OF BENEDICT

Reading should never be lacking during meals. Not just anyone who happens to pick up a book should read there. Rather, let the one who is going to read for the whole week begin on Sunday. . . . Let him ask all to pray for him, so that God may divert the spirit of pride from him.

RULE OF BENEDICT

And let there be the deepest silence, so that no one's whispering or voice is heard there except that of the one who is reading.

RULE OF BENEDICT

At all seasons of the year, as soon as supper is over they should all sit together and someone should read the *Conferences* or *Lives of the Fathers* or something else that will edify the hearers, but not the Heptateuch or Kings, because it is not useful for untempered minds to hear these writings at that hour. They ought to be read at other times.

RULE OF BENEDICT

During Lent, they should each receive a book from the library that they are to read straight through to the end.

RULE OF BENEDICT

On Sundays, all should devote themselves to reading, except those who are assigned to special duties.

RULE OF BENEDICT

Let the divine law [i.e., the Bible] be read to guests for their edification.

RULE OF BENEDICT

For someone who is hurrying to the perfection of monastic living, there are the teachings of the holy fathers, whose observance leads one to the heights of perfection. For what page or word of the divine authority of the Old and New Testament is not a carefully honed guideline for human life?

And what book of the holy catholic fathers does not sound the way by which we may reach our creator? And the *Conferences* of the Fathers, their *Institutes* and *Lives*, and the *Rule* of our Father Basil—what else are they but tools of virtues for good and obedient monks?

RULE OF BENEDICT

We have a consoler, our Lord Jesus Christ. Although we cannot see him with bodily eyes, we keep in written form in the Gospels the things he did and taught while he was bodily among us. If we take care to hear, read, and confer with each other about these things, which need to be preserved in our hearts and bodies, we will certainly conquer the obstacles of this age as surely as if the Lord were always standing by us and consoling us.

BEDE, *HOMILIES ON THE GOSPELS*

At Wulfstan's table edifying books were read. Silence was rigorously kept so that all might listen attentively. When the meal was over and the eating place quiet, he would explain what had been read in their native tongue, so that he could provide heavenly alms for those to whom he had already served bodily sustenance.

LIFE OF WULFSTAN

Nicholas was born of distinguished English parents. They had great reverence for the holy man [Wulfstan] and sought in many ways to earn his friendship. Wulfstan baptized Nicholas and saw to it that he was educated. As Nicholas grew up, Wulfstan always had him at his side. In order that learning might be perfected in Nicholas, Wulfstan sent the young man to Kent to be educated under the guidance of Lanfranc. Afterward, in the time of Bishop Thiulf, Nicholas was made prior of Worcester. Within a short time, he had given ample proof of his energy. What I judge to be particularly profitable was that he poured letters and learning into the inhabitants of the place by word and example, so that it

was not exceeded in learning by those great English
churches that are larger than Worcester.

LIFE OF WULFSTAN

When you read, bring a friendly simplicity to the divine law
. . . do not interpret it in novel or erroneous ways. Do not
struggle with questions that do not edify but arouse strife
and the downfall of the listeners. Read to understand; understand to do the commands of God. . . . What lies dead
and deformed in the letter on the dead parchment comes to
life when what is read is put into practice.

PETER OF CELLE,
THE SCHOOL OF THE CLOISTER

Reading is bound to silence. . . . Constant and attentive
reading done devoutly purifies our inner self.

PETER OF CELLE,
THE SCHOOL OF THE CLOISTER

Even if the fruit of understanding and knowledge does not
result from reading, reading is still always useful because
our minds are occupied, and exempted from vain and
useless thinking, which weighs them down and stubbornly
intrudes itself.

PETER OF CELLE,
THE SCHOOL OF THE CLOISTER

Reading should not be vain and garrulous, but quiet and
marked with the seal of meditation.

PETER OF CELLE,
THE SCHOOL OF THE CLOISTER

The Gospel of Matthew . . . begins: "The book of the generation of Jesus Christ" [Mt 1.1]. By this beginning we are
told: "Come and see in this book the mystery hidden from
the ages, revealed and manifest through the generation of

Christ. Come and see the Word incarnate, which has hitherto lain hidden with the Father under the seal of divinity."

> PETER OF CELLE,
> *THE SCHOOL OF THE CLOISTER*

I consider a room without reading to be a hell without consolation, an instrument of torture without relief, a prison
without light, a tomb without ventilation, a ditch swarming
with worms, a strangling noose, the empty house of which
the Gospel speaks.

> PETER OF CELLE,
> *ON AFFLICTION AND READING*

[Reading] continuously tells of the clash of virtue and
vices. . . . Reading is the food, light, lamp, refuge, solace
of the soul, the spice of all spiritual flavors. It feeds the
hungry, gives light to the one sitting in darkness, offers bread
to the one fleeing shipwreck or war, comforts the contrite
heart.

> PETER OF CELLE,
> *ON AFFLICTION AND READING*

Reading seeks a lover to whom she can give not just food,
but offspring; not any sort of lover, but one who is noble,
handsome, thoughtful, healthy, and holy. What is contained
in reading is holy, because holy Scripture contains nothing
that is not holy, since it is inspired by the Holy Spirit.

> PETER OF CELLE,
> *ON AFFLICTION AND READING*

[Gertrude] passed beyond the study of the liberal arts and
became a theologian. She pondered untiringly whatever
theological works she had or could obtain and filled the
vault of her heart with the most useful and sweet verses of
holy Scripture. Thus, she always had at hand the divine and
edifying word. Hence, she could always help those who

came to consult her, and she could refute any false idea with scriptural witnesses that were so to the point that no one could argue with her.

GERTRUDE THE GREAT,
THE HERALD OF DIVINE LOVE

She worked tirelessly to collect and transcribe whatever she thought could be useful to others. She did this solely for the honor of God. She was concerned about the salvation of souls, without any thought to human thanks. When people whom she hoped could profit from her writings asked for them, she gave them promptly. If Gertrude discovered that copies of the holy Scriptures were lacking in certain places, she collected as many as she could, in order to gain all for Jesus Christ.

GERTRUDE THE GREAT,
THE HERALD OF DIVINE LOVE

[Gertrude prayed:] May you be glorified if others, in reading these pages, are delighted by the gentleness of your love and are drawn to enjoy in intimacy with you an even greater happiness. Those who study begin by learning the alphabet in order ultimately to arrive at the study of logic. So may these descriptions and these images lead others to taste in themselves this hidden manna, which cannot be known by means of pictures, but for which only those have a hunger who have already tasted it.

GERTRUDE THE GREAT,
THE HERALD OF DIVINE LOVE

[Gertrude concluded:] The more simple readers of this book, who are not strong enough to swim in the river of divine love, can use these pages as a vehicle to help them on the way toward God. May the sight of the graces granted others lead them by the hand, to reading, to meditation, and to contemplation, so that they may begin to taste how sweet is the Lord, and how truly happy is the person who hopes in God and places all his cares in him.

GERTRUDE THE GREAT,
THE HERALD OF DIVINE LOVE

Every interval of time seems short to me, if I am devoting my time to the reading and study of Sacred Scripture. However, if I am not reading or studying, every hour seems tedious and interminable to me. There [in the Bible], I find what I want, I learn what I seek, I am strengthened in hope and taught how to lead my life. There, divine love is announced, the deeds of the saints arouse us to imitate Christ, we develop an avid taste for dwelling in eternal beatitude, and charity enflames the soul.

JOHN TRITHEMIUS, *RULE*

Idle reading corrupts a holy mind.

JOHN TRITHEMIUS, *RULE*

You should listen to the word of God and salutary teaching with a ready and eager mind, no matter who is the speaker. . . . When you want to devote yourself to sacred reading, seek only the honor and glory of God, not idle pleasure or to satisfy vain curiosity or to know many things. In order not to lose your calm and peace of mind by becoming weighed down inside, do not read too much at one time. Read carefully and with an inner desire, not negligently and halfheartedly. Good and salutary things you should always accept as fresh and interesting, even though you have often read or heard them. If you read such things humbly, devoutly, simply, carefully, and reverently, you will derive great utility from them, even if you did not understand them very well. After reading, give thanks to the Lord, and offer to him the things that you have read or heard in eternal praise and in the union of divine love. Ponder these things within yourself, if time is available, and

petition God that you might arrange your life in accord
with them.

LOUIS DE BLOIS, *SPIRITUAL DOCTRINE*

When you properly devote yourself to holy reading, or you
do something else correctly for the praise of God, you often
take away not less but more fruit than if you prayed. For not
only prayers but other salutary words read or heard for the
glory of God, as well as devout actions and thoughts, won-
drously adorn the soul. The mind of a good person receives
from spiritual teaching much that is outstanding and suitable: spiritual teaching preserves from stain, casts out ignorance, makes peaceful, enlightens, nourishes, arouses,
strengthens.

LOUIS DE BLOIS, *SPIRITUAL MIRROR*

Do not imitate those who follow no order in their reading
but are content to read whatever reading chances to come
their way. They are interested in nothing except what is new
and unheard of. Whatever is familiar and everything old,
however useful, bores them. Avoid such instability, for it
does not build up the spirit but scatters it.

LOUIS DE BLOIS, *MIRROR FOR MONKS*

Each day from noon to at least 12:30, if there is no legitimate excuse, a regular public reading should be held in the
chapter room or in the cloister or in some other suitable
place. The readings should include the books of Lawrence
Justinian or the short works of Thomas à Kempis or other
similar devout treatises suitable to monks. When these books
are read through completely, they should be repeated from
the beginning. . . . As regards the readings that are heard
during the community meals, the following plan should
be followed. At the beginning of lunch and dinner, a chapter of the Bible is read. . . . After the reading from holy
Scripture . . . there is added a reading from the holy Doc-

tors, which lasts until the end of the meal. . . . Likewise, each day before compline there should be reading for about a quarter of the hour in the chapter room, cloister, or some other suitable place. . . . At this gathering there should be readings from the accounts of the martyrs and the lives of the saints, and the *Conferences* and *Acts* of the Fathers.

LOUIS DE BLOIS, *MONASTIC STATUTES*

While it is true that studies were never the principal purpose of monks and that they are not necessary for each individual monk in order for him to reach perfection in his state in life, one can also say that without studies it is impossible for monastic communities to maintain order and economy for a long time.

JEAN MABILLON,
TREATISE ON THE STUDIES OF MONKS

If monasteries cannot last without superiors, one can also say that in the ordinary course of things there cannot be good superiors without knowledge. Learning is the superior's guide. . . . That is why all the ancient monastic rules always put knowledge and wisdom in parallel with goodness of life among the qualities required of an abbot. . . . It is not sufficient that a superior have acquired knowledge before undertaking government over his brothers; he must continue to deepen and augment his knowledge by study and reading.

JEAN MABILLON,
TREATISE ON THE STUDIES OF MONKS

The spirit in which Scriptures should be read: search first to know God and the mysteries of our religion, and to know oneself; and to understand the ways to travel to God, and how to make good use of creatures. In a word: seek in this reading only truth and justice and the practice of charity and the other virtues. The particular qualities needed are purity of heart, humility, simplicity, control of curiosity, and enthusiasm.

JEAN MABILLON,
TREATISE ON THE STUDIES OF MONKS

If the reading of Scripture is necessary for monks, the reading of the holy Fathers—who are Scripture's true interpreters—is no less important.

JEAN MABILLON,
TREATISE ON THE STUDIES OF MONKS

The two principle goals of monastic studies are knowledge of the truth, and charity or love of justice. . . . It is not only monks who must have these two principal ends in view in their studies, but all Christians. . . . Besides these two principal ends . . . one can also propose some others that are equally advantageous. One of these is to make good use of one's time. . . . In the second place, study can take the place of work, and hence of penance. . . . A third goal of study is to fill one's spirit with holy thoughts and one's heart with devout feelings.

JEAN MABILLON,
TREATISE ON THE STUDIES OF MONKS

In their studies, monks can have the aim of preaching or writing. . . . However, it seems to me dangerous that young religious have this sort of goal in view before they have been filled with truths that they must teach to others. One could say, perhaps, that in working for others, they will fill themselves. But if one considers this more closely, one will see that the things one studies in order to preach or write do not ordinarily enter deeply in the heart of the one studying. . . . I believe therefore that . . . young religious should be occupied in their reading and studies only with care for themselves, that they have in view only to fill their own spirit and heart with the truths they need, and that they leave to Providence and their superiors concerns about applying these truths to others in the future.

JEAN MABILLON,
TREATISE ON THE STUDIES OF MONKS

The contemplative life should liberate and purify the imagination which passively absorbs all kinds of things without our realizing it; liberate and purify it from the influence of so much violence done by the bombardment of social images. . . . The training of the imagination implies a certain freedom and this freedom implies a certain capacity to choose and to find its own appropriate nourishment. Thus in the interior life there should be moments of relaxation, freedom and "browsing." Perhaps the best way to do this is in the midst of nature, but also in literature. Perhaps also a certain amount of art is necessary and music.

THOMAS MERTON,
CONTEMPLATION IN A WORLD OF ACTION

The Rule is totally scriptural. The purpose of the monastic life is to shape life according to the Scriptures. Benedict cites the Bible at every moment.

ESTHER DE WAAL, *A LIFE-GIVING WAY*

The reading of the Word is an essential element of the night office. But Benedict is not content with merely listening to Scripture. He also wants a deepening of our understanding of it. How can we be fed if we do not stretch our minds? It is only too easy to let familiar passages from the Bible drift over me. Benedict wants me to make use of my intellect in my prayer. This means I should study them, use my mind critically, see what others have to say about them, and let myself be humble enough to learn from their interpretation.

ESTHER DE WAAL, *A LIFE-GIVING WAY*

The purpose of reading at meals is a reminder of the whole purpose of the life that Benedict is laying before us: it is so that we should be listening to God at all times. . . . I have been made aware of the attention paid to the needs of the body, but it is no less vital to think of the needs of the mind. It is important to nourish, feed, and enrich the intellect.

ESTHER DE WAAL, *A LIFE-GIVING WAY*

Benedict wants us to do more than read the Scriptures. He wants us to study them, to wrestle with them, to understand them, to make them part of us, to let them grow in us through the work of traditional and contemporary scholarship so that the faith can stay green in us.

SR. JOAN CHITTISTER, *THE RULE OF BENEDICT*

Benedict considers reading such an important part of the meal, in fact, that he insists that the person doing the reading be a good reader, someone who would inspire rather than irritate the souls of the listeners. The reading was to be an artistic event, an instructive experience, a moment of meditation.

SR. JOAN CHITTISTER, *THE RULE OF BENEDICT*

Study is hard work. It is so much easier to find something else to do in its place than to stay at the grind of it. We have excuses aplenty for avoiding the dull, hard, daily attempt to learn. There is always something so much more important to do than reading. There is always some excuse for not stretching our souls with new ideas and insights now or yet or ever.

SR. JOAN CHITTISTER, *THE RULE OF BENEDICT*

CHAPTER 3

Work

The readings in this section are sparse. This may be mere chance, but the small number of quotations does seem to reflect the amount of reflection that monastics have devoted to work. In the realm of monastic theory, work is almost always taken for granted. Saint Benedict insisted that all work was valuable in itself. As Hildegard explains, work engages the monk in God's ongoing work of creation and salvation. Tools deserve the same reverence as chalices and other vessels of the altar. Whether the tool is a shovel or a pen really doesn't make any difference. Both are instruments of good work—of sharing in God's creative activity and of providing for the needs of others.

Monk-workers should be conscientious and reverent; they should use their talents, but be humble about it. Except in dire necessity, they should not be asked to work so much that they are worn out or unhappy. Help should be provided when a task becomes overwhelming. Granted these parameters, monks should work without complaining. Work is natural and necessary. Work is also a way of serving Christ with Christ. Work in which human beings pool their talents and efforts toward a common cause is also a way of uniting us in the Spirit who calls and heals us all.

Benedict and his followers could legislate a benign workload because their primary concerns were neither production nor consumption. If a monastery aimed at sufficiency and no more, the monks would not have to work long hours to produce things to sell or trade. Moreover, monasteries were often the beneficiaries of gifts and donations that helped support the monks and nuns. This enabled them not only to meet their own needs without heroic effort, but also to help others.

Once again one comes back to Benedict's horarium, with its division of the day into prayer, reading, and work. If during the early Middle Ages and often since, prayer has tended to usurp the place of reading and to a lesser degree of work, in recent times it is work that has threatened Benedictine balance. Especially in North American monasticism, work has tended to overshadow all else. The reasons for this are not hard to find. Benedictines came to the United States in the last half of the nineteenth century. They came to serve a immigrant church that was short of personnel and money. Those pioneer monks and sisters generously sacrificed the comforts of the cloister for the challenges of missionary life. They accomplished great feats of evangelization and education. Work was their asceticism. They did not mind working hard, for the tasks were necessary and noble. They established a tradition of hard work that was not without merit. Their intensity and dedication could well serve later generations as examples of how to work hard in the service of others.

In the last half of the twentieth century, when monastics could realistically look to reestablishing a better balance in their lives among work, prayer, and reading, the number of vocations suddenly fell drastically. The population of monasteries became older and older; the number of able-bodied men and women became fewer. In many monasteries it is the heroic efforts of the few that enable the elderly to spend their last years quietly, without fear for the morrow. These able-bodied few are working very hard, and they are very tired.

Unfortunately, the frenetic work schedule of such monastics is matched in our society by the equally inhuman work schedules of many other men and women, especially those with families. For several decades, real income for half or more of the people in our country has risen very little. To compete in the capitalist marketplace, many companies are forcing people to work part-time with partial or no benefits. The new high-tech industries may be glamorous and full of opportunity for the few, but those on the assembly line who are paid eight dollars an hour can support their family only if there are two incomes and minimal expenses. Something similar is happening in universities, where full-time and tenured professors are being replaced with part-time, ill-paid Ph.D.'s who must race from job to job to make a living.

At the other end of the scale, those who hold salaried positions are often expected to work sixty or seventy hours instead of the standard forty. When both spouses work at that pace, family life is minimal at best. All one's best energies go to the job; there is little left for God, for family, for oneself.

In such extreme situations, both monastics and non-monastics have to carve out a life as best they can. One way to take some of the pressure off is to make do with sufficiency rather than abundance or luxury. If this means owning one less car, using the library more, eating simpler, less expensive food and eating at home rather than in restaurants, making fewer trips to the theater, it is perhaps a blessing in disguise. At least necessity and social obligation—to conserve resources, avoid pollution, strengthen the family—will often coincide.

Our pace of work is in part a symptom of very bizarre values. Perhaps if monastics and others could find ways to slow down and work less, they would have time not just for prayer and reading, but also for considering the state of our society and trying to change what is wrong. When one ponders a society where people are tempted to spend most of their waking hours in frantic work or mindless television viewing, ordering time to make a place not just for work, but for reading, reflection, and prayer—and some social activism—seems eminently rational.

An old man said: "Never have I desired a work that was useful to me but that caused harm to my brother, for I have this firm hope: that my brother's advantage is for me a work full of fruit."

SAYINGS OF THE DESERT FATHERS AND MOTHERS

In whatever work that you do, you should say to yourself at every moment: "If God looks at me, what does he see?" Then see how you answer yourself. If you condemn yourself, leave immediately. Stop the work that you were doing and take up something else in order to be sure to reach your destination. For it is necessary that the traveler be always ready to continue his journey. When you are seated at manual labor, when you are walking along the road, when you are eating, tell yourself this: "If God called me now, what would happen?" See how your conscience answers and hurry to do what it tells you.

SAYINGS OF THE DESERT FATHERS AND MOTHERS

If you are at your manual labor in your room and it comes time to pray, do not say: "I will use up my supply of branches or finish weaving the little basket, and then I will rise," but rise immediately and render to God the prayer that is owed him. Otherwise, little by little you come to neglect you prayer and your duty habitually, and your soul will become a wasteland devoid of every spiritual and bodily work. For right at the beginning your will is apparent.

SAYINGS OF THE DESERT FATHERS AND MOTHERS

A monk was working on the feast day of a martyr. Another monk saw him and asked: "Are we allowed to work today?" The other answered: "On this day the servant of God was tortured and died a martyr. And should I not tire myself a bit by working?"

SAYINGS OF THE DESERT FATHERS AND MOTHERS

The old men said of one of the brothers that he never stopped his manual labor but his prayer ascended continually before God. He was very humble and very stable.

SAYINGS OF THE DESERT FATHERS AND MOTHERS

The brothers should serve one another.

RULE OF BENEDICT

Let all have help according to the size of the community and the circumstances of the place.

RULE OF BENEDICT

If the community is large, the cellarer [business manager, in charge of material goods] should receive helpers to assist him so he can fulfill the office committed to him with an untroubled mind. Requests should be made and supplies handed out at the proper hours so that no one will be disturbed or unhappy in the house of God.

RULE OF BENEDICT

An hour before mealtime, the weekly servers should receive an extra portion of bread and drink over and above the regular allotment, so that then they may serve the rest of the community at mealtimes without murmuring or heavy fatigue.

RULE OF BENEDICT

At the end of Sunday lauds, those beginning or completing a week of table service should bow down in the oratory before all the community and ask them to pray for them.

RULE OF BENEDICT

This principle pertains to all tasks in the monastery: when they need help, let it be given them, and when they have nothing to do, they should do what they are told.

RULE OF BENEDICT

The house of God should be wisely managed by wise people.

RULE OF BENEDICT

If there are artisans in the monastery, let them work at their arts with all humility.

RULE OF BENEDICT

If some of the work of the artisans is to be sold, let those who conduct the sale make sure there is no fraud. . . . They should make sure that the vice of avarice does not affect the prices. Let things always be sold somewhat more cheaply than they can be by secular people, so that in all things God may be glorified.

RULE OF BENEDICT

Let them direct to God the works that they do, because human work that is directed to God will shine in the heavens. . . . For God created human beings and placed other creatures under them so that they might act on other creatures in such a way that God's good works would not be destroyed.

HILDEGARD OF BINGEN, *BOOK OF LIFE'S MERITS*

When someone, through the gift of the Holy Spirit, rightly and properly imposes on himself labors to meet some need of the living or for the repose of the dead, God receives his toil as right and just, just as he heard Moses and Eli when they worked ceaselessly on behalf of those who had sinned against God. . . . Therefore, every believer should never stop working for God, on behalf of others as well as himself, because God will look into the hearts of men and reward their just labor and goodwill.

HILDEGARD OF BINGEN, *BOOK OF LIFE'S MERITS*

Just as the work of God, which mankind is, will not be exterminated, but will rather endure, so also human work will not fade away, because human work that is directed toward God will shine in the heavens. . . . When God created human beings, he enjoined them to work on created things. And just as he will not come to an end—he will be changed into ashes but afterward he will rise—so his good works will be seen unto glory.

HILDEGARD OF BINGEN, *BOOK OF LIFE'S MERITS*

When the excellence of God is praised by human beings, it is as if honor were shown to God by the earth itself in the just and holy works of human beings who arise from that earth. . . . Human beings, who are animated by the power of reason and the spirit of intelligence, are made from the earth. The material of God's work is in them who are the material of the humanity of the Son of God, because that handiwork which God made into human beings from the earth was also the material of that Virgin who brought forth the Son of God without any blemish in his pure and holy humanity. . . . The soul is the matter of good works and of a better life, which is a divine element in the powers of the soul, for it is from God and exists in human beings who prepare for just and well-ordered works in response to the divine command and then begin to do them; then the incarnate Son of God completes them in the perfection of his blessed virtues and in manifesting true holiness. Thus existent life gives life to those who believe in it.

HILDEGARD OF BINGEN, *BOOK OF LIFE'S MERITS*

Benedict's idea seems to be that the monk gives glory to God precisely by not working as others do, for material gain or for popular success. This can easily escalate and become competitive, in a search for more money, a better reputation.

ESTHER DE WAAL, *A LIFE-GIVING WAY*

Work done in the Benedictine tradition is supposed to be regular; it is supposed to be productive, it is supposed to be worthwhile, but it is not supposed to be impossible.

SR. JOAN CHITTISTER, *THE RULE OF BENEDICT*

CHAPTER 4

Mutual Support

Human relationships in a monastery are not quite the same as those in any other setting. Monastics take vows that bind them to their community for life. In this there is some analogy to marriage vows. A monastery is like a family, but it is not a family. The ties between monks are not ties of kinship. Nor are they for the most part ties of close friendship. Monastics are sometimes friends with each other, but a monk is more likely to have friends outside his cloister than inside it. This is mostly because of numbers: if a friend is one in a thousand, the chances of finding a close friend in a monastery are not very high. The closest analogue to the ties that bind a monastic community together is probably found among longtime neighbors, who get along with each other, who trust and can count on each other—people bound to each other by seldom examined but time-tested and sturdy ties.

The most important relationship in the monastery is that of the monk to God. Upon that relationship depends all the others. The bedrock of one's relation to God is faith: a firm conviction that God is there for each of us and all of us together. For the Christian and the Christian monk, this faith centers on Christ. For the *Rule of Benedict* Christ is the divine Son of God and Lord of Life and the sick person with special needs, the inconvenient guest, and each monk. So, ultimately, the relationship of monk to monk is the relationship of monk to Christ and, indeed, Christ to Christ.

In spite of the uniqueness and deeply Christian basis of the relationships in a monastery, monks have much to teach about how people can get along together in families, communities, and places of work. The Benedictine emphasis on community is rooted in a long-standing monastic conviction that if a person is not properly related to her neighbors, that person is not properly related to Christ. There is a provision in the *Rule of Benedict* for monks to go from the community to live a solitary life at a distance from the community. Such solitary life takes many forms, but it is universally agreed that leaving the community for a solitary life ought not be an escape from the need to relate to others or a way to avoid facing the selfishness and narcissism and fear and impatience that make others unbearable, that make well-meaning, flawed human beings seem like enemies.

Saint Antony said: "From our neighbor comes life or death." To prevent the possibility of death coming in this way, Benedict provided that every day, morning and evening, the abbot should lead the community in the Lord's Prayer, because in that prayer monks declare, "Forgive us our offenses as we forgive those who offend us." Equally important is Benedict's admonition that the sun should not go down on one's anger. He even provides somewhat ritualized procedures for dealing with anger and alienation. Medieval monasteries had some interesting ways of dealing with hostilities, including a daily meeting in which there was a ritualized opportunity to accuse oneself or others of faults against the peace and order of the community. Monasteries today are experimenting with new models of dealing with anger, irritation, and misunderstanding. Sometimes they have a counselor or psychological consultant help them. The goal, of course, is to have a community of honest and tolerant adults.

One of the key elements in living peacefully together is to avoid judging others. One can spend an entire vespers surveying the monks—evaluating their singing, their posture, their enunciation—then move to dinner and evaluate their table manners. Whatever criterion one uses, it will usually be one on which one scores very highly oneself. People who naturally wear old, cheap clothes mercilessly judge those who wear fancy clothes for their extravagance. People who dress nicely mercilessly judge those who wear inexpensive clothes for their sloppiness and embarrassing lack of style.

Hostility, unchecked, grows into sullen avoidance, silence, or, worse, retaliation. Several monasteries have stories about monks who liked to park their power mowers outside the room or classroom of a fellow monk to irritate him and thus gain revenge for some real or imagined slight. The next step is to gossip and criticize, to complain to people who share one's point of view and so divide the community into opposing camps.

All these sins against community are mentioned in the readings. For those who would like still more analysis of the psychological underlay of human conflict in community, there is the ruthless analysis in Saint Bernard's treatise *On the Stages of Humility and Pride.*

"From our neighbor comes life or death." Enough has been said of death; what about life? The monastic tradition makes much of the notion of mutual service. Where feasible, monks serve each other in the dining room, taking turns at cooking, serving, and doing the dishes. If that is not possible, they at least divide up cleaning tasks among themselves. In this way all the monks serve, and they work together, which can help cement the bonds that connect them.

Beyond such mutual service, there are the needs that arise unexpectedly. Someone suddenly has too much to do, or someone becomes ill. At that point, the monastic tradition says the rest of the community should be willing and able to help. Willing, because of the mutual commitment that binds the community together, and able, because people's schedules are not so inflexible and full that they cannot find time to help a brother, or sister, wife, or child, in need.

To share one's talents with the community and to value the talents of others as though they were one's own was perhaps easier in ages in which there was a stronger sense of community. Yet even today there seems to be no basis, other than our essential interconnectedness, upon which envy and selfishness can be eliminated, and scope given for each person's talents to unfold and contribute to the good of all.

Antony said, "From our neighbor comes life or death. If we win over our brother, we have gained God, but if we scandalize our brother, we have sinned against Christ."

ANTONY, *SAYINGS*

Some brothers came to the Abba Antony and said to him, "Speak a word that tells us how are we to be saved." The old man said to them, "You have heard the Scriptures. That should be enough for you." But they said, "We want to hear from you too, Father." Then the old man said to them, "The Gospel says, if anyone strikes you on the right cheek, turn to him the other also" [Mt 5.39]. They said, "We cannot do that." The old man replied, "If you cannot turn the other cheek, at least allow one cheek to be struck." "We cannot do that either," they said. So he said, "If you are cannot even do that, do not return evil for evil." Once more they said, "We cannot do that either." Then the old man said to his disciple, "Prepare a little brew of corn for these invalids." Then he said to the brothers: "If you cannot do this, or that, what can I do for you? What you need is prayers."

ANTONY, *SAYINGS*

[The evil spirits] envy us at all times. [They corrupt our relations with each other in three noteworthy ways:] the judgments which they sow in our hearts, causing us, when we are sitting alone, to judge the brothers who are not with us; the contempt they set in our hearts by pride when we are hard-hearted and despise each other, when we are bitter against each other with our hard words, grieving at every hour, accusing each other and not ourselves, thinking that our struggle is from our fellows, passing judgment on what appears outwardly, while the robbers are all inside our house; and the disputes and divisions we have with each other until we establish our own words to appear justified in the face of each other.

ANTONY, *LETTERS*

[The demons] know that our destruction is from our neighbor, and our life is also from our neighbor.

ANTONY, *LETTERS*

Whoever sins against his neighbor sins against himself.

ANTONY, *LETTERS*

Whoever knows himself knows all human beings. . . . But whoever can love himself loves all human beings.

ANTONY, *LETTERS*

And likewise if someone, being human, is found blamewor-thy, we do not judge him. God is the judge, and in each case he has, as judges under himself, the successors of the Apostles, able in Spirit to "judge according to what is right" [Jn 7.24]. As for us among the flock, we must be compas-sionate and merciful to each other.

LIFE OF PACHOMIUS

For what is greater than such a vision, to see the invisible God in a visible human being, his temple?

LIFE OF PACHOMIUS

One day Abba Pachomius himself told the brothers about this, which is a kind of vision: "I once saw a large place with many pillars in it. And there were in the place many men unable to see where to go, some of them going around the pillars, thinking they had traveled a long dis-tance toward the light. And a voice [resounded] from all di-rections: 'Behold! Here is the light!' They would turn back to find it, only to hear the voice again and turn back an-other time. There was great wretchedness. Afterwards I saw a lamp moving, followed by many men. Four of them saw it and the others followed them, each holding his neigh-bor's shoulder lest he go astray in the dark. And if anyone let go of the man in front of him, he would go astray with those following him. Recognizing two of them who had let go of their neighbor, I shouted to them, 'Hold on, lest you lose yourselves and the others.' And guided by the lamp, those who followed it came up to this light through an opening."

He told these things to some brothers in private. And we heard it from them much later, along with the following interpretation: "This world is the dark [place, which is dark] because of error, each heretic thinking to have the right path. The lamp is the faith of Christ, which saves those who believe aright and leads to the kingdom of God."

LIFE OF PACHOMIUS

It is essential, then, to be on guard against remembrance of wrongs, for many terrible consequences develop from it: envy, sadness, malicious talk. The evil of these vices is lethal, even if they seem to occur in small doses.

LIFE OF SYNCLETICA

[Those] courageous in disposition and strong in will, live with the weak and share their lives in their desire to save them. And, to be sure, they are censured by people on the outside and mocked by those who see them spending their lives with people less disciplined. [Their behavior] is like the Lord's for the Lord ate with tax collectors and sinners. Their attitude is characterized by brotherly love rather than self-love for they regard those who sin as houses on fire; giving no thought to their own interests, they apply their efforts to save what belongs to others. . . . Good people have placed their own possessions second to the salvation of others. This is the sign of genuine love. These people are the custodians of pure love.

LIFE OF SYNCLETICA

Give aid to the poor, clothe the naked, visit the sick, bury the dead, help those in difficulty, console the sorrowing.

RULE OF BENEDICT

Above all, the cellarer should have humility, and when he has no material goods to give someone who asks, he should at least offer a kind reply.

RULE OF BENEDICT

Let them serve one another, and let none be excused from kitchen duty, unless they are sick or occupied with some important business, because from such service a greater reward and charity are acquired. . . . Helpers should be provided for those who are weak so that they will not find their work depressing. In fact, let all have help according to the size of the community and the nature of the place. The rest should serve one another in love.

RULE OF BENEDICT

Before and above all else, care is to be given to the sick, for Christ is really served in them. . . . But let the sick keep in mind that they are served for the honor of God and not distress those who are serving them by their excessive demands.

RULE OF BENEDICT

The weakness of the elderly and of children should be kept in mind, and the rule should not be strictly applied to them in regard to food. Rather, let them be treated with loving consideration.

RULE OF BENEDICT

Special care is to be taken that on no occasion anyone presume to defend another in the monastery or, at it were, to take another under his protection.

RULE OF BENEDICT

Love your enemies.

RULE OF BENEDICT

Let them vie in giving one another honor. Let them patiently bear everyone's weaknesses of body and behavior. Let them compete in obeying one another. Let no one do what he judges beneficial to himself, but what is better for another. Let them practice chaste love in the community. Let them fear God out of love. Let them love their abbot with a sincere and humble love. Let them prefer nothing to Christ. May Christ lead us together to eternal life.

RULE OF BENEDICT

What can I, a beggar and a pauper, a worm and ashes, what can I return to my God, if not that I keep his command with all my heart? It is your command that we love one another.

ANSELM OF CANTERBURY,
PRAYERS AND MEDITATIONS

[Gertrude] was wont to say that as long as she kept them for herself and her own enjoyment, all the things that she, unworthy and ungrateful, received unmerited from the overflowing goodness of the Lord seemed to her like treasures hidden in muck. However, if she shared them with a neighbor, these favors became like a precious stone set in pure gold.

GERTRUDE THE GREAT,
THE HERALD OF DIVINE LOVE

Do not look on others with too severe a countenance, nor let your mind be stern and bitter. Instead, be transformed by kindly feelings, and show yourself to have a gentle, benevolent, affable, and ready heart toward everyone. But if anger or indignation should suddenly move or provoke you, or you feel bitterness toward anyone, take care not to give in to this wicked impulse, but reprove, soften, and extinguish it as much as you can. Regret that your heart is still so bitter. Humble yourself and ask God's help. Once he has bountifully poured the sweetness of charity into you, you will no longer be bitter. Often God allows his chosen friends to be prone to anger, so that they may know themselves more deeply and stand fast more firmly in humility.

BLOSIUS, *SPIRITUAL MIRROR*

Be there with a ready will for those who need your help.

BLOSIUS, *SPIRITUAL MIRROR*

[Monastic community] has been from the beginning, a
grace of communion in shared quest and a participated
light. It is then a charism of special love and of mutual aid in
the attainment of a difficult end, in the living of a hazardous
and austere life. . . . Monastic work, obedience, poverty,
chastity, are all in some way colored and tempered by the
communal charism of brotherhood in pilgrimage and in
hope.

THOMAS MERTON,
CONTEMPLATION IN A WORLD OF ACTION

One is not absolutely alone, . . . one cannot live and die
for himself alone. My life and my death are not purely and
simply my own business. I live by and for others, and my
death involves others.

THOMAS MERTON,
CONJECTURES OF A GUILTY BYSTANDER

How glad I am to find this short chapter on the celebration
of Vigils or Matins on the anniversaries of the saints. It
adds another dimension to the sense of time and order that
Benedict is giving us. . . . I am inserted into a community
here on earth; I am also part of a community in the wider
context of the Church beyond time and space. It makes me
think in gratitude of what I owe to the saints, living and
dead, known and unknown.

ESTHER DE WAAL, *A LIFE-GIVING WAY*

There is to be acceptance of people who come from very
different places (using this metaphorically as well as literally). There is to be willingness to hear "reasonable criticisms or observations" and to learn from the example of
others. . . . In a world that builds barriers, puts up walls,

keeps the other out, and is looking for certainty, we turn to the Rule and find a man who insists on balance, mutual respect, reciprocity, openness. [Benedict] . . . refused to live with a closed mind.

ESTHER DE WAAL, *A LIFE-GIVING WAY*

Complaining is the acid that shrivels our own souls and the soul of the community around us as well.

SR. JOAN CHITTISTER, *THE RULE OF BENEDICT*

CHAPTER 5

Hospitality

A month ago a missionary priest from Mexico, on sabbatical from teaching in a seminary, asked if he could stay at our monastery for four or five weeks. The community gladly said yes. Today I received a letter from a longtime friend, who wrote that her son may write to ask if he can stay at our monastery for a while. He is searching and finds life somewhat mystifying. He would like a place of retreat where he could strive for perspective and a plan. If he writes, I hope we invite him to spend some time with us. Today such requests to monasteries are not uncommon, but they are hard to honor. There are so many factors: groups wanting to rent the guest house, guests who might be frightened by the presence of a stranger none of us knows, the costs of room and board, possible legal liability.

The situation in early monasticism was quite different. In a harsh desert environment, where hospitality was a much simpler issue, a matter of life or death, monks never hesitated to be hospitable. In such places people don't lock the doors to the storerooms when they leave home, and they welcome whoever comes. The desert fathers taught that monks should interrupt their prayers and break their fasts in order to welcome guests. Even when monasteries appeared in fertile lands and cities, they maintained this tradition of hospitality.

Benedict and the tradition after him struggled with treating all people fairly. Noble guests and bishops received one sort of hospitality, paupers and pilgrims another. Yet everyone knew that if Christ came to visit, he would be found among the paupers. So the ideal remained: treat all as though they were Christ.

Today, the great enemies of any such universal hospitality are busyness, fear, and professionalism. If I don't have time to talk to the person calling for help, hospitality is out of the question. The advent of a guest, like the unanticipated needs of fellow monks, is a gauge of our use of time. If we have no time for the guest, our day is too full. However, busyness can be an independent sin against the stranger, or it can be an excuse concocted because we don't want to say we are afraid or prefer to remain uninvolved.

We are afraid of violence and sexual assault, of robbery and vandalism. We want to avoid aggressive intrusions into our business and our privacy by salesmen and poll takers. Violence and intrusion are genuine dangers, but perhaps we have too much to lose, too many things clung to so tightly that the possibility of losing them looms too large. Professionalism becomes a problem when, rather than welcome needy strangers, I immediately think how to shunt them to the appropriate agency, get them a voucher from the food bank, or send them to the downtown mission.

Positively, hospitable people have more fun. They meet Christ in the strangest guises. Several years ago I was spending Lent at a mission in the high desert about five miles from a town of one hundred people. The enterprises of the town closed up on Sundays. Two vans of people drove up and knocked on my door. They were looking for a bathroom. There was none in the town and no trees in the desert. My little church and trailer looked semiofficial, so to me they came as their last hope. A string of fourteen people snaked from the inside of the trailer and out onto the porch. Nobody talked or made any fast moves until after they had reached the head of the line. Then we visited a bit, but I couldn't convince any of them to have some juice or a soft drink.

Observers tell us that contemporary American society needs to strengthen the communities that are intermediate between the government on the one hand and the family on the other: neighborhood, clubs, service organizations, parishes, and all the sorts of voluntary organizations. It is said that if each church in America would sponsor one family's housing, all involuntary homelessness would be eliminated. If neighbors could be hospitable to each other's children, some of the difficulties latchkey children experience would be solved.

Hospitality requires discipline on the part of the host. The host provides a place where the guest or stranger is secure and respected. The host may provide options, but it is not the host's task to fill up all the guest's time with activities or her space with noise or things. The good host has no ambition to control the space made available to strangers or to control the strangers themselves.

Presupposing the proper management of time, requiring that we overcome some of our fears and our need to control and that we invite people as equals and indeed as Christ, hospitality is an art and a school requiring the exercise of most of the qualities of character valued in the Benedictine tradition and discussed in the rest of this book.

⌒

A brother came to visit a hermit. As he was taking his leave, he said: "Pardon me, father, for I have caused you to violate your rule." But the hermit answered: "My rule is to refresh you and send you back in peace."

SAYINGS OF THE DESERT FATHERS AND MOTHERS

A hermit lived near a monastery. He lived a very austere life. Now it happened that some visitors came to the monastery and caused him to eat outside of the usual mealtime. After that, the brothers said to him: "Father, were you not distressed?" He said to them: "My distress is to do my own will."

SAYINGS OF THE DESERT FATHERS AND MOTHERS

There was talk of an old man who dwelt in Syria near a desert road. This was his task: whenever a monk came from the desert, he cheerfully provided him with refreshment. One day there came a hermit for whom he wished to provided refreshment. However, the other did not wish to accept anything, saying that he was fasting. The old man was saddened and said to him: "Do not neglect your servant, I pray you, nor despise me: let us pray together. See this tree

here? We will yield to whichever of us causes it to bow
when he places his knee to the ground and prays." The hermit knelt then in order to pray, and nothing happened. Then
the hospitable monk knelt and the tree bent over with him.
Reassured in this way, they gave thanks to God.

SAYINGS OF THE DESERT FATHERS AND MOTHERS

Two brothers came one day to see an old man. Now the old
man had the custom of eating only every other day. When
he saw the brothers, he rejoiced and said: "Fasting brings its
recompense; but whoever eats because of charity fulfills two
precepts: he abandons his own will, and he fulfills the law of
charity." And he gave refreshment to the brothers.

SAYINGS OF THE DESERT FATHERS AND MOTHERS

All guests who arrive should be received as Christ. . . .
When guests are announced, let them be met by the superior or some members of the community with every mark
of love. Let them first pray together, and so socialize in
peace. . . . All arriving or departing guests should be greeted
with profound humility. . . . One must adore Christ in
them, for he is in fact the one who is received.

RULE OF BENEDICT

Let all kindness be shown to guests. The superior should
break his fast for the guest unless it is a special fast day that
must be observed. . . . Let the abbot wash the hands of the
guests; the feet of all guests should be washed by both the
abbot and the community.

RULE OF BENEDICT

The greatest care is to be shown in the reception of the
poor and of pilgrims, because in them especially, Christ is
received; fear of the rich demands that the wealthy be
treated with respect.

RULE OF BENEDICT

[Wulfstan's hospitality to some high-ranking visitors from Rome] left nothing undone, so that they would know the bounteous hospitality of the English. . . . Every day Wulfstan took care of three poor people. At the Lord's command he gave them their daily bread and washed their feet.

LIFE OF WULFSTAN

O God, you visit the humble and you console us with mutual love. Stretch forth your grace to our community so that we may become aware of your coming into our midst through those in whom you dwell.

WULFSTAN OF WORCESTER, *PORTIFOLIUM*

For it is as though Christ is present when guests arrive and they receive them, or when guests depart and they bless them as they go, or they bow before the guests out of reverence for Christ or ask pardon from them. Benedict adds immediately: "And after this let all courtesy be shown him."

HILDEGARD OF BINGEN,
EXPLANATION OF THE RULE OF BENEDICT

When upright men and friends arrive, [the monks] can speak with them at suitable times about whatever is proper, even if it is outside the time for community conversation.

LOUIS DE BLOIS, *MONASTIC STATUTES*

What does it mean to receive another as Christ? I find that the story of Benedict at Subiaco, which St. Gregory records in the *Dialogues,* gives me an illuminating glimpse. Benedict has been alone in the cave for three years, in silence and in solitude, when he is visited by a priest—sent specially by God, who wished Benedict to have company at Easter. The scene is charming and really very humorous. Benedict is so deep in prayer and so far away from everything that he has no idea that it is Easter, but to the priest's greeting he replies: "Easter it is indeed since I have the joy of seeing you." In the face of the first person that he sees, Benedict finds the first fruits of the resurrection and of the new world to which he is called.

ESTHER DE WAAL, *A LIFE-GIVING WAY*

We cannot be too busy, too professional, too removed from the world of the poor to receive the poor and sustain the poor. . . . To practice hospitality in our world, it may be necessary to evaluate all the laws and all the promotions and all the invitation lists of corporate and political society from the point of view of the people who never make the lists. Then hospitality may demand that we work to change things.

SR. JOAN CHITTISTER, *THE RULE OF BENEDICT*

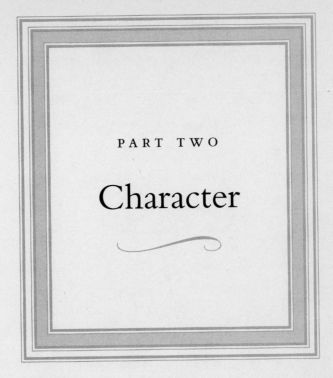

PART TWO

Character

HAVING LOOKED AT THE FIVE activities into which the Benedictine tradition divides the monk's day, we turn now to the sort
of person that tradition thought a monk should be. A monk was to
have certain qualities of character that guided the way he carried out
those five activities and were honed and strengthened in the process.

I am not the first person in Benedictine history to draw up a list
of desirable traits. Speaking in one of his homilies about the workings
of the Holy Spirit, Bede distinguished virtues that are stable character
traits, and unusual gifts that come and go. Bede's list has a monastic
ring to it:

> Note that the Holy Spirit always remained in the Lord, but in holy
> men and women, while they still bear their mortal bodies, the Spirit
> partly remains and partly leaves, perhaps to return again later. The
> Spirit remains within them so that they may be zealous for good deeds,
> love voluntary poverty, seek gentleness, mourn with desire for the
> eternal, hunger and thirst for justice, embrace mercy, purity of heart,
> and the tranquillity of peace, and also so that they may not be afraid to
> suffer persecution for the sake of acting justly and they may desire to
> dedicate themselves to alms, prayers, fasting, and the rest of the fruits
> of the Spirit. He withdraws for a time so that they do not always have
> the ability to cure the sick, raise the dead, cast out demons, or even
> prophesy. The Spirit always remains so that they can have virtue and
> live wondrously. The Spirit comes intermittently so that they can man-
> ifest to others through miraculous signs what they are within.

Saint Gertrude wrote in her *Spiritual Exercises:*

Dear Jesus, . . .
make me perfect in fearing you.
Make me pleasing to you
in humility of spirit,
in sisterly charity,
in chaste simplicity,
in humble modesty,
in purity of heart,
in the guarding of my senses,
in holiness of life,
in ready obedience,
in gentle patience,
in spiritual discipline,
in freely chosen poverty,
in holy leniency,
in maturity of conduct,
in cheerfulness of spirit, and
in all truth,
in good conscience,
in steadfast faith,
in holy perseverance,
in strength of hope,
in fullness of charity, and
in the blessed consummation of your cherishing-love:
so that the thornbush of my heart may be converted
into a paradise of all virtues and a red berry bush of total
perfection, as if it were a field blessed by the Lord, full
of all peace, holiness, and devotion.

Peter of Celle was fond of such lists also, although he listed components of cloistered life and not simply virtues. A composite of five of his lists in *The School of the Cloister* includes the following: simplicity and frugality in food, drink, clothing, sleep, and speech; external conduct that is humble and acceptable to outsiders; seclusion; fraternal love and obedience to superiors; fear and awareness of death and hell; fear, obedience, and love of God; confession and sorrow for sins; prayer in choir and in private; reading; and perseverance.

Thomas Merton, who agonized over the definition of monastic life and the role of the writer within it, also developed a list in the text of some conferences, printed in *Contemplation in a World of Action*: separation from ordinary life outside the cloister; charismatic freedom; asceticism (the price of freedom); the discipline of listening to God; community; prayer; and penance.

In the end, we are judged by who we have become rather than what we have accomplished. When we are young we may think that doing is more important than being, but time disabuses us of this notion. Most of us find we can accomplish much less than we'd hoped. More important, we discover to our horror that what we do is colored by who we are. Our every vice and defect tends to leave a smudge on the things we do and build and on the people we influence.

Benedict is almost entirely indifferent to material results. He doesn't ask whether the cellarer makes the monastery rich; he asks how the cellarer treats the monks. He does not ask if the abbot is popular, but whether he has helped his monks grow as sons of God and human beings. Monastic success is a matter of people-making for God, not of numbers or affluence or even influence. The monastery is a school of virtue or good habits and a school of divine service. In the end, virtue and divine service coalesce. For the glory of God, said Irenaeus, an early Christian writer, is a human being who is fully alive.

The school of virtue is the community in which one finds oneself. We are life or death for each other. From others we learn honesty. Their presence invites us to live for something greater than ourselves. They are, in fact, the abiding sacrament of Christ. So I must listen humbly to what they say, to what God tells me through them, and then put their message into practice. When life with these others—abbot and fellow monks in the monastery; wife, husband, parent, children, friends, neighbors, and colleagues elsewhere—becomes unbearable, then I will learn patience and the hard lessons of peace. Somehow, with and through them, I will find the strength to resist the lure of an indulgent, consumerist society that is confused about what makes people whole and happy.

Virtue does not give us easy answers or certainty. Virtue hones our skills so that in each situation we can listen carefully to our hearts, to the advice or commands of others, to the still whisper of God, and then act with discretion. Discretion, we shall see, is the pivotal monastic virtue. Rooted in self-knowledge and attentiveness, discretion guides us in each situation. There are rules and they are necessary, but they are secondary. Listening and wise choices are primary. Mozart couldn't have composed without staffs, and scales and tempo, but his genius was in how he composed something unique and beautiful within that framework. Each of us is called to compose a unique and beautiful person, with the rules of morality and the circumstances of our lives to provide parameters and the voice of God and the advice of others to inspire us.

⌒

[The Virtues declare:] The Word of God grew bright in human form, and therefore we shine with him, building up the members of his beautiful body.

HILDEGARD OF BINGEN, *ORDO VIRTUTUM*

The one who has set his foot on the way of the virtues lives more securely in the cloister than out of it, for as the proverb says: "Woe to those who are alone; when they fall, they have no one to help them up" [Eccl 4.9].

JOHN TRITHEMIUS, *RULE*

To attain the promises of God, we need above all continuous exercise in the virtues; for however firm one's commitment to some good may be, if it is not renewed daily, it quickly dies out.

JOHN TRITHEMIUS, *RULE*

This school of virtue—the monastic life!

JOHN TRITHEMIUS, *RULE*

This is the school of virtues, in which the reader-instructor is Christ, the book is conscience, and the rod is the fear of the Lord.

JOHN TRITHEMIUS, *RULE*

Benedict does not give me certainty. He does not give me easy answers. He gives me a focus, shows me the stance. He is forming me so that I can respond to each new situation, each new demand. He knows about the weakness and frailty of human nature and how we tend to cling when we are frightened and insecure. That sort of dependency is disastrous. Benedict has such a respect for each one of us that he pays us this compliment of refusing to stifle our freedom.

ESTHER DE WAAL, *A LIFE-GIVING WAY*

CHAPTER 6

Silence and Speech

Silence and speech are the two forms of communication that cement community. Writing for their fellow monks but with suggestions that could find a place in any human community from family to parish, Thomas Merton speaks of true and false communication and Jean Mabillon searches for ways in which speech could be formed into an instrument for sharing information.

The first word in the *Rule of Benedict* is "Listen!" Monastic life is a training in the art of listening, which begins in silence, develops in attentiveness, and is perfected in communication. The first seven chapters of Benedict's *Rule* are devoted to fundamental topics. Chapter 5 is on obedience (a form of active listening); and chapter 6 is on reticence. In chapter 4, Benedict urges monks to avoid much talking, evil or silly talk, and raucous laughter. These admonitions are repeated in chapter 7 regarding humility, which is itself a prerequisite for effective listening and communication.

Silence is a dwindling resource in the contemporary world. Rock music blasts at the onlookers at NBA games, country music played over loudspeakers entertains patrons at self-service gas stations, the insipid music in elevators and on phone answering systems is presumably designed to soothe those who find waiting an aggravation. Meanwhile, sirens provide an overlay of random noise that sounds above the ordinary buzzes and bangs and squeaks of daily life.

Silence is usually the first impression of visitors to a monastery. Such silence is not necessarily emptiness, a mere background to sound. Silence can be full and alert, or a static-free medium of communication.

The principal enemy of interior and exterior silence for most of us is our own tongue. Perhaps we fear the emptiness within us and take refuge in speech. Speech serving as an escape is likely to be speech devoid of serious content and full of ego.

Saint Benedict forbids laughter. This is startling, because among the most valuable members of any community are the cheerful people who can get others to laugh or to smile. Even practical jokers have a contribution to make. Perhaps Benedict was thinking of raucous laughter, or laughter at the expense of others, or laughter at off-color jokes, all of which may be implied by the Latin words he uses for "laughter." Certainly laughter, like silence and speech, can be used for purposes of ridicule and unhealthy social control. However, a genuine smile is almost always a grace, and an occasional all-out laugh can be very therapeutic.

Benedict was insistent that monks listen to each other. The abbot should not make decisions without consulting his advisers or even the whole community. Monks were to listen to the abbot, since he held the place of the Lord Christ among them. Elders were to lend understanding ears to the troubles of the neophytes and other members of the community. All were to listen respectfully to the ideas of the young, because God often reveals the best course of action to them. The applications of these admonitions beyond the monastery are obvious enough. The way to find out if we are really listening is to ask those who speak to us.

Listening requires selectivity. We should avoid gossip and chatter, flattery and deception, detraction and slander. Putting down others so that one might rise is a much-used strategy, and one that leaves speaker, listener, and victim violated. Syncletica was eloquent on the need to avoid malicious and quarrelsome talk.

Speech should arise from humility. It should be at the service of truth. From a truthful heart should come truthful words. Each of us should have someone with whom we can be completely honest about ourselves. The truths about ourselves that we conceal from everyone destroy our inner peace.

Complaining corrodes community life. Humility is one hedge against complaining: few of us deserve what we have, much less have a right to more. Some complaining is objectively justified and would not occur if there were legitimate avenues of communication through which people could make problems and difficulties known and find solutions to them. In fact, there are times when silence is sinful. One must speak up to protect the innocent or abused, to try to correct those who are wrecking their lives, to defend the truth from falsehood, to report that the king is wearing no clothes. An honest argument is better than passive-aggressive silence.

If the highest use of speech is the praise of God, teaching others cannot rank far behind. The monastic tradition emphasizes the superior's duty to teach by both word and example. Surely the same duty applies to every teacher, every parent, every mentor. Louis de Blois warns us: before giving an answer or advice, pray to God for guidance, then speak humbly, prudently, and wisely. Never answer harshly.

Some brothers were coming from Scetis to see Abba Antony. As they were boarding a boat to go there, they found an old man who also wanted to go there. The brothers did not know him. They sat in the boat, occupied by turns with the words of the Fathers, Scripture and their manual work. The old man remained silent. When they arrived at the place to disembark, they found that the old man was going to the cell of Abba Antony too. When they reached the place, Antony said to them, "You found this old man a good companion for the journey?" Then he said to the old man, "You have brought many good brethren with you, father." The old man said, "Certainly they are good, but there is no door on their house, and anyone can enter the stable and untie the ass." He meant that the brethren said whatever came into their mouths.

ANTONY, *SAYINGS*

Again the Spirit teaches the tongue its own purity, since the tongue is very sick. . . . But the mind is strengthened by the Spirit; first it is purified, then it learns discretion in the words it delivers to the tongue so that they are free of hypocrisy and self-will.

ANTONY, *LETTERS*

[Pachomius] called Theodore and said to him, "When the brothers come out from table in the evening, give your ministry to someone else and come to where we gather for the instruction on Sunday." And when Theodore came to the instruction, he told him, "Stand here in the midst of the brothers and speak the word of God to us"—as he used to do himself. He obeyed and stood up, though unwillingly, and he began to speak what the Lord gave him. All stood, including Abba Pachomius who listened as one of them. But some, out of pride, were vexed and they returned to their tents so as not to listen to him. The one who stood [to speak] was younger in human age.

After the instruction and prayer Pachomius sat down as was his custom and he began saying, "You have heard what was said. Whose was it? The speaker's or the Lord's? And those who were vexed, for what reason were they vexed? Because he is younger? But we find that the Lord said about a child, 'Anyone who receives a child like this in my name receives me.' Was I not standing and listening as one of you? And I tell you that I did not only pretend but I was listening with all my heart, as one thirsty for water. For worthy indeed of all acceptance is the word of the Lord, as it is written. Wretched are those who went away; they have estranged themselves from God's mercies."

LIFE OF PACHOMIUS

In the monastery of Phbow there were ten ancient brothers who, although they were chaste in body, often used to murmur and would not listen to the Man of God [Pachomius] with faith. Since he was patient and loved their souls, especially the ones for whom he had been toiling for a long time, admonishing and exhorting them, he did not want to neglect them. He mourned for them before the Lord, humbling his soul with fasting, spending six days without food and up to forty nights without sleep. And his body became extremely lean and feeble. Then the Lord heard him and each one of them received the understanding to be healed from his error as much as possible.

LIFE OF PACHOMIUS

Moreover, by closing her senses as if they were windows, Syncletica continued to converse in solitude with her bridegroom, referring to the following passage: "I belong to my beloved and my beloved belongs to me." If conversations of a questionable and unedifying nature were taking place, she avoided them, retreating to the inner treasure chambers of her soul; but where enlightened and helpful counsels were being offered, she concentrated her whole mind on receiving what was being said.

LIFE OF SYNCLETICA

Malicious talk, therefore, is a serious and troublesome matter, for it is the sustenance and recreation of some people. You should not, however, accept empty hearsay, lest you become a receptacle for other peoples' evils. Keep your own soul unlittered. For, by accepting the foul-smelling garbage of words, you will introduce stains to your prayer through your thoughts, and without cause you will hate your associates. For when your hearing has been drenched with the misanthropy of malicious talkers, you will look on all people without generosity, just as the eye has a blurred image of objects when it is inordinately obsessed with color.

LIFE OF SYNCLETICA

There is no need, then, to be quarrelsome. Do not spend long periods of time in extended conversations, for the Devil can actually do harm through inopportune chitchat.

LIFE OF SYNCLETICA

Listen, O child, to the commands of your master, and bend the ear of your heart.

RULE OF BENEDICT

With our eyes open to the deifying light and our ears at-tuned, let us hear the divine voice that calls to us each day and admonishes us: "If today you hear his voice, do not harden your hearts."

RULE OF BENEDICT

Offer advice with all the deference of humility, and do not presume to defend your point of view obstinately.

RULE OF BENEDICT

Utter truth from the heart and from the mouth.

RULE OF BENEDICT

Be neither a complainer nor a detractor.

RULE OF BENEDICT

Reveal to a spiritual elder evil thoughts that come to your heart.

RULE OF BENEDICT

Keep your mouth from evil or depraved talk, do not love much talking, do not talk mindlessly or in a way that prompts laughter, do not love much or violent laughter.

RULE OF BENEDICT

Confess to God daily with tears and sighs your past sins, and correct them for the future.

RULE OF BENEDICT

Do not wish to be called holy before you are.

RULE OF BENEDICT

To be silent and to listen befits the disciple.

RULE OF BENEDICT

The ninth step of humility is that the monk forbid his tongue to speak, and keeping quiet, not speak unless he is asked a question. . . . The tenth step of humility is that one not be quick and ready to laugh, because it is written: "The fool raises his voice in laughter." The eleventh step of humility is that when a monk speaks, he does so gently and without laughter, and that he speaks few and reasonable words humbly, with restraint.

RULE OF BENEDICT

If any brother is found to be defiant or disobedient or proud or murmuring or in some other way contravening the holy rule and the commands of his seniors, then, in accord with our Lord's command, he should be admonished a first and second time secretly by his seniors. If he will not amend, let him be corrected publicly.

RULE OF BENEDICT

Monks should strive for silence at all times, but especially during the night. . . . Exceptions to this may arise from the needs of guests or from a command of the abbot, but these should be taken care of with the utmost seriousness and gentle restraint.

RULE OF BENEDICT

If a visiting monk . . . reasonably and with loving humility singles out something in the community for criticism, the abbot should prudently consider the matter, because the Lord may have sent the visitor for this very purpose.

RULE OF BENEDICT

At the gate of the monastery there should be a wise old man who knows how to receive a message and respond, one whose age will keep him from wandering. This porter

should have a room near the gate, so that those who come
to the monastery will always find there someone who can
respond to them. As soon as anyone knocks or a poor man
calls, let him respond: "Thanks be to God," or "Bless you";
and let him answer him promptly with all the kindness of
the fear of God and with the fervor of charity.

RULE OF BENEDICT

If anyone . . . senses that a superior or anyone else is irritated
or angry with him, even slightly, let him immediately lie flat
on the ground before his feet making satisfaction, until the
disturbance is cured by a blessing.

RULE OF BENEDICT

I would like you to take a few moments to consider what
our pride does. When we notice that some of the mysteries
of the Scriptures that . . . we have learned with the Lord's
help and that we are discussing are beyond the grasp of some
of the more simple brethren, we are likely to immediately
extol ourselves and look down on them. We take pride in
our almost unique and wide-ranging learning, as if there
were not many people much more learned than we whom
we do not want to despise us. We enjoy ridiculing those
who are less educated than we and make no effort to remember that entry into the kingdom lies open not for those
who only learn the mysteries of faith and the commands of
the Creator by meditating on them, but for those who put
into practice the things they have learned.

BEDE, *HOMILIES ON THE GOSPELS*

Those who conceive the grace of heavenly inspiration in
their mind, those who have learned words of exhortation
by which they are able to comfort their neighbor, must not
hide in silence the good that they know. They should com-
municate it right away to their brothers by speaking
openly.

BEDE, *HOMILIES ON THE GOSPELS*

[As a boy,] Wulfstan rejected, first of all in himself, then in others, foolish talking, which is a source for temptations. He matured so quickly that he gathered boys of his own age and even older boys to pray that by living well they might provide each other the example of a good life. If he did something wrong, they would reprove him; he gladly accepted correction.

LIFE OF WULFSTAN

When Wulfstan noticed that the moral conduct of the people was declining because of lack of preaching, every Sunday and major feast in church, he poured out on them the counsels of salvation.

LIFE OF WULFSTAN

This is surely wisdom: if you live well, if your deeds precede your words.

LIFE OF WULFSTAN

We must not regard with contempt the rebuke of a just man, for such a rebuke is the destruction of sin and a healing for the heart, as well as a path for God to the soul. We should never neglect to listen to any discourse that supports piety, virtues, and good behavior, for it is a way by which the salvation of God is manifested. . . . If you are not only moved to compunction by the conversation, but even converted totally to the Lord, swearing and promising to keep the judgment of his justice, you will also know that he is already present, especially if you feel yourself burning with his love.

BERNARD OF CLAIRVAUX,
ON THE SONG OF SONGS

If a brother is addicted to some fault, a man of the church who already has received the Spirit will try to instruct him right away in the same spirit of gentleness, keeping an eye on himself lest he fall into the same sin.

BERNARD OF CLAIRVAUX,
ON THE SONG OF SONGS

[In accusing a brother of a fault,] if it is manifest, use the gentle words of the gentle lamb. . . . If it is hidden, correct it privately; don't make a public disclosure. If it is a powerful person or prelate, follow the example of Nathan's correction of David and Noah's two sons: proceed cautiously and indirectly.

PETER OF CELLE,
THE SCHOOL OF THE CLOISTER

Silence is neither mute nor talkative. . . . In such silence holy desires, peace and calm of heart, and true purity grow and multiply, in the absence of windy and vain talkativeness . . . which sows discord.

PETER OF CELLE,
THE SCHOOL OF THE CLOISTER

[There are seven reasons for silence:] tranquillity, profession, peace, to subdue feelings and inclinations of the heart, to detach oneself from secular affairs, to study the law of God, for the sake of contemplation.

PETER OF CELLE,
THE SCHOOL OF THE CLOISTER

True confession omits nothing, for in it one accuses oneself of all excesses both of the flesh and of higher reason. It is one thing to sin by the senses, which you have in common with the animal kingdom; it is another to sin by reason, which you have as proper to your humanity. . . . Sins of the senses are those that arise from weakness or surprise, for which you owe a lesser penalty and penance. Sins of the reason, which occur from deliberation and ambition, are subject to the more stringent penalty.

PETER OF CELLE,
THE SCHOOL OF THE CLOISTER

Here the human heart can be in possession of itself, for it has narrowed all questions to one. Having excluded all that is alien, your heart must devote its attention to its own affairs. That one question is great, but not insoluble, if you always zealously seek yourself in God and God in yourself. However, there is a preliminary question: to seek yourself in yourself. . . . Our solitary inquiry goes better in silence and is studied more deeply in solitude.

PETER OF CELLE,
ON AFFLICTION AND READING

Falsehood does not rejoice with the truth, but exaggerates about what is not and cannot be, and it does this with exaltation and unjust happiness. Falsehood tells no one the truth, but tells lies about strange things that no one could see. Falsehood tries to do this against God and his saints, in whom God works many miracles. That a person sins in fleshly desires is human, but when he resorts to lying he is inhuman. For lies entangle themselves with more lies, like a snake hiding itself in its lair.

HILDEGARD OF BINGEN,
BOOK OF LIFE'S MERITS

However, since it is almost inhuman for a person to be silent always and never speak, the same father [Benedict] left this matter, as he did many other things, in the power of the judgment of the abbot. He may provide a suitable time for the disciples to speak together about matters that are good and necessary, so that they will not be burdened with weariness because of excessive silence.

HILDEGARD OF BINGEN,
EXPLANATION OF THE RULE OF BENEDICT

If Gertrude had an opportunity to give some advice or suggestion to someone, she put aside all her usual modesty (a virtue that shone brilliantly among all her other virtues) and ignored all inordinate human respect. Confident in him who had armed her with the faith and to whom she wanted to subject the universe, she dipped the pen of her tongue in the blood of her heart, and fashioned words filled with such great love and profound wisdom that the most hardened and contrary people, if there was a spark of piety in them, felt themselves touched by what they heard, at least to the extent that they conceived the will or desire to amend.

GERTRUDE THE GREAT,
THE HERALD OF DIVINE LOVE

We are going to render an account to God, not only for our idle words, but also for our ill-considered silence.

JOHN TRITHEMIUS, *RULE*

For the devout mind, the first cause of ruin is lack of attention. . . . The cause of all evil is a negligent heart.

JOHN TRITHEMIUS, *RULE*

If anyone seeks advice from you, recognize in your heart that you cannot give a suitable answer on your own. Turn to God and pray silently: "O Lord God, who are in me, deign to speak through me whatever pleases you and is most suited to your honor and the salvation of souls." Then say humbly, prudently, and wisely whatever should be said. If you have spoken well, attribute that to God; if badly, ascribe that to yourself. At all times avoid unseasonable harshness in your speech. Be truthful in speech, and avoid both false show and flattery. Do not be eager to say anything that blames others.

LOUIS DE BLOIS, *SPIRITUAL DOCTRINE*

In speaking, be circumspect, polite, restrained, and without fault. Love reasonable silence. Do not say things that are utterly vain or useless, and that arouse unbridled laughter. . . . Avoid excessively sharp and biting words, and abominate the vice of detraction and slander. . . . Also, do not affirm as certain anything that you do not know for sure. . . . If it should happen that you hear someone saying mocking or wicked or unkind words, end the conversation politely, or even modestly and discretely correct the one who was speaking.

LOUIS DE BLOIS, *SPIRITUAL MIRROR*

Have a special love for solitude, silence, and restraint in speech. Always be more ready to listen to talking than to utter it. Don't be impatient, unruly, loud, or contentious in your words, but say true and proper things without any deception and modestly, humbly, and with goodwill.

LOUIS DE BLOIS, *SPIRITUAL MIRROR*

Conferences about spiritual matters are very useful; they have been held in religious communities from the beginning. There are two kinds. One sort consists in talks given by superiors to their subjects; the other consists in conversations among religious regarding matters of piety. . . . This sort of conference is no longer held in communities, but one could usefully reestablish it. Such conferences might be no less advantageous than the conferences given by superiors. . . . Let me indicate my thoughts about reestablishing this holy practice and propose two or three ways of conducting such conferences. . . . The first would be to undertake in common the reading of some important material . . . and to let each have the freedom to indicate what difficulties he found in the reading. . . . The second method would be to propose subjects or materials for conferences for the entire year or one by one. . . . A third method, no less useful, is that a qualified religious give a lecture on some determined subject, and that he respond to questions proposed to him.

JEAN MABILLON,
TREATISE ON THE STUDIES OF MONKS

To live in communion, in genuine dialogue with others is absolutely necessary if man is to remain human. But to live in the midst of others, sharing nothing with them but the common noise and the general distraction, isolates a man in the worst way, separates him from reality in a way that is almost painless.

THOMAS MERTON,
NEW SEEDS OF CONTEMPLATION

"Listen!" I could take that as a summary of the whole of
Benedict's teaching. I could spend the rest of my life pondering on the implications of that one word. It plunges
me at once into a personal relationship. It takes me away
from the danger of talking about God and not communing
with him.

ESTHER DE WAAL, *A LIFE-GIVING WAY*

[The three moments of the Prodigal's way back to his Father
are] first the listening and responding, obedience (for that
is what the word means, *obaudiens,* to listen intently), then
the *metanoia,* or turning (which is what *conversatio morum*
involves, continual conversion, journeying on), and then
the stability (from the Latin *stare,* to stand), being in the
place of firm ground.

ESTHER DE WAAL, *A LIFE-GIVING WAY*

Anyone who loves words will tend to let themselves be
satisfied by them, and as a result stop short of true satisfaction. For true satisfaction . . . comes when I am silent and
listen. . . . When God's voice is drowned out by incessant
clamor, whether inner or outer, in whatever shape or form,
then continuous dialogue with God becomes impossible.
An inner monologue with myself, constant chatter with
others, the invasion of the spoken word through the press
and television are all the ever-present realities in my daily
life over which I need to exercise some sort of discipline if
I am to keep any quiet inner space in which to listen to the
Word.

ESTHER DE WAAL, *A LIFE-GIVING WAY*

Speaking is something that must be undertaken reverently
and responsibly. If I reflect on what Benedict is saying, I
find guidelines for my own situation. This is not a call for
absolute silence (silence can after all become an instrument
of the passive aggressive, and it can be isolating, hurtful), but

for a restrained, disciplined, and thoughtful approach to speech.

ESTHER DE WAAL, *A LIFE-GIVING WAY*

Clearly, for Benedict, God is not something to be achieved; God is a presence to be responded to but to whom, without that presence, we cannot respond.

ESTHER DE WAAL, *A LIFE-GIVING WAY*

The end of Benedictine spirituality is to develop a transparent personality. Dissimulation, half answers, vindictive attitudes, a false presentation of self are all barbs in the soul of the monastic. Holiness, this ancient rule says to a culture that has made crafty packaging high art, has something to do with being who we say we are, claiming our truths, opening our hearts, giving ourselves to the other pure and unglossed.

SR. JOAN CHITTISTER,
THE RULE OF BENEDICT

Silence is a cornerstone of Benedictine life and spiritual development, but the goal of monastic silence is not non-talking. The goal of monastic silence and monastic speech is respect for others, a sense of place, a spirit of peace. . . . Silence for its own selfish, insulating sake, silence that is passive-aggressive, silence that is insensitive to the present needs of the other is not Benedictine silence.

SR. JOAN CHITTISTER,
THE RULE OF BENEDICT

Humor and laughter are not necessarily the same thing. Humor permits us to see into life from a fresh and gracious perspective. We learn to take ourselves more lightly in the presence of good humor. Humor gives us the strength to bear what cannot be changed, and the sight to see the human under the pompous.

SR. JOAN CHITTISTER,
THE RULE OF BENEDICT

CHAPTER 7

Reverence

"Fear of the Lord is the beginning of wisdom" (Prv 1.7) is an often repeated assertion of the sages of the Old Testament. The *Rule of Benedict,* which borrows much from the sages' writings, reiterates the same truth. On the one hand, Benedict urges the monk to find Christ in the needy guest and neighbor, but at the same time Benedict warns that God and Christ know our every thought and action and will judge us from them. It is difficult to know which aspect of Benedict's Christology is more demanding and more frightful.

Fear of the Lord is not a sentiment widely acknowledged in our society. For us, God is a merciful God, and nothing more need be said. Hell has become an abstract possibility, not a threatening reality. Our convictions about divine mercy are surely justified by the New Testament. However, a God who is completely and merely merciful is neither just nor justifying. Before such a God, human responsibility does not seem to count for much. Benedict takes God and the possibility of hell very seriously.

A useful first step in dealing with this wide difference between Benedict's *Rule* and modern religious sentiment is to note that the fear Benedict has in mind seems to be closely connected with reverence. Benedict wants his monks to be reverent toward God, reverent toward the community and its possessions, reverent toward visitors. In a passage quoted in conjunction with Benedict's teaching on prayer, Gregory the Great reports that Benedict once saw a vision of the whole world in a single sunbeam. Gregory draws the conclusion that to one who has seen God, the world appears to be very small. Perhaps. However, Benedict seems to have found the world and all that it is in it sacred, worthy of care and cultivation, too precious to claim as one's own property. Benedict does not contrast the sacredness of church space and church time to the insignificance of secular places and secular activities. His inclination is to extend the reverence one should feel in liturgical settings to the whole of reality. Hence Hildegard's declaration that all of God's creatures are pleasing and none should be injured.

After God, it is human beings who deserve our honor. All human beings—elderly, young, strangers or neighbors, the productive and the seemingly unproductive.

Had I chosen to discuss chastity, this would probably be the place to do it. For chastity, whether celibate or married, is very much a matter of reverence for ourselves and for other persons embodied and alluring, whom we are tempted to possess or control and so to violate. For the monk or nun, sexual relations are one path to God not taken because they have chosen other paths instead. That said, the thesis of this book is that the paths to God of monk and non-monk are very much alike. As one friend of mine said: husband and wife become each other's monastery. Their life together is a sacrament, holy to the church because of what it teaches about faithfulness and steadfastness and compassion and holy hilarity and tenderness and hospitality and the sanctity of everyday things. Their marriage is a continual conversion to their life together, to listening to one another, to care of one another and others.

Honor all people, and do not do to another what you do not want to happen to yourself.

RULE OF BENEDICT

Venerate the elders; love the younger people.

RULE OF BENEDICT

The first degree of humility is "to keep the fear of God always before one's eyes" [Ps 36.2], and to avoid all forgetfulness, always mindful of all that God commands. One should always be pondering in one's mind how hell burns for their sins those who hold God in contempt, while eternal life has been prepared for those who fear God.

RULE OF BENEDICT

When the cantor begins to say, "Glory be . . . ," all should immediately rise from their seats out of respect and reverence for the Holy Trinity.

RULE OF BENEDICT

We believe that God is present everywhere, and that the eyes of the Lord behold good and evil people everywhere; we believe this especially without any hesitation when we assist at the work of God.

RULE OF BENEDICT

When the work of God is finished, all should leave [the chapel] in deep silence and show reverence for God.

RULE OF BENEDICT

Juniors [in the time of entry into the monastery] should honor their seniors, and seniors should love their juniors. . . . Whenever they meet one another, the junior should ask a blessing from the senior. When a senior walks by, the junior should rise and give him his seat. The junior should not presume to sit down again unless the senior bids him. Thus, they may fulfill what is written: "They should strive to honor one another" [Rom 12.10].

RULE OF BENEDICT

The prior [second-in-command] must perform with reverence whatever is enjoined on him by the abbot and do nothing against the will or arrangements of the abbot. Just as he has been placed before others, so it is required of him that he observe the precepts of the rule more carefully.

RULE OF BENEDICT

The first glimpse of wisdom is fear of the Lord, just as the dawn precedes the sun. For when a person understands that she has been created by God, she begins to fear God. What is feared is honored, and what is honored is loved; if it is loved rightly, it is also honored rightly.

HILDEGARD OF BINGEN,
BOOK OF LIFE'S MERITS

Reverence declares: "All the things God established please me. I do not hurt any of them."

HILDEGARD OF BINGEN,
BOOK OF LIFE'S MERITS

As [Benedict's *Rule*] says: "When the work of God is finished, let all go out with the greatest silence; and let a reverence be made to God" [*Rule of Benedict* 55.2]. Let them bow reverently as they go out, and let them have reverence in their other works that are done in the service of God, and not rush into anything wanton or excessive.

HILDEGARD OF BINGEN,
EXPLANATION OF THE RULE OF BENEDICT

[Gertrude's] tender compassion extended not only to human beings, but reached out to every creature. When she saw little birds or other animals suffering from hunger, thirst, or cold, she was moved with intense pity for the work of her Lord. Then, desiring that God have mercy on his creature and deign to relieve its misery, she strove to offer devoutly to the Lord's eternal praise this suffering of irrational creation, in union with the dignity by which every creature is supremely perfected and ennobled in God.

GERTRUDE THE GREAT,
THE HERALD OF DIVINE LOVE

There is this difference between filial and servile fear: the child fears to offend; the servant shudders at the thought of being whipped. Filial fear is virtuous because it shows reverence for one's parent; servile fear is good, because it shows forth the power of the Lord. However, it is better to have filial fear and love than to fear and fail to love.

JOHN TRITHEMIUS, *RULE*

In the midst of the multiple activities of the day, you should stay free of multiplicity and preserve oneness of spirit within yourself. Let your mind form an idea of God and of his supreme majesty and goodness. Keep his lovable presence before your mind's eye.

LOUIS DE BLOIS, *SPIRITUAL DOCTRINE*

It was because the saints were absorbed in God that they were truly capable of seeing and appreciating created things and it was because they loved Him alone that they alone loved everybody.

THOMAS MERTON,
NEW SEEDS OF CONTEMPLATION

[Benedict] writes about the elderly and children and about their need for special understanding. . . . When society seems increasingly to say that productivity and usefulness are the qualities by which we judge the worth of the individual, here Benedict is telling us that respect should be shown to those who apparently contribute little or nothing to the community in these terms.

ESTHER DE WAAL, *A LIFE-GIVING WAY*

Benedict has a deep belief and respect for each one of us as sons and daughters made in the image of God. It is up to each of us to take due and proper responsibility for the handling of this amazing gift of our sonship or daughterhood.

ESTHER DE WAAL, *A LIFE-GIVING WAY*

[Benedict] knew that the secret of the holy life was not so much a holy reputation as it was a holy attitude toward all of creation: reverence for God, reverence for the body, reverence for the other who is younger and unimportant, or older and useless now, or in opposition to us and an irritant now.

SR. JOAN CHITTISTER,
THE RULE OF BENEDICT

In a society that depends on reputation to such a degree that people build themselves up by tearing other people down, the chapter on mutual obedience turns the world awry. Monastic spirituality says that we are to honor one another. We are to listen to one another. We are to reach across boundaries and differences in this fragmented world and see in our differences distinctions of great merit that can mend a competitive, uncaring, and foolish world.

SR. JOAN CHITTISTER,
THE RULE OF BENEDICT

CHAPTER 8

Humility

Saint Antony saw the world as something like a minefield that only humility can safely traverse. Benedict's teaching on humility is also a difficult minefield for interpreters. I do not know that a person can or should think he is lower and baser than all others (Benedict's seventh degree of humility). Humility is truth. In truth, it is statistically very unlikely that anyone is the lowest of all. Nor do I think we should work at looking humble (twelfth degree of humility). Humility is truth. One should not try to appear as anything, least of all as a foot-shuffling nobody.

Antony and Benedict knew that a true monk could accept insults and humiliations, in part because he deserved them, but, I suspect, also because they knew that a truly humble person cannot be humiliated. Someone who knows her own weaknesses and accepts them will not be terrified by the prospect of humiliations. Someone who does not pretend to be anything other than what she is will not be afraid of what people say about her.

Merton saw clearly that the ultimate basis of humility is grace: whatever one is or has or accomplishes is a gift from God and others. As the Eucharist is the offering of God's gifts back to God, so monastic life and any Christian life is an offering of God's gift of oneself to God.

Bede's homilies are thoroughly Christological. He is particularly given to citing the incarnation of the Son of God in the humanity of Christ as a supreme example of humility. For Christ, humbling himself was a way to share the lives of his human brothers and sisters. For us, humility is an acknowledgment that we share the weaknesses and the sins of our human brothers and sisters. Humility is also a recognition that we form one living system with the plants and animals, for all physical things, living and dead, arise ultimately from the *humus*, the moist ground of virgin earth. Try as we may to forget it, we will always need to share water and air and sunlight with the plants and the animals.

Humility is an essential part of listening. Only someone who believes he has something to learn is an attentive listener. The *Life of Pachomius* tells about Silvanos, who learned humility by imitating and obeying a humble man, and in that way Silvanos became "a living man." The beast of pride, which wars against each of us, Silvanos slew.

Humility is not about comparisons with other people, but if we are inclined to make too much of our virtues or achievements, we should remind ourselves of how many people have been able to exceed any accomplishment of ours. The more we know ourselves, the more we discover we are lower than our image of ourselves. In knowing ourselves and avoiding making comparisons between ourselves and those we know less well, we should be ready to do them any service or accept any assignment. Christ did the same.

Because humility avoids comparison, envy is a sure sign of its absence. Humility can rejoice in the gifts of all, because it recognizes the fundamental oneness of all people in their humanity and in Christ. Envy thinks of gifts as private property. Not only did Gertrude not think of her gifts as private property; she thought they were given her only so she might pass them on to others.

When a person has walked consciously in the presence of God and with God's help discovered how merciful God has been to him even in his sin, that person loves God more and more until this love casts out fear. For Benedict, love overcame and cast out fear not because he came to believe there was no hell, but because he discovered how good God had been to him and he had no reason to think God would ever act differently toward him. Fear helps keep us on the straight and narrow during the early and laborious days of our seeking to become what God wills for us. As we acquire virtue, we come more and more to do the good spontaneously out of good habit, delight in virtue, and love of Christ.

Humility is the truth about ourselves, the whole truth—about our weaknesses, our failures, our history, our virtues, our gifts. Once we are truthful about ourselves before God and others, we can deal gently with others who are afraid to face the truth about themselves or who fancy themselves our competitors. Christ humbled himself out of compassion; out of humility grows our compassion for one another.

[Abba Antony said:] I have seen all the snares of the enemy spread out over the world, and I said with a groan, "Who can get through such snares?" Then I heard a voice say to me, "Humility."

ANTONY, *SAYINGS*

The brothers praised a monk before Abba Antony. When he had received the monk, Antony wanted to learn how he would bear insults. When he saw that he could not bear them at all, he said to him, "You are like a building magnificently decorated on the outside, but pillaged within by robbers."

ANTONY, *SAYINGS*

Therefore, let this word be clear to you: you are not to think that your progress and entry into God's service has been your own work, but rather understand that you have always been helped by a divine power. Strive to offer yourself as a sacrifice to God always.

ANTONY, *LETTERS*

Except through humility in your whole heart and mind and spirit and soul and body, you will not be able to inherit the Kingdom of God.

ANTONY, *LETTERS*

Therefore, Jesus emptied himself of his glory, and took upon himself the form of a slave [Phil 2.7–8], that his bondage might make us free. And we became foolish, and in our foolishness committed every kind of evil. Again, He

took the form of foolishness, that by his foolishness we
might be made wise.

ANTONY, *LETTERS*

And so I also, the poor wretch who writes this letter, having
been awakened from the sleep of death, have spent most of
the time I have been upon earth mourning and weeping,
saying "What can I render to the Lord for all the benefits he
has done for me?" For nothing is lacking to us which he has
not done for us in our humiliation.

ANTONY, *LETTERS*

One of the brothers asked me, "Tell us about one of your
visions," and I said to him, "A sinner like me does not ask
God to see visions." It is against God's will and a mistake.
But in everything he does by God's will, even if he should
raise a dead man, the servant of God remains unhurt by
pride or boasting. For without God's permission, he would
not even see that Providence governs all things.

LIFE OF PACHOMIUS

One day [Pachomius] was weaving a mat in Tabennesi. A
boy who was doing the weekly service in the monastery
came by, and seeing him weaving said, "Not so, father. Do
not turn the thread this way, for Abba Theodore has taught
us another way of weaving." He got up at once and said,
"Yes, teach me the way." After the boy had taught him, he
sat down to work with joy, having forestalled the spirit of
pride in this, too.

LIFE OF PACHOMIUS

There was a boy called Silvanos. Our father Pachomius
had given him instructions before receiving him into the
monastery, but afterwards Silvanos became negligent. . . .
Pachomius was patient with him; he called a great monk
named Psenamon and told him in the boy's absence, "We
know that you have labored in ascesis for a long time. Now,

for God's sake, take this boy and suffer with him in all things until he is saved.". . . And so they worked together making mats, and they fulfilled the fast and the prayers properly. The boy obeyed Psenamon in everything as he had been commanded. He would not eat even a vegetable leaf without asking. And so he was humble, great [in virtue] and meek, keeping his mouth closed. . . . And to say it in short, he became a living man.

One day when the brothers were seated, Abba Pachomius began to tell them, "There is a man among us as I have not seen ever since I became a monk. . . . By his deep humility and the purity of his conscience he is great. The beast that wars against you, you have bound and put under your feet; and if you are negligent it will be set loose again and rise up against you. But Silvanos has slain it."

LIFE OF PACHOMIUS

Even if you were . . . successfully practicing the most extreme asceticism, do not make too much of it! For demons have in fact done and are doing more ascetic acts than yours. They do not eat, nor drink, nor sleep. They also spend their lives in a desert—in case you think that you are doing something great by living in a cave.

LIFE OF SYNCLETICA

So great a virtue is humility that, although the Devil seems to mimic all virtues, he does not begin to understand the nature of this one. . . . Just as it is impossible for a ship to be built without nails, so it is impossible to be saved without humility.

LIFE OF SYNCLETICA

Because humility is good and salutary, the Lord clothed himself in it while fulfilling the work of salvation [economy] for humanity. For he says: "Learn from me, for I am gentle and humble of heart" [Mt 11.29]. Notice who it is who is speaking. Learn his lesson perfectly. Let humility become for you the beginning and end of virtues. He means a humble heart. He refers not to appearance alone, but to the inner person, for the outer person will also follow after the inner.

LIFE OF SYNCLETICA

Humility, then, is formed through rebukes, through insults, through blows; you hear yourself called mindless and stupid, poor and a beggar, weak and worthless, ineffectual in what you do and irrational in what you say, contemptible in appearance, weak in power. These insults are the sinews of humility. These our Lord heard and experienced, for they said he was a Samaritan and was possessed. He took on the form of a slave, he was beaten, he was humiliated with blows.

LIFE OF SYNCLETICA

They know that what is good in themselves could not have come about except for the Lord. They heap praise on the Lord working in them, saying with the prophet: "Not to us, Lord, not to us, but to your name give the glory" [Ps 115.1].

RULE OF BENEDICT

The sixth step of humility is that a monk is content with every sort of mean and extreme condition, and judges himself a bad and unworthy worker in all the things that are enjoined upon him.

RULE OF BENEDICT

The seventh degree of humility is that one not only says with his tongue but believes with the deepest feeling of his heart that he is lower and baser than all others.

RULE OF BENEDICT

The twelfth degree of humility is that a monk always shows himself to be humble not only in his heart but also to those who see the way he carries himself at the work of God, in the chapel, in the monastery, in the garden, on the road, in the field, wherever he sits, walks, or stands. With his head always down, his eyes on the ground, at every moment thinking himself guilty of his sins, let him consider himself to be already presented before the fearful judgment, always saying to himself in his heart what the publican in the Gospels said with his eyes fixed on the ground: "Lord, I, a sinner, am not worthy to raise my eyes to the heavens."

RULE OF BENEDICT

Having ascended all these steps of humility, the monk will soon arrive at that perfect love of God that casts out fear, through which all those things that previously he did not observe without fear he will begin to keep effortlessly, as though practice had made them second nature, no longer out of fear of hell, but out of love for Christ, and good habit and delight in virtues. These things the Lord will deign to show by the Holy Spirit in his workman now cleansed of vices and sins.

RULE OF BENEDICT

Since, when we wish to propose something to powerful persons, we do not presume to do so except with humility and reverence, how much more ought we petition the Lord God of all things with all humility and pure devotion.

RULE OF BENEDICT

[Priests in the community] should give a better example of humility than anyone else.

RULE OF BENEDICT

The physician [Christ] came to visit the sick. In order to heal the chronic weakness of our pride, he offered us the fresh example of his humility.

BEDE, HOMILIES ON THE GOSPELS

Although Wulfstan excelled all others in virtues, he showed humility toward each person. He was constantly doing menial tasks that another would have found disgusting.

LIFE OF WULFSTAN

Certain ones said that the humility he loved was beneath the dignity of a bishop. Wulfstan answered: "Whoever is the greatest among you will be your servant. I am your bishop and teacher; therefore I must be the servant of you all, according to the Lord's command."

LIFE OF WULFSTAN

See, blessed Benedict, how vigorously this soldier of Christ fights under your leadership! See how effectively this student of yours advances in your school. See the good monk who, having mortified his evil ways and fleshly desires, is so eager and lives solely for virtue. No! Behold a false monk who, having lost the virtues, is ruled by a crowd of vices and smothered under a heap of sins!

ANSELM OF CANTERBURY,
PRAYERS AND MEDITATIONS

Many of those who are humiliated are not humble. Some react to humiliation with anger, others with patience, and others with freedom. The first are culpable, the next harmless, the last just. While innocence is part of justice, its consummation is found in the humble. The humble person who can say "It is good for me that you humbled me" is really humble. Someone who bears humiliation unwillingly cannot say this, much less someone who complains. We promise no grace to either of these because of their humiliation. Nevertheless, the two are quite different: one will possess his soul in patience; the other will perish in his complaining. Although one arouses anger, neither merits grace, for it is not to the humiliated but to the humble that God gives grace.

BERNARD OF CLAIRVAUX,
ON THE SONG OF SONGS

When people are proud, they envy the accomplishments of others and then stir up every kind of evil.

HILDEGARD OF BINGEN,
BOOK OF LIFE'S MERITS

[In her humility, Gertrude] thought herself so unworthy of God's gifts that she could not accept that they might be for her benefit alone. Instead, she saw herself as a channel through whom grace could flow to God's elect by the mysterious ways of Providence.

GERTRUDE THE GREAT,
THE HERALD OF DIVINE LOVE

Since my tongue is incapable of recounting the abundant favors you have given me by the continuous gift of your presence, accept, I beg you, O my God, the sentiment of my heart. From the depths of the abyss of humility where I have been gently drawn by your downward-bending charity, grant me to recognize and render thanks to your infinite goodness.

GERTRUDE THE GREAT,
THE HERALD OF DIVINE LOVE

Vainglory is a love of our own excellence. Vainglory gives birth to self-exaltation, pride, arrogance, contention, affront, contempt, presumption, disobedience, irreverence, and very often to factions, the worst of plagues. To avoid these things, we must glory in the Lord and not in ourselves.

JOHN TRITHEMIUS, *RULE*

Our Teacher . . . appeared with the humble, for he was the most humble of all. Let us remain in his teaching. Whatever he taught by word and example, let us fulfill by deed.

JOHN TRITHEMIUS, *RULE*

Have a humble and submissive heart. Acknowledge your nothingness, your weakness and lack of power. Acknowledge your ingratitude toward God, your wickedness and vileness. . . . Attribute to the mercy and kindness of God whatever good you have and do; in this, seek not your own praise and glory but God's. . . . Forgive from your heart every offense of those who trouble you or injure you.

LOUIS DE BLOIS, *SPIRITUAL MIRROR*

The things we really need come to us only as gifts, and in order to receive them as gifts we have to be open. In order to be open we have to renounce ourselves, in a sense we have to die to our image of ourselves, our autonomy, our fixation upon our self-willed identity.

THOMAS MERTON,
CONJECTURES OF A GUILTY BYSTANDER

A humble man is not disturbed by praise. Since he is no longer concerned with himself, and since he knows where the good that is in him comes from, he does not refuse praise, because it belongs to the God he loves, and in receiving it he keeps nothing for himself but gives it all, with great joy, to his God.

THOMAS MERTON,
NEW SEEDS OF CONTEMPLATION

A humble man can do great things with an uncommon per-fection because he is no longer concerned about incidentals, like his own interests and his own reputation, and therefore he no longer needs to waste his efforts in defending them.

THOMAS MERTON,
NEW SEEDS OF CONTEMPLATION

[Benedict's chapter on humility] is asking of me the honesty that means that I cease to play games, whether with myself, with others, with God. Unless I desire this with the whole of my being, to the extent that I am willing to undergo a holocaust to achieve it . . . it is hardly worth beginning.

ESTHER DE WAAL, *A LIFE-GIVING WAY*

Lack of contentment lets me become trapped in the coils of the competitive society, competing for material goods,

social status, the sort of car I drive, the place in which I
live.

ESTHER DE WAAL, *A LIFE-GIVING WAY*

If I accept myself as ordinary, weak, frail, in other words,
totally human and totally dependent upon God, then I am
stripped of any sense of being in some way set apart, different, superior. It is then that the genuine, real self may begin
to emerge.

ESTHER DE WAAL, *A LIFE-GIVING WAY*

The key to my growth in humility is that it brings me closer
to God as it subjects me more and more to the pull of the
gravitational force of God's love.

ESTHER DE WAAL, *A LIFE-GIVING WAY*

[Humility is] a proper sense of self in a universe of wonders.

SR. JOAN CHITTISTER,
THE RULE OF BENEDICT

Benedict wants us to realize that accepting our essential
smallness and embracing it frees us from the need to lie,
even to ourselves, about our frailties. More than that, it lib-
erates us to respect, revere, and deal gently with others who
have been unfortunate enough to have their own smallness
come obscenely to light.

SR. JOAN CHITTISTER,
THE RULE OF BENEDICT

CHAPTER 9

Simplicity

The *Life of Syncletica* presents a paradox. When Syncletica decided to build, she didn't gather materials from outside sources. Instead, she emptied out what she had within, getting rid of possessions and anti-social emotions. Thus she was able to build a solid tower on a rock foundation. Johannes Tauler, a German mystic of the fourteenth century, said simply: God cannot resist a vacuum. God is drawn irresistibly to a soul emptied out of possessions, pride, and hostility. More prosaically, when Syncletica converted to the monastic life, she gave her possessions to the poor and her body to God. In fact, she realized, everything belonged to God anyway.

The primary inspiration for voluntary Christian poverty has been the example and teaching of Christ and the example of the early church as described in the first chapters of Acts.

Syncletica thinks of possessions as tools for a certain kind of life, a life devoted to pleasure or to keeping up with the neighbors. If we renounce that sort of life, we won't need the tools anymore. Once divested of the tools, we don't need to worry about breaking or losing them. We are free. The one who has unlimited needs is never satisfied. Avarice is insatiable. The one who needs only what is sufficient is seldom in need.

While the Benedictine tradition renounces private property, it insists that the goal is for the community to have and distribute to its members what is necessary. What is necessary varies from person to person. So each does not receive exactly the same amount, though no one should receive anything superfluous.

The monastic tradition is convinced of the goodness of creation. We go to God in and through his world. However, the monastic tradition is of several minds about beauty in buildings, liturgy, and artifacts. Generally, the mainstream of Benedictine spirituality has not rejected the enjoyment of beauty, especially when that beauty is associated with the praise of God. Whatever possessions a monastery or an individual happens to have, they are on loan from Christ. They are to be treated with great respect.

Communal superfluity is no more licit than individual luxury. One of the most important lessons of monastic economy is that one can enjoy beauty in many forms without possessing it.

Monastic apparel is a controversial subject, especially because of historical differences in expectations placed on men and women. The best of the tradition was aimed at avoiding ostentation, the ostentation of fine clothes and the ostentation of rags. Benedict says to wear inexpensive clothes found in your area.

The real riches of the voluntary poor are their shared virtue, itself a gift. In the end, all one can give to God is his gift, oneself, a gift endowed with many gifts. Having offered all to God, one is dependent on God, which is to say, one is thoroughly human.

⟶

Upon his parents' death, Antony was left alone with an only sister, who was very young. He was about eighteen or twenty years old at the time and took care of the house and his sister. Less than six months had passed since his parents' death when, as usual, he chanced to be on his way to church. As he was walking along, he collected his thoughts and reflected how the Apostles left everything and followed the Savior [Mt 4.20], also how the people in Acts sold what they had and laid it at the feet of the Apostles for distribution among the needy [Acts 4.35], and what great hope is laid up in heaven for such as these [Eph 1.18]. With these thoughts in his mind, he entered the church. And it so happened that the Gospel was being read . . . in which

the Lord says to the rich man: "If you wish to be perfect,
go sell all that you have and give it to the poor; and come,
follow me and you shall have treasure in heaven" [Mt
19.21]. . . . Antony immediately left the church and
gave to the townspeople the property he had from his fore-
bears. . . . He did not want it to encumber himself or his
sister in any way whatever. He sold all the rest . . . keeping
back only a little for his sister. But once again as he entered
the church, he heard the Lord saying in the Gospel: "Be
not solicitous for the morrow" [Mt 6.34]. He could not
bear to wait longer, but went out and distributed those
things also to the poor. His sister he placed with known
and trusted virgins, giving her to the nuns to be brought
up. Then he himself devoted all his time to ascetic living,
intent on himself and living a life of self-denial near his
own home.

LIFE OF ANTONY

Unless each of you hates earthly possession and renounces it
and all its workings with all his heart, and stretches the hands
of his heart to heaven to the Father of all, he cannot be
saved.

ANTONY, LETTERS

[Pachomius] used to teach the brothers not to give heed to
the splendor and the beauty of this world in things like good
food, clothing, a cell, or a book outwardly pleasing to the
eye. "For the beauty of the faithful," he said, "lies in the
commandments of God"; as the psalmist says, "Lord, in
your will grant strength to my beauty" [Ps 30.7]. Although
Joseph was extremely handsome and came to rule over
Egypt, he paid no attention to these perishable things, having chastity for splendor and prudence for power. But others
who took their delight in these things perished by an evil
death, like Ammon and Absalom.

LIFE OF PACHOMIUS

[After distributing all her possessions to the poor, Syncletica said:] I have been judged worthy of a great title. What worthy return shall I make to the giver? I do not have anything. If in the outside world, for the sake of a transitory distinction, people throw away their whole substance, how much more necessary is it for me who have been granted so great a grace to offer my body along with what are regarded as possessions? But why do I talk about giving possessions or body when all that belongs to him? "For the Lord's is the earth and its fullness" [Ps 24.1]. Once she had clothed herself with humility [cf. Col 3.12] by means of these words, she entered upon a solitary life.

LIFE OF SYNCLETICA

Now the construction of buildings is traditionally carried out with materials from without, but Syncletica went about it in the opposite way. She did not gather all her building materials from without, but rather she emptied herself of what was within. For by giving her possessions to the poor, by relinquishing anger and vindictiveness, and by driving away envy and ambition, she built her house on rock, its tower visible from afar and its structure storm proof.

LIFE OF SYNCLETICA

[Voluntary poverty] is good for those women who are able to endure it. For the women who persevere in this condition have suffering in the flesh, but peace in the soul. For just as heavy clothing is washed and bleached by treading and vigorous wringing, so also the strong soul is strengthened to a greater degree through voluntary poverty.

LIFE OF SYNCLETICA

For possessions are the "tools" of a life devoted to pleasure. Take away first the "trade" (i.e., gluttony and soft living), and you will also be able easily to dispense with its material aspect represented by your possessions. For it is difficult, in my opinion, if the "trade" is going on, for the "tools" to be absent. For if a woman has not given up the first, how will she be able to reject the second?

LIFE OF SYNCLETICA

The Enemy, moreover, is more soundly vanquished in the case of those who live without possessions. For he lacks the means to do harm, since the majority of our griefs and trials originate in the removal of possessions. What course of action does he have against those without possessions? None! Can he burn their estates? Impossible! Destroy their livestock? They do not even have any! Lay hands on their dear ones? To these too they long ago said good-bye. And so voluntary poverty is a powerful retribution against the Enemy as well as a precious treasure for the soul.

LIFE OF SYNCLETICA

Let the cellarer regard all the utensils of the monastery and everything that belongs to it as if they were vessels consecrated for the altar. Let him not consider anything as having no importance. He should not burn with avarice, nor be wasteful and squander the goods of the monastery, but let him do all things with moderation and as the abbot bids.

RULE OF BENEDICT

Let all things be common to all, as Scripture [Acts 4.32] says, so that no one should say or presume that anything is his own.

RULE OF BENEDICT

In particular this vice is to be rooted out of the monastery: that anyone . . . have anything at all as his own.

RULE OF BENEDICT

As it is written: distribution was made to each as each had need [Acts 4.35]. We certainly do not mean there should be favoritism, but there should be a consideration for weaknesses. Thus, those who need less should thank God and not be upset, whereas those who need more should be humbled because of their weakness and not exalted by the mercy shown them.

RULE OF BENEDICT

Clothing should be given them suitable to the circumstances and the climate of the place where they live.

RULE OF BENEDICT

They should not worry about the color or quality of their clothes, but be satisfied with what can be found in the area where they live and can be purchased inexpensively.

RULE OF BENEDICT

To completely root out the vice of private ownership, the abbot will need to provide all the things that are necessary: cowl, tunic, sandals, shoes, belt, knife, stylus, needle, handkerchief, and writing tablets. In that way, all pretext of want will be eliminated.

RULE OF BENEDICT

[Wulfstan] always avoided every sort of ostentation; even when he was wealthy, he wore only lambskins. So, one day, Geoffrey, bishop of Coutances, good-naturedly criticized him. He showered him with friendly jibes. He asked Wulfstan why he wore lambskins when he could and should have had sable or beaver or fox. Wulfstan answered with good grace that Geoffrey and men schooled in worldly wisdom should use the skins of clever animals; he himself, unaware of trickery, would be content with lambskins. Geoffrey came back at him by saying he should at least wear catskins. Wulfstan answered: "Believe me, we sing 'Lamb of God' more often than we sing 'Cat of God.' " Geoffrey heard this and started laughing, delighted that he had the worst of the jest and that Wulfstan could not be budged.

LIFE OF WULFSTAN

Oh how spacious is that soul, and how privileged in her
merits, that she is found both worthy to receive the divine
presence into herself and sufficient to contain that presence.
She provides spacious walkways for the use of the divine
majesty. She is certainly not involved in lawsuits and worldly
cares, not a devotee of the stomach or of sensual pleasures,
nor is she curious to look around, nor avid to command, nor
proud in the power she has. It is necessary that the soul first
be empty of all these things, so that it can become the
heaven and dwelling place of God. Otherwise, how could
she be quiet enough to see that it is God himself? She certainly cannot give herself to envy or rancor, because wisdom
will not enter the wicked soul. Hence, it is necessary that
she grow and expand so that she is able to receive God. Her
expanse is her love, as the Apostle indicates: expand in love
[2 Cor 6.13].

BERNARD OF CLAIRVAUX,
ON THE SONG OF SONGS

In affliction, two things should be checked regularly, the
manner and the fruit: the manner, so that nothing is in excess; the fruit, so that the effort is not in vain. To afflict oneself without measure is tyranny; to do so without fruit is
stupid. Affliction without measure causes breakdown, not
conditioning; demolition, not upbuilding; wearing away,
not perfecting. Such affliction merits mockery, not con-
gratulations. The proper measure in affliction works against
indulgence, not nature, against the cause of sin, not the creation of God. . . . The proper measure is to show kindness
to the body, not to serve it.

PETER OF CELLE,
ON AFFLICTION AND READING

Those who love the world neither fear nor love God, but
gather to themselves all the things that please them. What
they like in creatures they excuse before God, saying it was

created for their use. Not fearing God, whom they should fear, they put their own will before God. Not loving God, they do not let go of their fleshly desires, nor do they rein themselves in for love of God, but with all their desire they embrace the world.

HILDEGARD OF BINGEN,
BOOK OF LIFE'S MERITS

Abstinence says: "No one should strike the lyre in such a way that its strings are damaged. But if its strings are damaged, what sound will it make? None. You, gluttony, fill up your belly so much that your veins are unhealthy. . . . I set a measure to food, so that a person neither dries up nor bloats."

HILDEGARD OF BINGEN,
BOOK OF LIFE'S MERITS

[Those who share all things in common (Acts 4.32)] rejoice because they want to be poor, not rich. Because they spurn riches as ashes that are dead because of avarice, none of them has anything according to his own will. Whatever each has through the gift of God, let her possess with God. She says that nothing is hers by her own strength, but all is from God who gives all good things to the good. And what are these? Truth and justice, which interweave with all good things.

HILDEGARD OF BINGEN,
BOOK OF LIFE'S MERITS

Greed says: "I snatch all things to myself. I hug all things to my breast; the more I have gathered the more I have. . . . When I have whatever I need, I have no worries about needing anything from someone else." Simple sufficiency replies: "You are harsh and devoid of mercy because you do not care for the advancement of others. Nothing is sufficient to satisfy you. I, however, sit above the stars, for all of God's

good things are sufficient for me. . . . Why should I desire
more than I need?"

HILDEGARD OF BINGEN,
BOOK OF LIFE'S MERITS

Because of her inner freedom, Gertrude could not bear to
keep anything that she did not need. If she received presents,
she almost always distributed them quickly to others, with
this distinction: she favored the needy, and did not prefer her
friends to her enemies. . . . In clothes and other things she
used, she always preferred what was necessary or useful to
what was unusual or pleasurable.

GERTRUDE THE GREAT,
THE HERALD OF DIVINE LOVE

O God of my life, I do not know how I may worthily praise
you or what I may give you in return, my beloved, for all the
good things that you have granted me. Consequently, I offer
you in me and me in you, my cherished Jesus, as a holocaust
of praise to you. I have nothing else. This itself, that I am
and live in you—this I give to you totally.

GERTRUDE THE GREAT,
SPIRITUAL EXERCISES

It is easy to be poor when we want nothing, to be humble
when we are despised by no one, to be patient if we never
suffer injury.

JOHN TRITHEMIUS, *RULE*

Spiritual and ascetic persons must learn to relinquish themselves and all things out of love of God. They should possess
nothing with a clinging affection of heart. They should
cling to no visible and perishable thing, to no mortal creation. They should seek the friendship, acquaintance, or
presence of no human beings, however holy, simply for the
pleasure of their company. Let them remember that not

only evil things, but even good ones, can be an impediment
if they are loved and sought inordinately. . . . Never in time
or in eternity should they seek something as their own.
Having rejected all personal property, they should strip and
deprive themselves and die to themselves and to all things.

LOUIS DE BLOIS, *SPIRITUAL DOCTRINE*

The charism of the monastic vocation is one of simplicity
and truth. The monk . . . is one who abandons the routines,
the clichés, the disguised idolatries and empty formalities of
"the world" in order to seek the most authentic and essential
meaning of the dedicated life on earth. Ideally speaking,
then, the monastery should be a place of utter sincerity,
without empty and deceptive formalities, without evasions,
without pretenses.

THOMAS MERTON,
CONTEMPLATION IN A WORLD OF ACTION

The purpose of monastic detachment—which demands
genuine sacrifice—is simply to leave the monk unencum-
bered, free to move, in possession of his spiritual senses
and of his right mind, capable of living a charismatic life
in freedom of spirit.

THOMAS MERTON,
CONTEMPLATION IN A WORLD OF ACTION

In losing touch with being and thus with God, we have
fallen into a senseless idolatry of production and consumption for their own sakes. We have renounced the act of being
and plunged ourself into process for its own sake.

THOMAS MERTON,
CONJECTURES OF A GUILTY BYSTANDER

Each year the new tractors get bigger and bigger, louder and
louder. The one in the valley now sounds like a tank or a big
bulldozer. Round and round the alfalfa field in fury. What

thoughts it represents: what fury of man; what restlessness; what avidity; what desperation.

THOMAS MERTON,
CONJECTURES OF A GUILTY BYSTANDER

We do not detach ourselves from things in order to attach ourselves to God, but rather we become detached from ourselves in order to see and use all things in and for God.

THOMAS MERTON,
NEW SEEDS OF CONTEMPLATION

We are placed in this world, and it is in and through this world, not by the denial of it, that we shall come to God. But I need guidelines on this. I am surrounded by a materialistic culture and I need help in holding a balance between appreciating the material things in my life and finding myself trapped by them. Since the abbot holds the place of Christ for the community, I now translate what that means for my own self, and I then find that I am being given a most practical and immediate example of how to approach this. All the good things in my life are lent to me by Christ. They are to be cared for. Each is important and Christ has kept a list. They are on loan so that I can fulfill the assigned tasks, and they are to be collected at the end of my life, the day of judgment.

ESTHER DE WAAL, *A LIFE-GIVING WAY*

If we are foolish enough to let avarice into our hearts, it will become an insatiable tyrant.

ESTHER DE WAAL, *A LIFE-GIVING WAY*

Benedict is splendidly precise. Everything matters, down to the last detail. There is such loving and careful respect and care for clothes in the way in which they are to be washed and stored after use. There is respect for the person, too. Ill-fitting clothes are unworthy and so there is care about size and fit. . . . He picks up the theme of stewardship, and handling with a sense of responsibility.

ESTHER DE WAAL, *A LIFE-GIVING WAY*

Living in relationship with the actual place in which one finds oneself means being earthed in the immediate reality not only of time and seasons, but of the very ground itself.

ESTHER DE WAAL, *A LIFE-GIVING WAY*

Benedict wants the cellarer to be someone who knows the difference between needs and desires, who will see that the community has what is necessary but does not begin the long, slippery road into excess and creature comforts and indolence and soft-souledness.

SR. JOAN CHITTISTER,
THE RULE OF BENEDICT

Dependence on God may be what is lacking in a society where consumerism and accumulation have become the root diseases of a world in which everything is not enough and nothing satisfies.

SR. JOAN CHITTISTER,
THE RULE OF BENEDICT

Waste is not a Benedictine virtue. Planned obsolescence is not a Benedictine goal. Disposability is not a Benedictine quality. A Benedictine soul is a soul that takes care of things . . . and "treats all utensils and goods of the monastery like the sacred vessels of the altar."

SR. JOAN CHITTISTER,
THE RULE OF BENEDICT

CHAPTER 10

Discernment

Possibly no quality has been more characteristic of the monastic tradition than discernment or discretion. Even today, Benedict is praised for his discretion and Benedictines for their moderation. To profit from this tradition, it is necessary to sort out the range of meanings the term embraces. Almost all these meanings appear in the life and instructions of Saint Antony.

Antony was a veritable doctor of discernment. He was able to discern the hand of the devil in events and to distinguish which thoughts came from the devil and which from God. Antony also knew which defenses worked best against which temptations. Antony was a renowned ascetic, and according to Antony's biographer, Athanasius, he sometimes seemed ashamed of having a body, yet even in old age he remained youthful and healthy in appearance. The sayings of Antony are particularly emphatic about moderation in ascetic practices. Antony was also a man of stable character; he was not given to extremes of elation or dejection. Antony knew himself; self-knowledge is a prerequisite for discernment or a manifestation of its power.

Benedict urged moderation in food, clothing, horarium. He called discretion the mother of the virtues. Benedict's own discretion showed itself particularly in giving the strong something to strive for without discouraging the weak. Discretion identified or distinguished good and evil, both in one's own life and in the lives of others. Bede warns that those inclined to correct others should do so only if they know themselves thoroughly and have acknowledged their own faults. For Hildegard, discretion puts individuals in tune with themselves.

Discretion, then, is able to pick out the word and will of God amid all the conflicting voices emanating from the devil, from oneself, from others. The discerning, balanced person is that way partly because of natural, God-given endowment, partly through experience, and completely by grace. Experience teaches us the ways in which we fool ourselves or let ourselves be fooled. Experience teaches us when our asceticism or our self-indulgence is likely to be harmful. By discernment we know ourselves, and so humility presupposes discretion, just as discretion presupposes humility. None of this happens without experience and imagination. Through them, we learn the boundaries marked out by discretion. Discernment then is the opposite of naïveté; it is wisdom won at the risk of error.

⟨ornament⟩

On the next day Antony went out, inspired with an even greater zeal for the service of God. . . . He set out at once for the mountain by himself. But there was the Enemy again! Seeing his earnestness and wishing to thwart it, he projected the illusion of a large disk of silver into the road. But Antony, seeing through the trickery of the Hater of Goodness, stopped, and, looking at the disk, exposed the Devil in it, saying: "A disk in the desert. Where does that come from? This is not a well traveled highway, and there is no sign that any people have come this way. It is of great size, it could not have been dropped unnoticed. Indeed, even if it had been lost, the loser would have turned back and looked for it. He would have found it because this is desert country. This is a trick of the Devil. You will not thwart my resolution by this, Devil. Let this thing perish with you." As Antony said this, the disk disappeared like smoke leaving fire.

LIFE OF ANTONY

[Antony] spent nearly twenty years practicing the ascetic life by himself, never going out and seldom seen by others. After this, as there were many who longed and sought to imitate his holy life, some of his friends came and forcefully broke down the door and removed it. Antony came forth as out of a shrine, as one initiated into sacred mysteries and filled with the spirit of God. . . . When they saw him, they were astonished to see that his body had kept its former appearance. It was neither obese from want of exercise, nor emaciated from his fastings and struggles with the demons. He was the same man they had known before his retirement.

Again, the state of his soul was pure, for it was neither contracted by grief, nor dissipated by pleasure nor pervaded by jollity and dejection. He was not embarrassed when he saw the crowd, nor was he elated at seeing so many there to receive him. No, he had himself completely under control—a man guided by reason and stable in his character.

Through him the Lord cured many of those present who were afflicted with bodily ills, and freed others from impure spirits. He also gave Antony charm in speaking; and so he comforted many in sorrow, and others who were quarreling he turned into friends. He exhorted all to prefer nothing in the world to the love of Christ.

LIFE OF ANTONY

For all the monks who came to him, Antony had the same advice—to place their confidence in the Lord and to love him, to keep themselves from bad thoughts and pleasures of the flesh, and not to be seduced by a full stomach, as is written in Proverbs [24.15]. They should flee conceit and pray continually, sing Psalms before sleeping and after, commit to heart the commandments enjoined in the Scriptures. . . . He counseled them, "the sun must not go down, not merely on our anger [Eph 4.26], but on any other sin of ours. . . . To assure ourselves of this, it is well to hear and treasure what the Apostle says: 'Judge yourselves and prove yourselves' [2 Cor 13.5]. Wherefore, let all, daily, make an accounting of the day's and the night's activity, and if they have sinned, let them stop sinning. . . . Often we are not aware of what we are doing—we do not know it, but the Lord notices

everything. Therefore, leaving judgment to Him, let us have
sympathy with each other and 'bear one another's burdens'
[Gal 6.2]. Ourselves let us judge; and where we fall short, let
us be earnest about making up our deficiency."

LIFE OF ANTONY

This was also unique in Antony's practice of asceticism that
. . . he had the gift of discerning [evil] spirits. He recognized
their movements and was well aware in what direction each
of them directed his effort and attack. Not only was he not
fooled by them, but encouraging others who were harassed
in their thoughts, he taught them how they might ward off
their designs, describing the weaknesses and wiles of the
spirits practicing possession. And so each went down as
though anointed by him and filled with confidence against
the designs of the devil and his demons.

LIFE OF ANTONY

Abba Pambo asked Abba Antony, "What should I do?" The
old man told him, "Do not trust in your own righteousness,
do not worry about the past, and be master of your tongue
and your stomach."

ANTONY, *SAYINGS*

Antony also said, "Some have afflicted their bodies with
asceticism, but they lack discernment, and so they are far
from God."

ANTONY, *SAYINGS*

A hunter in the desert saw Abba Antony enjoying himself
with the brothers and he was scandalized. Wanting to show
him that sometimes it is necessary to take care of the needs
of the brethren, the old man said to him, "Put an arrow in
your bow and shoot it." So he did. The old man said, "Shoot
another," and he did. Then the old man said, "Shoot yet
again," and the hunter answered, "If I bend my bow too
much I will break it." Then the old man said to him, "It is

the same with the work of God. If we stretch the brethren beyond measure they will soon break. Sometimes it is necessary to come down to meet their needs." When he heard these words, the hunter was pierced by compunction.

ANTONY, *SAYINGS*

My beloved in the Lord—I speak to you as wise people, able to know yourselves—we know that those who know themselves know God. . . . Prepare yourselves while we have some who pray for us that the fire that Jesus came to send upon the earth [Lk 12.49] may be enkindled in your hearts, so that you may be able to exercise your heart and senses to discern the good from the bad, right from left, the eternal from the passing.

ANTONY, *LETTERS*

I want you to know, my children, that I never cease praying to God for you night and day, so that He may open the eyes of your hearts to see the principal hidden evils which the evil spirits now pour upon us daily. I ask God to give you a heart of knowledge and a spirit of discernment, so that you may be able to offer your hearts before the Father as a pure sacrifice in great holiness, without blemish.

ANTONY, *LETTERS*

Truly, my children, I want you to know that there are many who have pursued asceticism throughout their life, but lack of discernment killed them.

ANTONY, *LETTERS*

They lived a cenobitic life. So he established for them in a rule an irreproachable lifestyle and traditions profitable for their souls. These he took from the holy Scriptures: proper measure in clothing, equality in food, and decent sleeping arrangements.

LIFE OF PACHOMIUS

At another time, holy though he was, he became physically sick. . . . Another brother, sick to death, was lying in another cell nearby. He had been ill so long his body was mere bones. He had asked the father of the monastery to be given a little meat, and it had not yet been given to him. [He asked to be taken to Pachomius and repeated his request to him.] Pachomius, understanding that he deserved what he had asked for, sighed. And when at the hour of the brothers' meal they brought to the monk to eat exactly what all the others had, Pachomius did not eat but said: "Respecters of persons, where is [the precept of] the Scripture, 'You shall love your neighbor as yourself?' Do you not see that this man is a corpse? Why did you not take good care of him before he made his request? And why did you overlook him after he made it? But you will say, 'We neglected his request because this sort of food is not customary among us.' Are there no differences among sick persons? Are not 'all things pure to the pure' [Ti 1.15]? And if you were unable to discern by your own judgment that this was good, why did you not tell me?" And saying this he wept.

LIFE OF PACHOMIUS

Once Pachomius was sailing with two other brothers in a boat to Thomousons, and at evening, at mealtime, they prepared [food]. As they sat down to eat, he saw the great variety of food on the table: cheeses, figs, olives, and many other things, and he began to eat only bread. But they indiscriminately laid hands on everything there. One [brother] looked up and saw him weeping. After they got up, they queried him on the meaning of this; but he said nothing. As they asked him a second time, he said, "It is because of you that I am grieved, because you are not abstinent. . . . For surely it is not a sin to eat, especially the cheap things; but it is good not to be dominated by anything, as the Apostle says [1 Cor 6.12]. As for me, a sinner, finding the bread good, I

was satisfied with it. Another time I will eat according to the
Lord's gift.

LIFE OF PACHOMIUS

It is a great evil not to confess one's temptation quickly to
someone who has knowledge, before the evil has matured.
Here is the therapy through discernment of spirits that the
Lord has taught us. "If I grieve my neighbor with a word,
my heart becomes contrite when convinced by the word
of God, and if I do not persuade him quickly I have no
rest. Unclean demons! How shall I join you apostates in a
thought of blasphemy against the God who created me? I
will not give in even if you should pull me to pieces in suggesting these things to me. These thoughts are not mine but
yours who are going to be chastised in unquenchable fire for
ever and ever. As for me, I shall not cease blessing, praising,
and thanking the One who created me when I did not exist,
and cursing you, for cursed indeed are you apart from the
Lord." When one says these things with faith, the demon
vanishes like smoke.

LIFE OF PACHOMIUS

We who have chosen this way of life must obtain perfect
temperance. This is also true among seculars, but intemper-
ance cohabits with it, because they sin with all the other
senses. They gawk shamelessly and they laugh immoderately.

SYNCLETICA, SAYINGS

At all times a lack of moderation is destructive. Do not ex-
pend all your defensive weapons at one time; you will be
caught unarmed and will become a prisoner in the war. Our
armor is the body and our soul is the soldier; take care of
both against the time of need.

LIFE OF SYNCLETICA

It is essential for us to govern our soul with all discretion,
and, since we live in community, not to seek our own

interest, or to be slaves to our own will, but to obey our
spiritual mother in faith.

LIFE OF SYNCLETICA

Deny yourself in order to follow Christ. . . . Chastise the
body, do not cling to pleasures, love fasting.

RULE OF BENEDICT

Love chastity.

RULE OF BENEDICT

Beware of evil desire, because death sits at the entrance to
delight.

RULE OF BENEDICT

We think two cooked dishes are sufficient for the main daily
meal, whether it is at the sixth or ninth hour, at all times of
the year. . . . If fruit or fresh vegetables are available, let a
third dish be added. A generous pound of bread should be
enough for the day. . . . But if the work be heavy, it lies in
the power and judgment of the abbot to increase the daily
food, if that seems helpful, provided that there be no gluttony. . . . Frugality is to be maintained in all matters. All
should abstain from eating meat, except those weak from
illness.

RULE OF BENEDICT

All persons have a gift from God, one this, another that
[1 Cor 7.7], and so it is with some hesitation that we regu-
late the amount of food for others. However, taking into account the limitations of the weak, we think a *hemina* [a unit
of measure of unknown quantity] of wine per day is sufficient for each. Those to whom God gives the capacity for
abstinence should know that they will have their own reward. But if the local conditions, the work, or the summer's
heat requires more, it is up to the superior to decide, taking
care in every situation that gluttony and drunkenness do not

creep in. . . . But if local conditions are such that the measure of wine prescribed above is not obtainable, but only much less or none at all, those who live there should bless God and not murmur.

RULE OF BENEDICT

The sick who are physically weak are allowed to eat meat to restore their strength; but when their health has improved, all should abstain from meat as usual.

RULE OF BENEDICT

The abbot should arrange all things moderately, so that souls may be saved and the community may do what they do without justifiable murmuring.

RULE OF BENEDICT

All things should be done in moderation for the sake of the fainthearted.

RULE OF BENEDICT

Monastic life should always have a Lenten character, but since few are capable of that, we urge all of them together to guard the purity of their lives during these days of Lent and efface the negligences of other times during these holy days. This will happen properly if we restrain ourselves from all evil, and devote ourselves to prayer with tears, reading, compunction of heart, and abstinence.

RULE OF BENEDICT

Taking into account these and other examples of discretion, the mother of the virtues, the abbot should arrange all things so that the strong have something to strive for and the weak are not driven away.

RULE OF BENEDICT

Three days a week he ate nothing, but fasted continuously day and night. On these days he enjoined his tongue to silence, so he would not slip in even a single word. On the other three weekdays his food was leeks or boiled cabbage and a crust of bread. On Sundays, out of reverence for the feast, he expanded his spare diet to include fish and wine.

LIFE OF WULFSTAN

Before we correct a sinning neighbor and after we render our neighbor the service of a deserved correction, we should consider with a properly humble investigation whether we ourselves are enmeshed in the very things we condemn in him or in other crimes like his. For it often happens, for example, that people judge a murderer who sins publicly more harshly than the evil hatreds they fail to recognize are despoiling them secretly, or that those who accuse a fornicator fail to notice the plague of pride by which they extol themselves for their chastity, or that those who condemn a drunken person do not see the virus of envy that consumes them.

BEDE, *HOMILIES ON THE GOSPELS*

The virtue of discretion lies dormant without the fervor of charity; and intense fervor runs wild without the guidance of discretion.

BERNARD OF CLAIRVAUX,
ON THE SONG OF SONGS

Zeal without knowledge is unbearable. Where there is fervent zeal, there discretion—the ordering of charity—is most necessary. Zeal without knowledge is always less effective, less useful. Often it is found to be very harmful. Wherever zeal is most fervent and the spirit most vehement, there the need for knowledge's oversight is all the greater. Knowledge restrains zeal, tempers the spirit, orders charity.

BERNARD OF CLAIRVAUX,
ON THE SONG OF SONGS

When the stomach hears the voice of insistent hunger, it
confuses necessity and pleasure in a deceptive tangle. It is a
rare person who can erect a wall or divider to distinguish in
his appetite between necessity and excess.

PETER OF CELLE,
THE SCHOOL OF THE CLOISTER

Rationality is surrounded by divine protection. It produces,
arranges, and distinguishes all the things that God has given.
There is nothing that it cannot subtly penetrate and discuss.

HILDEGARD OF BINGEN,
BOOK OF LIFE'S MERITS

People think they have the beauty of prudence when they
walk about in complete foolishness.

HILDEGARD OF BINGEN,
BOOK OF LIFE'S MERITS

You who wish to be sharers in the heavenly Jerusalem, praise
your creator in the sound of faith that rings through all
God's works with a praiseworthy tone of comprehending
rationality, so that from each thing it sounds praise to the
good God. Rationality is like a trumpet with a living voice
that has tasks below itself that it dispenses in creatures
through the various arts. Then the same creatures can assist
it by returning a good, strong sound. Rationality through
the sound of its living voice makes those things that do not
have living sound resound with reason. From the first breath
by which God breathes it into the human soul, it has a jubilant mode. Therefore, praise God in that pure and fitting
knowledge that makes the creature in tune with itself, and in
the gentle and deep wisdom that arranges all things wisely in
a just dispensation—namely, when it discerns heavenly matters wisely in the minds of human beings and senses earthly
matters smoothly. For the human soul has harmony within
it and is symphonic.

HILDEGARD OF BINGEN,
BOOK OF LIFE'S MERITS

Benedict was a closed fountain [Song 4.12] who poured forth his doctrine in the discretion of God. For he drove in the sharp nail [spigot] of his doctrine neither too high nor too low, but in the middle of the wheel, so that each one, whether strong or weak or sick, would be able to drink according to his capacity.

HILDEGARD OF BINGEN,
EXPLANATION OF THE RULE OF BENEDICT

Superiors, for the love of God do not burden human weakness with more new ceremonies and observances than it can bear. Remember the warning of our holy Father in the *Rule:* ponder and temper the works you enjoin, remembering the discretion of Holy Jacob, who said: "If I drive my flocks too much, they will die in a single day." Therefore, so moderate everything that the strong have something to strive for and the weak are not forced to flee [cf. *Rule of Benedict* 64.20]. See, then, beloved fathers, how pleasing discretion is to God.

LUDOVICO BARBO, *LETTERS*

It is better to do good by abstinence than to eat without sinning.

JOHN TRITHEMIUS, *RULE*

One should not heedlessly embrace unusual austerity. Genuine love of God joins a person much more closely to God, and more quickly and effectively restrains and conquers the wantonness of the flesh. God customarily exercises and burdens those who fully resign themselves to him and are prepared to accept any troubles from his hand and to bear them patiently as long as it pleases him. Dedicated persons should therefore not oppress their bodies with excessive abstinence, vigils, and austerities of their own choosing, nor should they treat them too gently. Instead, let them observe the moderation of holy discretion in all things and accept the sane advice of others.

LOUIS DE BLOIS, *SPIRITUAL DOCTRINE*

In refreshing the body with food, drink, or sleep, one
should aim at sustaining nature, not at pleasure. One should
take each morsel of food and each swallow of drink with
moderation and self-control, with holy fear and self-
mortification for the glory of God. . . . One should seek
simple rather than sumptuous things for one's use. Do not
seek superfluous things, but prefer want to abundance.

LOUIS DE BLOIS, *SPIRITUAL DOCTRINE*

Authentic renewal is going to demand a great deal of variety
and originality in experimentation.

THOMAS MERTON,
CONTEMPLATION IN A WORLD OF ACTION

One cannot simply open his eyes and see. The work of
understanding involves not only dialectic, but a long labor
of acceptance, obedience, liberty, and love.

THOMAS MERTON,
CONJECTURES OF A GUILTY BYSTANDER

As the seasons change and the nights grow shorter, Benedict
chooses to shorten the time of prayer rather than the time
of sleep.

ESTHER DE WAAL, *A LIFE-GIVING WAY*

The key word is moderation. Just as the brothers are to have
sufficient, not superfluous goods. . . so also the cellarer is to
steer a mid-point between being either extravagant or mean.
It is waste in particular that Benedict warns against.

ESTHER DE WAAL, *A LIFE-GIVING WAY*

[Benedict's concern regarding food] is not simply about
having sufficient food, enough but not superfluous, but
about the right handling of these good things. That is why
there is a choice of dishes, so that all can expect to eat with
enjoyment. That is why when there are fruits and fresh
vegetables in season, they are to be added to the table. That

is why he is not mean with the bread allowance. To look forward to a meal because it is carefully chosen and carefully presented gives to every meal something of a sacramental quality.

ESTHER DE WAAL, *A LIFE-GIVING WAY*

The purpose of fasting is simply to center on God. The discipline of fasting will reveal to me more than any other discipline what really controls me. It is no longer possible to cover up my interior dependencies—food, good things, praise, anger, envy. Fasting, therefore, plays its part in the movement of freedom, of dissociation and non-possession.

ESTHER DE WAAL, *A LIFE-GIVING WAY*

CHAPTER II

Peace

The nineteenth-century refounders of Benedictine monasticism mistakenly selected "Ora et Labora" (Work and Pray) as their motto. A more venerable and accurate motto would be "Pax," the Latin word for "peace." Monasticism is a many-sided effort at peace, within the individual monk, between monks, between the monastery and the surrounding communities, and ultimately in the whole of church and society. We have learned enough from Gandhi and the civil rights movement to know that peace is not a ploy of the weak, but an achievement of the strong and the courageous.

Beginning with Antony and the desert monks and nuns, a favorite symbol of monastic peace was the harmony monastics established with wild animals. Antony made peace with the wild animals who disturbed his garden, Benedict was served by crows, and in Switzerland, the Irish monk Saint Gall established good relations with a bear. The lamb and lion lay down together as the desert or the wilderness was transformed into a new Eden.

Not only was Antony at peace with the world of nature and with the people around him; he was at peace with himself. He radiated a peace and joy that attracted strangers to him. The inner peace of his heart was somehow etched on his face.

Good monastic leaders are able to maintain peace within their communities. Pachomius, who seems to have been a brilliant leader of men, worked hard to develop a potential successor. In the end, his efforts were partially foiled, and we hear the author of his biography lamenting the loss of the peace that the communities enjoyed during his lifetime.

Peace was an important concept for Saint Benedict, in part because of this earlier monastic tradition. Peace also figured prominently in the Bible, where it was a state of earthly plenty and of harmony with God, people, and nature. Biblical peace is God's gift, but also a central goal of human effort. For Saint Augustine and the classical Christian writers of the centuries before Benedict, peace was the tranquillity of order, based on observance of the laws God established for the world he created.

In the prologue of the *Rule of Benedict* Jesus is quoted using the words of a psalm (Ps 33.16) to tell those who desire life to seek peace and pursue it. Benedict wanted his monks to make peace with each other before sundown, and several times the *Rule* warns against making a feigned or insincere peace. He designed his rules on the distribution of goods so that "all the members of the family shall be at peace." Guests are to be given the sign of peace when they arrive, just as if they were Christ. Benedict's rules on rank in the community are for the sake of peace.

Read in the light of its biblical and classical background, Benedict's most basic requirement for peace is the tranquillity of order based on the observance of the laws of nature—for example, getting enough sleep, avoiding workaholism, taking care of the sick. Second, there should be a harmony between being, thought, word, and action; for example, an abbot should be what he is called, the mind should be in harmony with the voice. Third, the atmosphere of the monastery should be quiet and orderly, so that those who are there may also be at peace. Peace of soul means avoiding worry, excessive needs and wants, inflexibility, envy. Peace of soul presupposes that we seek to be content with life as we find it. To do that we must learn to control our desires, develop equanimity of character, and achieve unity with God. That is a lifetime's work—the summit of virtue, Benedict calls it. Even so, any peace on earth will be partial and fragile; lasting and perfect peace is for heaven.

The monastic enterprise is to create people and communities of peace, so it is not surprising that authors indicate that peace presupposes almost every other activity and virtue mentioned in this book. Peace can be achieved only where conflict is honestly acknowledged. To acknowledge such conflict takes courage and humility and an uncommon readiness to forgive. To honesty, courage, humility, and forgiveness must be added workable mechanisms of conflict resolution. Genuine peace is not easily or painlessly achieved. However, the alternative is open conflict, or worse yet, a false peace, a facade of order fronting a house at odds with itself.

At first, wild animals in the desert coming for water often would damage the beds of Antony's garden. But he caught one of the animals, held it gently, and said to them all: "Why do you do harm to me when I harm none of you? Go away, and in the Lord's name do not come near these things again!" And ever afterwards, as though awed by his orders, they did not come near the place.

LIFE OF ANTONY

[Antony's face] had a great and indescribable charm in it. And he had this added gift from the Savior: if he was present in a gathering of monks and someone who had no previous acquaintance with him wished to see him, as soon as he arrived he would pass over the others and run to Antony as if drawn by his eyes. It was not his stature or figure that made him stand out from the rest, but his settled character and the purity of his soul. For his soul was not perturbed, and so his outward appearance was calm. The joy in his soul expressed itself in the cheerfulness of his face.

LIFE OF ANTONY

Now it is not yet five years since he [Pachomius] passed away and we have forgotten that very great joy and peace which we then had with each other. For in the days of our father, we did not have either in heart or in mouth anything but the word of God which is sweeter than honey and the honeycomb [Ps 19.10]. We were not conscious of living on earth but of feasting in heaven.

LIFE OF PACHOMIUS

Hate no one. Do not be jealous. Do not act out of envy. Do not love quarreling.

RULE OF BENEDICT

If there is discord, make peace before the sun goes down.

RULE OF BENEDICT

Wulfstan spent much of the day in preaching. He tried to inculcate in his hearers that which he knew they needed most—peace. For mortal men can hear of nothing sweeter, seek nothing more desirable, find nothing better. Peace is the beginning and the end of human salvation, the ultimate goal of God's commands. The angelic music sang of it at the first sign of our redemption, the Lord gave it to his disciples when he had foreseen the impending Crucifixion, and at the Resurrection restored it to them as a trophy of victory.

LIFE OF WULFSTAN

"What then will you give us, Lord? What are you going to give us?" "Peace I give you. My peace I leave for you," says the Lord. That is enough for me: gratefully I accept what you leave, and I let go of what you retain. If it pleases you, I do not doubt that it is for my good. . . . I want peace, I desire peace, and nothing more. If there is anyone unsatisfied with peace, they will be unsatisfied with you.

BERNARD OF CLAIRVAUX,
ON THE SONG OF SONGS

In you, O Jesus, true peace, may I have peace upon peace forever, so that through you I may come to that peace which surpasses all understanding, where happily I may see you in yourself forever. Amen.

GERTRUDE THE GREAT,
SPIRITUAL EXERCISES

I urge you, above all, if you want to obtain the true fruit of prayers, strive to be in charity and peace with all by

forgiving those who offend you, by loving the virtuous, by
serving all with humility, and by obeying your superiors in
all things with a ready will, so that true peace may arise in
your minds, and our Lord God, whose place is the peace in
our minds, may reside in a peaceful place. I am confident in
saying that in a short time you will reach these virtues and
this peace through the use of [vocal] prayer.

LUDOVICO BARBO, *FORM OF PRAYER*

Humility is at the service of peace and concord.

JOHN TRITHEMIUS, *RULE*

There is nothing good where there is no peace. God is a
lover of peace and dwells only in peaceful hearts. No matter
what one has, it gives no joy if peace is lacking.

JOHN TRITHEMIUS, *RULE*

If you want to keep peace in the community, judge yourself
and no one else. Be careful never to disturb the peace of
your brothers, for whoever destroys the peace of just people
makes himself a persecutor of God.

JOHN TRITHEMIUS, *RULE*

Blessed are those to whom Jesus speaks inwardly, saying,
"Come up to a desert place." Blessed, I say, are those whom
the Lord carries across the great, wide sea through countless
dangers of this world to the port of monastic life. There life
is truly quiet and secure; there tranquillity, peace, and spiritual joy abound; there, day and night, holy people freely
serve the king of the ages without care or concern about
passing things. They have only one concern, that they may
please their great God through a firm commitment to obedience, through pleasant devotion in prayer, through sweet
exercises of holy reading, through gentle baptism in holy
tears.

LOUIS DE BLOIS, *MIRROR FOR MONKS*

Father, I beg you to keep me in this silence so that I may learn from it the word of your peace and the word of your mercy and the word of your gentleness to the world: and that through me perhaps your word of peace may make itself heard where it has not been possible for anyone to hear it for a long time.

THOMAS MERTON,
CONJECTURES OF A GUILTY BYSTANDER

[The cellarer] is indeed a model of non-violence, and the very way in which he handles people demonstrates a profound spiritual truth: people are to be handled with respect and reverence. But the cellarer is to handle himself with gentleness. He is to show these same qualities toward himself in the way in which he takes care of his own body and spirit. . . . The cellarer is not too proud to admit that he may need help. He is prepared to delegate, not seeing himself as indispensable. He knows the importance of drawing lines so that he is not endlessly accessible. He makes himself available at established times. . . . Handling with care applies just as much to my own self as it does to other people and to the material world. . . . And the purpose? So that he remain calm. Peace is fundamental in the Rule.

ESTHER DE WAAL, *A LIFE-GIVING WAY*

Benedictinism simply sets out to gentle a universe riddled with violence by being a peaceful voice for peace in a world that thinks that everything . . . is accomplished by force.

SR. JOAN CHITTISTER,
THE RULE OF BENEDICT

[Benedict extended the use of Alleluia in the liturgy of the hours to every day of the year except during Lent.] The prescription is a telling one. To the Benedictine mind, life in all its long nights and weary days is something to be praised, death is the rivet of joy, there is no end to the positive. Even

life in hot fields and drab offices and small houses is somehow one long happy thought when God is its center, and
blessings, however rare, however scant, are blessed.

SR. JOAN CHITTISTER,
THE RULE OF BENEDICT

CHAPTER 12

Patience

Patience comes from the Latin verb *pati,* which means "to suffer, to undergo, to endure." Gertrude's fanciful etymology of *pax* plus *scientia* (knowledge) is correct to the extent that knowing the purpose of suffering goes a long way toward making suffering bearable. Syncletica suggests that if monastics think they are burdened with much suffering, they should think about the burdens of their married sisters out beyond the protection of the cloister walls.

The Christian monastic tradition connects patience with Christ's sufferings, his "passion," another derivative of *pati.* A telling example is Benedict's statement in the prologue to his *Rule:* "We will share by patience in the sufferings of Christ, so that we may deserve to be sharers in his kingdom" (*Rule of Benedict* prologue 50). Christian efforts to understand suffering inevitably lead to the paschal mystery, the dying and rising of Christ, the seed that must die if it is to bear fruit. Hence suffering can coexist with joy, not because suffering is either unreal or invariably mild, but because it is a path to life.

Patience is essential, since the road to virtue is a long one. Only repeated effort and practice establish a habit, and a firm habit is frequently exercised. Especially at the beginning, the road is difficult. Amma Syncletica's comparison with lighting a fire mirrors the reality nicely.

There are some injustices we must accept since they are unavoidable. Others we might protest, but shouldn't, because the disruptive effects of such a protest outweigh any good effects it might achieve. In some cases we are obligated to protest. In all but the last case, one should bear persecution for justice's sake. Such patience is a gift, rooted in the faith that God is in charge of the universe, and that

God's Providence can and will bring good out of bad. As a friend reminded me recently, suffering entered into willingly leads us to the will of God, which may not be what we wanted or hoped for. Accepting annoyances and suffering as special gifts of God who loves us to perfection may take us out of ourselves and show us, in other people, the face of Christ turned toward us.

Perhaps the most difficult exercise of patience is to maintain it with our own failings. Our struggle to practice virtue often takes place on the verge of defeat, or it consists of trying to get back on our feet after falling yet again. God is patient with us, so we can afford to be patient also. Esther de Waal makes the wise observation that the *Rule* provides for the complete range of human weakness, but is neither cynical nor pessimistic. This patience of the *Rule* reflects the patience of God. We are saved not by our perfection, but by our identification with the dying and rising of Christ.

⌒

An old man said: "If you become sick from a bodily illness, don't lose courage. If your Lord wishes to afflict your body, why should you be upset? Does not his concern for you include everything? Can you live without him? Be patient then and pray that he will give you what you should have. His will is that you stay in your room with patience and that you eat what is given to you as alms."

SAYINGS OF THE DESERT
FATHERS AND MOTHERS

A brother, irritated with another, prayed, asking to be patient toward this brother. He prayed that the temptation would pass without causing him any harm. Immediately he saw smoke leave his mouth.

SAYINGS OF THE DESERT
FATHERS AND MOTHERS

Let us women not be misled by the thought that those in the world are without cares. For perhaps in comparison they

struggle more than we do. For towards women generally
there is great hostility in the world. They bear children with
difficulty and risk, and they suffer patiently through nursing,
and they share illnesses with their sick children—and these
things they endure without having any limit to their travail.
For either the children they bear are maimed in body, or,
brought up in perversity, they treacherously murder their
parents. Since we women know these facts, therefore, let us
not be deluded by the Enemy that their life is easy and care-
free. For in giving birth women die in labor, and yet, in failing to give birth, they waste away under reproaches that they
are barren and unfruitful.

LIFE OF SYNCLETICA

For those who are making their way to God there is at first
great struggle and effort, but then indescribable joy. For just
as those who wish to kindle a fire are at first choked with
smoke, suffer watery eyes, and in this way achieve their purpose (indeed Scripture says: "Our God is a consuming fire"
[Heb 12.29]), so we too must kindle the divine fire within
us with tears and effort.

LIFE OF SYNCLETICA

Let us also understand this profitable thing we heard from
our father [Theodore], from his interpretations of the holy
Scriptures, about a man wishing to be purified from a sin
such as anger. Unless he says in himself when he is reviled
the first time, "Behold, today I have gained a golden coin,"
and unless he considers it a further gain when he is reviled a
second time, and so on until he has an abundance of gold, it
is impossible for him not to get angry. . . . Such are the men
of God. Not only did they bear those who persecuted them
and did them evil, but they even prayed for them, according
to the commandment of the Savior, whose gold they were
going to inherit according to the Scripture, "Heirs of God,
and coheirs with Christ" [Rom 8.17].

LIFE OF PACHOMIUS

Bear persecution for the sake of justice.

RULE OF BENEDICT

Those who show patience in adversities and injustices fulfill the command of the Lord that says: "Those who are struck on one cheek should offer the other" [Mt 5.39].

RULE OF BENEDICT

Never departing from his instruction, but persevering in his teaching in the monastery until death, we will share by patience in the sufferings of Christ, so that we may deserve to be sharers in his kingdom.

RULE OF BENEDICT

[We ought] to be of help to all, to refrain from hurting others out of bitterness, to bear whatever injuries are inflicted on us, and even ask pardon from the Lord for those who inflict them.

BEDE, HOMILIES ON THE GOSPELS

People who are committed to praying frequently have experienced what I am talking about. Often we approach the altar with a lukewarm and arid heart in order to devote ourselves to prayer. If we are persistent, our heart is suddenly filled with grace.

BERNARD OF CLAIRVAUX,
ON THE SONG OF SONGS

Heavenly joy declares: I give all my works to God, because in some sadness there is joy, and in some pleasure there is no prosperity.

HILDEGARD OF BINGEN,
BOOK OF LIFE'S MERITS

[Gertrude] firmly believed that everything, external or internal, worked together for her good.

GERTRUDE THE GREAT,
THE HERALD OF DIVINE LOVE

The Lord told M[echthild] in prayer: "The *patientia* (patience) that I like in Gertrude comes from the words *pax* (peace) and *scientia* (knowledge). The fervor of her patience should be such that in adversity she does not lose her peace of heart, but always strives to think why she is suffering— namely, out of love as a sign of true faithfulness.

GERTRUDE THE GREAT,
THE HERALD OF DIVINE LOVE

Christ says: "Deny yourself, so that you can follow me," and "Take up your cross daily" [Mk 8.34]. Those who patiently and freely suffer all adversities for God take up their cross daily. Our cross consists of the difficult obstacles of this life through which we travel to God. "Take up,"—that is, bear them cheerfully and willingly. "Take up your cross and follow me." It is of no use to deny ourselves and bear the cross unless we also follow Christ.

JOHN TRITHEMIUS, *RULE*

For all the living, life is the most desirable thing. We all want to live and reign with Christ, but we do not all want to suffer with Christ.

JOHN TRITHEMIUS, *RULE*

Nothing is hard for the advanced person or for the one who loves or is perfect. But for beginners, even easy things are hard, for they invite the mind spiritually to acts that are contrary to its usual way of acting.

JOHN TRITHEMIUS, *RULE*

Whatever happens to them, let them refer it to the divine will and accept it just as it comes from the hand of God, without whose Providence not even a leaf falls from a tree to the earth. . . . Let them bear with patient and tranquil minds internal abandonment and disaster as well as any afflictions, and let them praise God, believing that he is willing and able to promote their salvation in all circumstances.

LOUIS DE BLOIS, *SPIRITUAL DOCTRINE*

Persist in your holy purpose, even if you fail a thousand times a day.

LOUIS DE BLOIS, *SPIRITUAL MIRROR*

When you are afflicted with sensory distractions, depression, dryness of heart, headache, or any other misery and temptation, beware of saying: "I am abandoned. The Lord has cast me off. My service does not please him." These are things that the faint-hearted often say. Instead, bear all things patiently and cheerfully for the sake of him who called and chose you. Believe for certain that he is near to those who are troubled in heart.

LOUIS DE BLOIS, *MIRROR FOR MONKS*

Benedict is always showing me the patience of God waiting and working for the return of his children. Throughout the prologue, he never fails to situate our lives in the context of this patience of God which is no less than the paschal mystery working in us through the *patientia,* the suffering of Christ.

ESTHER DE WAAL, *A LIFE-GIVING WAY*

What I have increasingly appreciated as I have stayed with the Rule is finding how it provides for the whole range of human weakness and inadequacy, yet with a complete absence of cynicism or pessimism. This is what the human condition is, and this is where God's grace is encountered and the paschal mystery happens. . . . Benedict would seem to be saying that weakness and failure are not necessarily a handicap or a disqualification but can, with help, be made the place in which the power of the crucified and risen Christ can be manifested in our lives.

ESTHER DE WAAL, *A LIFE-GIVING WAY*

CHAPTER 13

Separation

Monasticism is by definition a countercultural movement, not because monastics make it a point to define themselves against any existing culture, but because they try to maintain their own values and virtues, whatever values the surrounding culture may exhibit. At their best and wisest, monastics listen to and learn from existing culture, but they do so critically, with a preexisting understanding of who they are and who they want to be.

To maintain monastic culture, monks limit their contact with the surrounding culture by means of cloister or separation from the world. In part, cloister is spatial; a wall beyond which the monk usually does not go except for brief and necessary forays. More essentially, cloister is a matter of mind and heart. Monastics monitor what they read, watch, and hear, and learn to make sure that they can hear God's voice and that the Biblical tradition pulses as the heart of their community.

Peter of Celle may be somewhat sanguine about the correlation between staying in a cloister and stretching the mind. However, the mind that withdraws from gossip, useless news, potboiler novels, and surfing the Internet will have much more time and energy for God, and for praying, reading, thinking, and listening to and caring for other people—activities that do stretch the mind. The monastic writers spoke of dispersal and collection. People serious about living deeply should gather the rubble of their lives and glue themselves back together.

It is one thing to love one's room because one is so stressed out by work, crowds, talking, rushing from one appointment to the next, answering phone messages, that one's room is a place where one can collapse in peace. It is another thing to find somewhere a place of silence and creativity, where one can listen for the voice of God and think one's own thoughts and be one's own self.

⌒

Once when Antony had been importuned by people who needed assistance and the military commander had sent numerous messengers asking him to come down, he came and spoke a few words on the subject of salvation and in behalf of those who wanted him, and then hastened to leave. When the duke, as he is called, begged him to stay, he said he could not spend any time with them, and satisfied him by a beautiful comparison: "Just as fish exposed for any length of time on dry land die, so monks go to pieces when they loiter among you and spend too much time with you. Therefore, we must be off to the mountain, as fish to the sea. Otherwise, if we tarry, we may lose sight of the inner life."

LIFE OF ANTONY

Abba Antony said that a time is coming when men will go mad, a time when, if they will see someone who is not mad, they will attack him saying, "You are mad, because you are not like us."

ANTONY, SAYINGS

Abba Antony once went to visit Abba Amoun in Mount Nitria. During their visit Abba Amoun said, "Since by your prayers the number of the brethren increases, some of them want to build their cells at a distance where they may live in peace. How far away from here do you think we should build their cells?" Abba Antony said, "We will eat at the ninth hour and then go for a walk in the desert and explore the country." So they went out into the desert and walked until sunset. Then Abba Antony said, "Let us pray and plant

the cross here, so that those who wish to do so may build
here. Then when those who remain behind want to visit
those who have come here, they can come after taking a
little food at the ninth hour. If they do this, they will be
able to keep in touch with each other without distraction."
The distance is twelve miles.

ANTONY, *SAYINGS*

Not all courses are suitable for all people. You should have
confidence in your own disposition. For many it is profitable to live in community; for others it is helpful to with-
draw on their own. . . . Many people have found salvation
in a city while imagining the conditions of a desert. And
many though on a mountain, have been lost by living the
life of townspeople. It is possible for one who is in a group
to be alone in thought, and for one who is alone to live
mentally with a crowd.

LIFE OF SYNCLETICA

We have committed ourselves to exile, that is, we are outside secular boundaries; we have, then, been banished—
let us not seek the same ends.

LIFE OF SYNCLETICA

Make yourself a stranger to the world's activities.

RULE OF BENEDICT

Keep death daily before your eyes.

RULE OF BENEDICT

If possible, the monastery should be located so that all ne-
cessities—that is, water, mill, garden, and various crafts—
are provided within the monastery, so that there will be
no need for monks to wander forth, which is not good for
their souls.

RULE OF BENEDICT

Those who are about to set out on a journey should com-
mend themselves to the prayer of the community and
abbot. . . . Nor should they presume to tell anyone else what
they saw or heard outside the monastery, because this has
caused great harm.

RULE OF BENEDICT

It feels good to rest after working. After having been
troubled all year with painful and unrelenting problems, I
am thirsting mightily for the modest silence of my room
as a desirable haven. I draw deeply from the silence now
granted. My mind finds a more expansive rest by being
within these four walls than by traveling around outside to
the four corners of the earth. In fact, the smaller the place,
the more the mind stretches, for when the body is held in
check, the mind rises up; curbing the body brings expansion
of the mind.

PETER OF CELLE,
ON AFFLICTION AND READING

[Staying quietly in one's room] is not among those pleasures
that I find cloying once they are attained though they were
desirable before being possessed. A room is experienced in
two ways, depending on the lifestyle of the person who lives
in it. To carnal people it is a harsh environment, to spiritual
people a pleasant one. It is a prison to the flesh, a paradise
for the mind.

PETER OF CELLE,
ON AFFLICTION AND READING

The need for a certain distance from the world does
not make the monk love the world less. Nor does it
imply that he never has any contact with the outside
world. Certainly the monastic community has the right
and duty to create a certain solitude for the monks: it is
no sin to live a silent life. But at the same time the mo-

nastic community owes other men a share in that quiet and that solitude.

THOMAS MERTON,
CONTEMPLATION IN A WORLD OF ACTION

[Speaking of his affinity for Albert Camus, Merton says it is easy for him to take Camus's position:] that of a man who at once loves the world yet stands apart from it with a critical objectivity which refuses to become involved in its transient fashions and its more manifest absurdities.

THOMAS MERTON,
CONTEMPLATION IN A WORLD OF ACTION

The monk is by definition a man who lives in seclusion, in solitude, in silence outside of the noise and the confusion of a busy worldly existence. He does this because seclusion provides certain necessary conditions for his life: an interior freedom, silence, liberation from trivial concerns that arise from the overstimulation of the appetites and the imagination. The monk finally seeks solitude and silence, let us admit it, because he knows that the real fruit of his vocation is union with God in love and contemplation.

THOMAS MERTON,
CONTEMPLATION IN A WORLD OF ACTION

In Louisville, at the corner of Fourth and Walnut, in the center of the shopping district, I was suddenly overwhelmed with the realization that I love all those people, that they were mine and I theirs, that we could not be alien to one another even though we were total strangers. It was like waking from a dream of separateness, of spurious self-isolation in a special world. . . . Though "out of the world" we are in the same world as everybody else, the world of the bomb, the world of race hatred, the world of technology, the world of mass media, big business, revolution, and all the rest. . . . It is a glorious destiny to be a member of the human race, though it is a race dedicated to many absurdities and one which makes many terrible mistakes: yet, with all that, God Himself gloried in becoming a member of the human race.

THOMAS MERTON,
CONJECTURES OF A GUILTY BYSTANDER

Benedictine spirituality goes into the heart in order to embrace the world. It forms us differently than the world forms us but it does not attempt to shape us independently of the real world around us.

SR. JOAN CHITTISTER,
THE RULE OF BENEDICT

CHAPTER 14

Stability

A healthy human life is a combination of fidelity to commitments on the one hand, and growth, change, and development on the other. One thinks of the Israelites, who made their covenant with God, then entered the promised land, took up settled agriculture, and developed structures of government and cohesion. Or of Ruth, who, having committed herself to Naomi with the promise "I will go where you go," did so, met Boaz, married, and started life afresh. Jesus himself was fundamentally committed to doing his father's will. For thirty years this kept him in Nazareth, probably working at his father's trade, learning it better, and growing in grace and wisdom. Then when he was almost thirty Jesus came to see that his fidelity to God's will for him required a radical change in his life, a change that involved a year or two as a wandering preacher, and then a momentous journey to Jerusalem, where he was tortured and executed, and rose again.

The *Rule of Benedict* endorses fidelity and change by the two vows of stability and conversion. Stability commits one to a certain community and its way of life; conversion calls one to continuously grow and follow the lead of God's will as this appears in one's deepest desires, in one's circumstances, and in the advice and authority of other people (listening and obedience). There is clearly a tension here, one that can be resolved only in dialogue, prayer, and love: in dialogue, to help the individual and community discern; in prayer, because it is God's will they are seeking; in love, because love is an unselfish and caring affirmation of the being and goodness of another. The tension is less when communities that value and respect the gifts and callings of individuals try to give them scope for growth and change. The same tension between fidelity and change occurs in almost every significant human relationship.

The vow of stability attaches the monk to a single community or monastery. There is very little that ties one Benedictine monastery to another. Almost all are in congregations of monasteries that provide member communities with regular visitations, meetings, and support but leave the individual monasteries autonomous. The advantage of this is that the monk has to learn to live with and for the community he has chosen. He cannot just move from place to place as he becomes discouraged with one community and then another. He has to face the situation and learn the truth about himself and the human condition. A disadvantage is that the monk is very deeply defined by his community; any dysfunction in that community will affect him either directly or indirectly.

For the most part, monasteries are not in the vanguard of change. They may call into question the certitudes of the dominant culture, but they are slow to change their own ways of doing things. For one thing, most of the customary ways of doing things are in place precisely so that the monks do not have to think about them. One knows when to eat lunch, where to sit, whether to talk, what prayers to say, and so one can concentrate on doing them well rather than think about what to do next. These customary ways of doing things are second nature, a second nature defined in part by the requirements of community living, in part by the values monks espouse. That is why Ludovico Barbo, for one, says that customary observances should not be changed readily.

However, conservatism in monastic customs may gradually turn to fossilization. Monastic education, monastic work and economy, monastic organization, and monastic recruitment are all in great flux today. These and other issues call for imagination and experimentation. One needs to decide what is the best possible course of action and then do it, leaving the results in God's hands. Stability must provide a ground for innovation, for continual renewal of *conversatio*. Barbo was an example of such innovation in his time.

Here, too, discernment is the key. The monastic vows aim at a subtle combination of stability and openness to change. Innovation on a foundation of stability, and firm commitment in the midst of renewal or innovation, are not easy. They seem to be the principal challenge of our time. Hence, we probably should be kinder to those who seem out of tune with the rest of us; they may be in tune with the future.

Similarly, as Bede points out, discernment helps us to know ourselves and to perceive where we need to grow in virtue and integrity. The acquisition of virtue is the moral equivalent of physical stability. One becomes morally stable by acquiring virtue. The Benedictine tradition suggests that a certain stability of place and lifestyle is an advantageous setting for moral growth and stability.

Someone asked Abba Antony, "What should I do in order to please God?" The old man answered: "Pay attention to what I am going to tell you: wherever you go, always have God before your eyes; do everything you do according to the testimony of the holy Scriptures; wherever you live, do not leave it easily."

ANTONY, *SAYINGS*

An old man said: "The fathers did not leave the place where they were except for one of three causes: if there was someone there who was angry with them and they were unable to win him over; if they were praised too much; or if they risked falling into temptation."

SAYINGS OF THE DESERT
FATHERS AND MOTHERS

A brother asked one of the old men: "What should I do? My thoughts torment me, saying: 'You can neither keep a fast nor work; at least go and visit the sick, for that is a work of charity.'" The old man told him: "Go, eat, drink, sleep, only don't leave your cell. Know that perseverance in his room keeps the monk in his regular routine." When he has passed some days, he became bored, and, finding some small branches of palm, he split them; then the next day he wove them. After having worked, he said: "There are still some other small branches that I will prepare before I eat." He prepared them; then he said: "I will go read a little, then I will eat." After having read, he said: "I will recite my brief psalmody, then I will eat quietly." Thus he progressed little by little with the help of God until he restored his regular routine. In acting confidently against his tormenting thoughts, he conquered them.

SAYINGS OF THE DESERT
FATHERS AND MOTHERS

Do you live in a cenobitic monastery? Do not change your location, for you will be greatly harmed. For just as a bird that abandons its eggs renders them empty and unfruitful, so a nun or a monk grows cold and dies to faith by moving from place to place.

LIFE OF SYNCLETICA

We must follow in [the] footsteps [of our predecessors in the faith] in our own time, my brothers, directing the ordering of our life according to the example of good people and persisting until death in our commitment to an upright life.

BEDE, HOMILIES ON THE GOSPELS

By digging deeply they alertly examine their consciences so that nothing sordid may lie hidden within them. They carefully probe all the depths of their hearts for the hiding places of empty thoughts and draw them out with the hand of conscientious discretion so that they can prepare a firm and restful throne within themselves for that strong rock, who is Christ. And through his presence they persevere amid the fearful adversities of this world and amid its allurements as well.

BEDE, HOMILIES ON THE GOSPELS

Albero, a man of noteworthy virtue and age, skilled in book decoration, saw something at the time of calamity and anguish when the father [Abbot Hugh] died that deserves mention. It happened that a certain uncle of his had chosen him to be his companion on a pilgrimage to Compostela. But when he came to the gate, blessed Hugh met him with a serene and angelic face and chided him with the words: "Where are you going, Albero? Stay! Why are you going away?" Albero said to him: "How can I remain here when I do not find you here anymore, you who were sent here as a tower of David, a column, a wall for the upright of Israel. Like a sheep without a shepherd wanders a monk deprived of his abbot." The abbot, whom Albero saw in his spirit's imagination, replied: "Those whom God raises in heaven are not taken down from their assigned place. Those who stay in their rightful place in this world receive a higher place above."

LIFE OF HUGH OF CLUNY

When you are feeling strong, do not be complacent, but call to God with the prophet and say: "When my strength fails me, do not abandon me" [Ps 70.9]. And in time of temptation be consoled and say with the bride: "Draw me after you, and we shall run in the odor of your ointments" [Ps 33.2]. Thus you will not lose hope in bad times, nor will foresight desert you in good times, and amid both the prosperity and adversity of changing times you will retain a certain image of eternity—that is, this inviolable and unshakable constancy of a stable soul—blessing the Lord at every moment. In this way you claim for yourself, even amid the doubtful events and inevitable deficiencies of this changing world, a certain status of lasting unchangeability while you begin to renew and reform yourself according to the ancient pattern of likeness to the eternal God, "in whom there is neither alteration nor the shadow of change" [Jas 1.17].

BERNARD OF CLAIRVAUX,
ON THE SONG OF SONGS

People who wish to dispel from themselves the wicked spirits who urge them to be constantly changing and desire to flee their punishments should, if they be laypeople, collect themselves to lead a spiritual life, and if they be claustrals, let them confine themselves more strictly than usual in their way of life with all the discipline that truth requires, so that they can cast off the wickedness of this vice.

HILDEGARD OF BINGEN,
BOOK OF LIFE'S MERITS

Our conversion is pleasing to God when we persevere to the end and complete the good that we have begun.

JOHN TRITHEMIUS, *RULE*

[To people outside of a monastic community, the three Benedictine vows of stability, obedience, and conversion of life appear to be] three promises that together form one whole process. They ask me to enter into a dynamic commitment that simultaneously holds me still (stability) and moves me forward (continual conversion) with all the time God, and not my own self, as the point of reference (obedience, listening intently).

ESTHER DE WAAL, *A LIFE-GIVING WAY*

In the end I am brought back, of course, to Christ himself and to his example, the willingness to endure faithfully and with patience, *patientia,* reminding me that this means both waiting and suffering. What makes this possible? The faithfulness of God. God is faithful to the covenant, and I know I can rely on him. . . . My stability is possible in the end because of the certain, guaranteed, steadfastness of God.

ESTHER DE WAAL, *A LIFE-GIVING WAY*

It is not perfection that leads us to God; it is perseverance.

SR. JOAN CHITTISTER,
THE RULE OF BENEDICT

No one . . . has a call simply to a particular place, as good as it may be. The call of God is to the Will of God. Consequently, though every institution mediates the call of God for us, every vocation transcends any particular institution.

SR. JOAN CHITTISTER,
THE RULE OF BENEDICT

CHAPTER 15

Obedience

Obedience *(ob-audire)* is related to listening *(audire)*. The obedient person listens to others to discover what is true and what is good and what should be done. Among those others who should be listened to, some are leaders with authority in the community. They hold the place of Christ in the community. Quite apart from theology, in any community the leaders are likely to be better informed than anyone else, so their decisions have a certain a priori weight. Moreover, the community good is promoted far more often by ready implementation of the leader's orders than by stubborn resistance to them. Benedict says monks should make their ideas known, and if they think they cannot do something they should say so. The abbot should consider their statements, then repeat or reformulate his orders. The monk should obey them. At worst, he will fail; at best he will be stretched beyond his self-defined limits.

Hierarchy and obedience are logically distinct. Neither word has a nice ring to it. Hierarchy makes one think of kings; obedience conjures up the Gestapo. In fact, Benedict says monks should obey each other. Three monks should be able to arrange a room without arguing, because their aim is to listen to each other and do God's will, not enforce their own.

Thus obedience looks to the good both of the community and of the individual. For Saint Benedict, one cannot be obedient unless one is also cheerful, and perhaps a bit bemused by the tremendous authority with which people, oneself included, invest their opinions and desires about almost anything, from liturgical minutiae to how to wash the dishes.

Christ is the model of obedience. He sought his father's will and followed where it led. In his case, it led to the cross. Hildegard's personified obedience speaks with the voice of Old Testament Wisdom, and the New Testament Word.

The Benedictine tradition prefers listening to ascetic feats, simple obedience to arrogant ecstasy. The important thing, again, is not what one does, but how one does it.

～〜

Truthfully, my children, I tell you that everyone who delights in his own will and is subdued to his own thoughts, and takes up the things sown in his own heart, and rejoices in them, and supposes in his heart that these are some great chosen mystery, and justifies himself in what he does—the soul of such a man is the breath of evil spirits.

ANTONY, *LETTERS*

When we live in community, let us choose obedience over discipline; for the latter teaches arrogance, while the former calls for humility.

LIFE OF SYNCLETICA

Willingly accept the advice of a loving father and put it into action. In that way you will return by the labor of obedience to him whom you left by the inertia of disobedience.

RULE OF BENEDICT

Hate your own will. Obey the commands of the abbot even if he act otherwise.

RULE OF BENEDICT

The primary path to humility is prompt obedience. This befits those who hold nothing dearer to them than Christ. . . . It is a desire for eternal life that motivates them.

RULE OF BENEDICT

Obedience extended to one's superior is given to God, for he himself said: "Whoever listens to you listens to me" [Lk 10.16]. This must be done by disciples with a willing mind, because "God loves a cheerful giver" [2 Cor 9.7].

RULE OF BENEDICT

The second step of humility is reached when someone who does not love his own will does not delight in fulfilling his own desires, but imitates with his deeds the saying of the Lord: "I have not come to do my own will, but the will of him who sent me" [Jn 6.38].

RULE OF BENEDICT

The third step of humility is that someone, out of love for God, submit himself in all obedience to his superior, imitating the Lord, of whom the Apostle says: "He was made obedient unto death" [Phil 2.8].

RULE OF BENEDICT

We rightly learn not to do our own will when we are frightened by what holy Scripture says: "There are ways that seem right to men, but whose end is plunged in the depths of hell" [Prov 16.25].

RULE OF BENEDICT

The eighth step of humility is that the monk do nothing that is not enjoined by the common rule of the monastery or the examples of the elders.

RULE OF BENEDICT

When someone is newly come to monastic life, easy entrance should not be granted him. . . . One should take note whether he really seeks God, if he is serious about the work of God [liturgical prayer], obedience, and hardships. . . . One to be received [into the community] must promise stability, fidelity to the monastic lifestyle, and obedience in front of all in the chapel.

RULE OF BENEDICT

If burdensome or impossible tasks are enjoined on a brother, let him accept the command of the superior meekly and obediently. But if the burden of the task seems to exceed completely the limits of his strength, let him mention to the one giving the order the causes of his incapacity and do so patiently and at the proper time, without pride, obstinacy, or refusal. But if, after his suggestion, the superior does not change his mind, let him know that it is for his own good, and obey out of love, trusting in God's help.

RULE OF BENEDICT

Not only is the blessing of obedience to be shown to the abbot by all, but they are also to obey each other, knowing that by this road of obedience they will go to God.

RULE OF BENEDICT

[Obedience says:] Just as a human being's will perfects whatever she desires, so am I the will in God, by bringing to fulfillment what God commands. I was with God in his primordial council. God arranged all things through me, whatever he wanted to do. For I responded to the command of his word just like a lyre, because I am his command. I touch nothing, wish nothing, desire nothing, except what is in God, for I came forth from him, and I grew through him; I want nothing besides God.

HILDEGARD OF BINGEN,
BOOK OF LIFE'S MERITS

Whoever wishes to offer God an acceptable sacrifice has nothing more precious to offer than his own will.

JOHN TRITHEMIUS, *RULE*

It is better to sweep up leaves out of simple obedience than to engage in the sublime contemplation of heavenly things out of self-will.

LOUIS DE BLOIS, *SPIRITUAL MIRROR*

Monastic obedience exists not to make yes-men and efficient bureaucrats who can be used in institutional politics, but to liberate the hearts and minds into the lucid and terrible darkness of a contemplation that no tongue can explain and no rationalization can account for.

THOMAS MERTON,
CONTEMPLATION IN A WORLD OF ACTION

The monastic vocation really allows quite a lot of scope for individual differences, at least it should allow quite a lot of scope for the individual to follow a personal call, to follow something that he feels is especially relevant to him.

THOMAS MERTON,
CONTEMPLATION IN A WORLD OF ACTION

Mere outward compliance will not do. Obedience should come cheerfully, freely, and gladly. It is only when I remind myself that obedience is *ob-audiens,* listening intently to God rather than listening to my own self, that what Benedict is telling me—even though it may still seem difficult—is not impossible, for it is a response of love to love.

ESTHER DE WAAL, *A LIFE-GIVING WAY*

Christ's obedience was obedience unto death. This gives me the perspective. I am being asked to let go of something in me that must die before the new can be born. Two things help to make this possible: that the motive force is love; that I do it in imitation of Christ.

ESTHER DE WAAL, *A LIFE-GIVING WAY*

Obedience depends on listening so totally and openly to the other that through them we discern the face, the voice of

Christ himself. This is the root of that obedience that we show to one another.

ESTHER DE WAAL, *A LIFE-GIVING WAY*

No one grows simply by doing what someone else forces us to do. We begin to grow when we finally want to grow.

SR. JOAN CHITTISTER,
THE RULE OF BENEDICT

Obedience, Benedict says—the willingness to listen for the voice of God in life—is what will wrench us out of the limitations of our own landscape.

SR. JOAN CHITTISTER,
THE RULE OF BENEDICT

CHAPTER 16

Authority

A whole theory of effective management could be derived from the monastic tradition. Christian monasticism could also provide countless examples of good and bad managers. Benedict himself seems to have failed when, with no experience of community life, he was made abbot of an existing community. By the time he established Monte Cassino, he had learned management by study and by trial and error. For example, when in the *Rule* he becomes strident about the dangers of having a prior, especially one appointed by the same people who appoint the abbot, he seems to be animated by some unpleasant memories.

The authority of the desert fathers and mothers who served as guides to other hermits was based on their perceived wisdom and virtue. The disciple whose needs were no longer met by one spiritual guide could move on to another. With the advent of community life, relations between *abba* or *amma* and the individual monastics under them were transformed. The *abba* or *amma* was now the leader of a community, and the monastic's commitment was now to a community to which he or she was permanently attached. Moreover, the *abba* or *amma* was now responsible for both the spiritual and temporal welfare of the community. Many an abbot would experience tensions between institutional and personal need—for example, between the need to appoint an administrator for some important monastic enterprise and the felt need of the only possible appointee for solitude or manual work or serving others directly and personally in the infirmary or the guest house or the school.

When they became abbots or bishops or popes, the responsibilities of some monks became enormous. Saint Bernard's protégé Eugene III found the papacy almost overwhelming. Bernard advised him to use his time wisely, to delegate, to surround himself with trustworthy helpers, and above all to take time to examine himself to make sure he was acting thoughtfully and fairly.

The *Life of Pachomius* offers the example of a very skillful leader and manager who could read hearts, organize communities, and plan for the future. Pachomius could deal effectively with people because he was not handicapped by concerns for his own dignity or prerogatives. Although Pachomius's efforts to train a successor were only partially successful, he did make the attempt. He knew, as any abbot or parent knows, that one must share responsibility if one is to nurture leadership for the next generation. One of Pachomius's immediate successors enunciated a principle that is applicable in most ecclesiastical settings: if a person desires power, that person probably should not be given authority.

The entire monastic tradition teaches that whoever is in charge should teach by word and example. She must adapt herself to different temperaments, but not play favorites. She should be especially devoted to the delinquent and the needy. Positions of responsibility should be awarded according to the merit of the candidates' behavior and wise teaching. Benedict insists that his subordinate officials treat the rest of the community fairly. They are not to meddle in what is not their concern. Like the abbot, they should seek to be loved rather than to be feared.

Although the *Rule of Benedict* gives great authority to the abbot, there are evident limits. Benedict's *Rule* places the abbot under the *Rule,* while making the *Rule* and the abbot the normative guides for the monks. The *Rule* legislates that the abbot should not make decisions without consulting members of the community, and that he should not make major decisions without consulting all of the community. Thus does the community help the abbot discern what is God's will. Deliberate deception through manipulative internal or external public relations, privileged access to information or to the seats of power, disdain for procedures, and all the other tricks of political expediency are diametrically opposed to this communal effort at discernment.

The *Rule* says that the abbot *"is believed* to hold the place of Christ." Effective monastic government is rooted in faith not in the abbot primarily, though trust between abbot and monks is crucial, but in the God of the covenant who leads the people according to the divine promises. The God who inspired Syncletica and Benedict and the members of their communities inspires their successors today.

⌒

Remembering the promise he had made to God, Pachomius began with his brother to build a larger monastery to receive those who would come to this life. As they were building, Pachomius was extending the place with this aim in view while his brother, thinking of withdrawal apart, was making it smaller. And once John, who was older according to the flesh, was vexed and said to him, "Stop being conceited!" When Pachomius heard this he became angry as if for a good cause, but did not say anything in reply to him. As he kept control of his heart, he went down to a little cavern during the following night and began to weep in sorrow. He prayed, "O God, the mind of the flesh is still in me. . . . But I believe that if your many mercies help me I will be taught henceforth to walk in the way of the saints, 'stretching out towards what lies ahead' [Phil 3.13]. For with your help they put the enemy to shame as they ought. And how will I teach those whom you call to choose this life with me, O Lord, if I have not first conquered myself?"

LIFE OF PACHOMIUS

The father of a nearby monastery used to visit the holy father, Pachomius. One of his monks was asking for the rank of steward, but he did not consider him worthy of that task. Not being able to persuade him, he told him guilefully, "Our father Pachomius warned me not to do this, knowing well that you are not yet worthy of your request." When he

heard this, the brother dragged him along angrily, saying,
"Come, let us go to him, and he shall have to prove what he
says against me!" The other followed him in fear and sorrow,
wondering what the result of that affair would be.

When they arrived, they found Pachomius with the
brothers, building a wall for the monastery. That brother
approached Pachomius and told him very angrily, "Come
down, liar, and give me a proof of my sin!" As [Pachomius]
kept silent, he said to him again, "Is your mouth silenced,
finding nothing in your defense? Who compels you to lie,
you who claim to be clairvoyant, when you are stone-
blind?" When he had said this, the Great Man answered,
knowing nothing of what the other was talking about, "I
have sinned against you: forgive me. Have you never trans-
gressed?" When he heard this his anger calmed down.

The Old Man came down from his work and sought the
father of the other monastery. He found him weeping and
heart-broken, and he asked him, "What is going on?" He
answered, "This brother has asked us for a ministry beyond
his worth. I knew I could not make him give up his claim,
for he does not listen to me. So I used your name to quiet
him down, for we know that the Lord has granted you
the gift of discovering guile swiftly. And behold this fool
has added to his evil deeds by reviling a righteous man."
Pachomius said to him, "Have you not come to seek from
me the will of God? Listen to me. Grant him his request
that by this means we may snatch his soul away from the enemy. For it happens when good is done to a bad man he may
come to some perception of the good. This is God's love, to
have compassion for each other."

When that brother had got what he wanted, he returned
immediately to the great Pachomius, greatly sobered. He
embraced him and confessed, "O Man of God, you are
much greater than we had heard. We have seen how you
have conquered evil with good by sparing a foolish sinner
like me. If you had not been truly patient and had said
something against me, I would have rejected the monastic

life and become estranged from God. Blessed are you, for thanks to you, I live."

LIFE OF PACHOMIUS

Another time the brothers were with [Pachomius] cutting rushes. And as they were transporting the rushes to the boat, Pachomius suddenly fell into ecstasy. He saw some of the brothers surrounded by a fiery circle with flames licking them, and they were unable to pass over it. Others were barefoot on top of thorny pieces of wood, pierced by splinters, and they had no way out. And others were standing half-way up a steep precipice, unable either to climb up or to throw themselves into the river, for there were crocodiles below, watching them and leaping up at them. As he was still standing there, taken by his vision, the brothers passing by saw him. They cast their burdens down and they stood by him in prayer.

When he returned to himself after a long hour, he ordered food to be given to the brothers, for it was already evening. Then he told them to gather around him. He told them about his vision and they all wept with great fear. And as they asked him what this meant, he said, "I perceive that after my death this will happen to the brothers, who will not find anyone capable of comforting them rightly in the Lord from their afflictions."

LIFE OF PACHOMIUS

Abba Pachomius loved Theodore because he bore the life well. . . . He appointed him housemaster of the Alexandrians and foreigners who came after him. And his house was full of piety.

The holy Pachomius did many things with him, instructing him how to govern men. He would say, "It is a great thing! If you see someone of the house negligent of his salvation, admonish him privately with patience. If he once gets angry, leave him until God moves him to repentance. It is just like when someone wants to extract a thorn from somebody's foot. He digs around it, and if it bleeds and is painful, it is better to leave it and to put on it a softening plaster or something similar. Then after a few days it comes out by itself and easily. A man who is angry even against someone who does not argue with him will gain more after this from the one who is teaching him according to the Law. But if the offense is serious, report it to us and we will do as the merciful Lord wants. Care also for the sick as for yourself. Practice continence and bear the cross more than they do, since you hold the rank of father. And be the first to keep the rules of the brothers so that they also may keep them. And if after this there is anything else you want to decide and you do not know how, by the grace of God tell me about it. Together we shall try to find the exact answer to each one of the problems."

LIFE OF PACHOMIUS

Here is also what our father Horsiesios used to say, "I see some of you wanting to receive titles and to rule. . . . In the past, in the time of our father [Pachomius], except in obedience, nobody wanted to be called great, fearing to be found least in the kingdom of heaven [Mt 5.19]. And when Abba Petronios appointed me, I wept copiously, in fear of the danger to souls. Not only I, but the saints also. Moses, being sent by God for the sake of the people, first declined in his humility, and then accepted that ministry only when God was angered at him because of this. As for us, brothers, hearing what is written, "He who exalts himself will be humbled" [Lk 18.14], let us watch ourselves. It does not belong to all to govern souls, but only to perfect men. Here is a parable: if an unbaked brick is set in a foundation near a river, it does not last a single day; but if it is baked, it endures like stone.

LIFE OF PACHOMIUS

The abbot is believed to hold the place of Christ in the monastery.

RULE OF BENEDICT

When someone receives the title "abbot," he must direct his disciples with a twofold teaching; that is, he should show all that is good and holy more by his deeds than by his words.

RULE OF BENEDICT

There should be no playing favorites in the monastery.

RULE OF BENEDICT

Let the abbot be aware what a difficult and arduous task he has taken up: to govern souls and put himself at the service of many different temperaments, one with encouraging words, another with rebukes, another with persuasion.

RULE OF BENEDICT

Fearing always the judgment that awaits the shepherd regarding the sheep entrusted to him, let the account [the abbot] must give of others make him careful about himself, so that when he admonishes others he will also amend his own bad inclinations.

RULE OF BENEDICT

Whenever some important matters are to be dealt with in the monastery, let the abbot convene the entire community and tell them what is to be considered, and hearing the council of the brothers, let him ponder the matter and do what he judges is most expedient. The reason we said all should be called to council is that the Lord often reveals to the youngest what is best.

RULE OF BENEDICT

In all things let all follow the rule as master, and let no one depart from it rashly. No one in the monastery should simply follow the will of his heart.

RULE OF BENEDICT

If the community be larger, let there be chosen from it brothers of good repute and holy life, and let them be

appointed as deans who will take care of their deaneries
in all things according to the commands of God and the
precepts of their abbot. Those chosen to be deans should be
such that the abbot can confidently share his burdens with
them. They should be chosen . . . for their deserving lives
and wise teaching.

RULE OF BENEDICT

The abbot should exercise great care regarding delinquent
brothers, for it is not the healthy who need a doctor but
those who are sick [cf. Mt 9.12]. . . . He should understand
that he has undertaken to care for the weak and not to dominate the strong. . . . Let him imitate the devoted example
of the good shepherd, who left the ninety-nine sheep in the
mountains, and went to seek the one sheep that had wan-
dered off [cf. Lk 15.4–5].

RULE OF BENEDICT

A cellarer of the monastery should be chosen from the community—a person wise, of mature character, and sober in
judgment. He should not be given to excessive eating, nor
proud, nor unfair, nor stingy, nor wasteful. He should fear
God and be like a father to the whole community. He
should care for the needs of all, but he should not do anything without the abbot's command.

RULE OF BENEDICT

The cellarer should not embarrass the brothers. If a brother
should make an unreasonable request, he should not brush
him off and hurt his feelings, but deny the unjustified request reasonably and humbly.

RULE OF BENEDICT

In the installation of an abbot, the proper procedure is always to appoint whoever is chosen by the whole community in accord with the fear of God. Let the candidate be

selected because of his worthy life and wise doctrine, even if
he is the last in seniority.

RULE OF BENEDICT

The abbot should keep in mind what kind of burden he has
accepted and to whom he is going to render an account of
his stewardship. He should know that it is more important
for him to be of profit to his monks than to preside over
them. It is necessary therefore that he be learned in the divine law so that he may know how to bring forth things
new and old; that he be chaste, temperate, and merciful . . .
He should hate vices and love the community. In correcting, he should act prudently and not overdo it.

RULE OF BENEDICT

Let the abbot strive to be loved more than to be feared.

RULE OF BENEDICT

The abbot should not be restless and worried, nor extreme
and stubborn, nor jealous and overly suspicious, because
then he will never have peace.

RULE OF BENEDICT

He should be farseeing and thoughtful, discerning and
moderate.

RULE OF BENEDICT

[Young Wulfstan] was serious of mind and speech, reverent,
cheerful; he wore the clothes of a layman, but lived like a
monk. If he saw someone in need of correction, he always
tempered his speech, so that the rigor of harsh correction
might be followed by some reason for praise. He could
hardly appear harsh, because although what he said might be
strict, it was inwardly scented with love.

LIFE OF WULFSTAN

[When Wulfstan was made prior] he showed striking zeal in
solidifying the external possessions of the monastery, which

his predecessors had let deteriorate, and he reformed the internal life within the boundaries of the *Rule*. In order to do this effectively, he offered to those under him the devout example of his own life. He was ashamed to preach anything that he hesitated to put into practice.

LIFE OF WULFSTAN

The holy man Wulfstan was presented at the court of the king. He was ordered to accept the gift of the office of bishop. He resisted, saying he was unworthy to receive such an honor. Meanwhile, all the rest called out that he was worthy. . . . The cardinals and archbishops would have labored in vain to convince him to accept the office if they had not countered his resistance with the duty to obey the pope. . . . The more he thought himself unworthy, the more insistent was the people's urging. For he showed more promise of being a wise administrator because he came to the task not without fear. A fool takes on a task heedlessly, ignorant of how much work it will require.

LIFE OF WULFSTAN

If someone came to him for advice, he thoughtfully gave it. If someone made a request, he was very approachable. When some request had to be answered, he deliberated fairly and announced his decision quickly. When he had to pass judgment, he sided with justice. He did not tap the rich for money, nor repulse the poor because of their poverty. He was unmoved by flattery, and not obliged to those who flattered him. He never swerved from justice because of fear of princes, nor did he, for love of them, give them any honor they did not deserve. When he was praised for his goodness, he attributed it to the grace of God and was not proud. When he was criticized, he forgave the error of those who criticized him, at ease with his conscience. Criticism came his way rarely, because he cherished every man with a father's love; in turn, all loved him as if he were a parent.

LIFE OF WULFSTAN

There are many who live peacefully under a superior until
the yoke is lifted. Then they cannot be quiet, nor keep
themselves from disturbing their equals. Similarly, you see
countless people who can live with their brothers without
any conflict, but when they are placed over their brothers
they are not only useless but foolish and wicked. People like
this must be satisfied with a moderate level of goodness, in
accord with the measure of grace that God has granted
them. They do not need a master, but they are not suited to
be masters, either. The latter excel the former somewhat in
character, but there are those who excel them both because
they know how to be superiors. Finally they are entrusted
with all the Lord's goods. But there are few who can preside
effectively, fewer yet who can preside humbly. The person
who is perfectly schooled in discretion, the mother of the
virtues, can fulfill both roles easily.

BERNARD OF CLAIRVAUX,
ON THE SONG OF SONGS

When you ponder your present state, you should also recall
how you used to be. Compare your present state with your
past one. Have you grown in virtue, in wisdom, in understanding? Are you easier to get along with? . . . Reflect
upon your zeal, your mercy, and also your discretion. . . .
Reflect on the way you forgive and punish injuries, and in
each consider how carefully you take into account manner,
place, and time. . . . In addition, I do not want you to overlook the way you act in tribulations.

BERNARD OF CLAIRVAUX,
ON CONSIDERATION

Preside in order to promote the good of those whom you
govern. . . . Provide rather than dominate. I fear for you, for
there is no poison more dangerous . . . , nor sword more
deadly, than the lust to dominate.

BERNARD OF CLAIRVAUX,
ON CONSIDERATION

Accept no secret and murmured accusations. Think of them rather as detractions. I would like you to make this a general rule for yourself, that you hold suspect everyone who fears to say openly what he has whispered in your ear.

BERNARD OF CLAIRVAUX,
ON CONSIDERATION

Good teachers . . . govern their students with discernment and with fair correction.

HILDEGARD OF BINGEN,
BOOK OF LIFE'S MERITS

Fathers, do not grow tired of caring for your sheep. Nothing is more acceptable to God than the service of pastoral care. God requires of pastors that, as a sign of Christ's love, they feed the sheep entrusted to them with diligent care. . . . Accept with fearless humility the talent given you. You can be *fearless* because you have as a helper the very one who sent you. You will be consoled by the one who urged the fearful Moses to assume care of a great and burdensome people: "Go, I will be with you." And Christ prayed for Peter: "I have asked on your behalf, Peter, that your faith not fail and that when you have devoted yourself to the care committed to you, you may strengthen them as I have already strengthened you." . . . You should be *humble,* for no one should presume he can feed the flocks on his own, for God foresaw that he would need great, divine prayers.

LUDOVICO BARBO, *LETTERS*

Never forget our holy Father [Benedict's dictum]: strive to be loved by your sons rather than feared. If you wish to be loved, love! A superior who loves fosters virtues with good and frequent exhortations and nurtures spiritual progress. He corrects the erring, not as an angry judge, but as a loving father.

LUDOVICO BARBO, *LETTERS*

Where there is mildness in the father (superior), there will
be no distrust; if mildness is combined with care, there no
sin can take root. Where these are combined with prudence,
there is no meaningless correction. For the correction given
by a kind, solicitous, and prudent father is received with
love, works in due time, and brings a suitable healing to
wounds.

LUDOVICO BARBO, *LETTERS*

Since "the art of arts is the government of souls," as Gregory
says in his *Pastoral Rule,* wretched is the one who is compelled to teach before he has a chance to learn, who is forced
to show to others a way he has never walked.

JOHN TRITHEMIUS, *RULE*

Who would not rather feed some farmer's pigs than have
governance over souls?

JOHN TRITHEMIUS, *RULE*

Just as the superior must be very diligent in correcting
faults, so he must be particularly discreet. Let him
always note what sort of fault it is, whether it was done
knowingly or ignorantly, whether it was committed
only once or often, whether it was humbly admitted or
proudly defended.

LOUIS DE BLOIS, *STATUTES*

Now there must be a very delicate balancing between the
superior and his personal gifts, the insights of the living
community and the Rule that is the bearer of the accumulated wisdom of tradition. . . . Openness to the working of
the Spirit in both individual and in community is vital, life-
giving. Without it, there will be a closed-up person, a
closed-up community, lacking the growth that Benedict
holds out so urgently in the prologue.

ESTHER DE WAAL,
A LIFE-GIVING WAY

The cellarer is said to be like *(sicut)* a father to the community. But that word *sicut* is important. He is not to take over the role of the head of the community; he is a man under orders. Benedict knows only too well that for anyone who has to deal with material possessions, there is always the danger of the abuse of power.

ESTHER DE WAAL,
A LIFE-GIVING WAY

The superior of a monastery of Benedictines will be a Christ figure, simple, unassuming, immersed in God, loving of the marginal, doer of the Gospel, beacon to the strong.

SR. JOAN CHITTISTER,
THE RULE OF BENEDICT

[Benedict] does not want people in positions simply to get a job done. He wants people in positions who embody why we bother to do the job at all. He wants holy listeners who care about the effect of what they do on everybody else.

SR. JOAN CHITTISTER,
THE RULE OF BENEDICT

It is not easy for honest people who hold their own failures in their praying hands to question behavior in anyone else. . . . Aware of what I myself am capable of doing, how can I possibly censure or disparage or reprimand or reproach anyone else? On the other hand, Benedict reminds us, how can those who know that conversion is possible, who have been called to midwife the spiritual life, for this generation and the next, do less?

SR. JOAN CHITTISTER,
THE RULE OF BENEDICT

Abbots and prioresses, good leaders and teachers, fine parents and mentors, tender husbands and gentle wives, good friends and quality administrators, who listen to us as much as we listen to them, are there to help us bear the heat of life that shapes us, not to escape it.

SR. JOAN CHITTISTER,
THE RULE OF BENEDICT

[People in positions of authority should] "keep watch over their own souls" guarding themselves against the pitfalls of any position: arrogance, disinterest, unkindness, aloofness from the very people the position is designed to serve. Then, to make the point clear, Benedict describes the people who are not to get overlooked for the sake of efficiency in the bureaucratic game of hurry up and wait. And they are everybody who cannot possibly be expected to want things when the office is open: the sick, the young, the guests, and the poor.

SR. JOAN CHITTISTER,
THE RULE OF BENEDICT

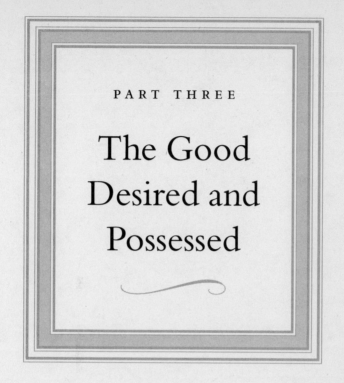

PART THREE

The Good Desired and Possessed

ONE OF THE MOST STRIKING things in monastic writings is the emphasis on desire and longing. A well-ordered, virtuous life was not enough for the monastic writers we have studied here. They desired something greater, someone greater. Their Christian faith guided their desire, but the desire itself seems to be implanted in every person. Order and virtue can become smug, closed, not a place of delight like the garden enclosed of the *Song of Songs,* but a prison. Saint Anselm is the most eloquent spokesman for this abiding discontent, but almost any monastic author would provide suitable texts. Such writers sometimes had recourse to the same *Song of Songs* to express the longing they felt: "I am faint with love." They believed that their desire, no matter how purified, would never be fully at rest in this life, and so they looked from earthly experience to ecstasy and heaven. Not every reader of this book will be able to join monastics on this part of their quest, but most readers will recognize the desire and perhaps join in their hope that love really is stronger than death.

We desire true and everlasting life.

RULE OF BENEDICT

There are all the great wonders that the faithful ponder with devotion constantly, because they proceed from God. The one who made these is God alone, because all good things arise from him and return to him. When God created human beings, God caused them to travel around him like a circle in the spirit of life, so that they also return to him often.

HILDEGARD OF BINGEN,
BOOK OF LIFE'S MERITS

God is like a blacksmith who kindles the fire with a bellows, turns the iron round and round to finish his work. When the human spirit is guided properly along the path of good deeds, it will return to eternal joy, see the purest light, and hear the songs of the angels.

HILDEGARD OF BINGEN,
BOOK OF LIFE'S MERITS

The true creative spirit must be fired with love and with an authentic desire of God. This means, in so many words, that the monastic vocation is one which implicitly, if not explicitly, seeks the experience of union with God.

THOMAS MERTON,
CONTEMPLATION IN A WORLD OF ACTION

[Benedict] does not want a collection of passive ciphers, but a dynamic and alive people. This primary spiritual energy which brings light and fire, passion and fervor and which prevents what might otherwise be simply plodding, he calls "a very ardent love." The Latin *ferventissimo amore* suggests a burning, white-hot love.

ESTHER DE WAAL, *A LIFE-GIVING WAY*

CHAPTER 17

Longing

In a poem about feeling and love, Hadewijch, a devout Beguine of the thirteenth century, echoes much of what the monastic tradition says about longing and desire. To desire many things, to prefer pleasurable feeling, is to aim too low. One must, she says, desire beyond reason. Love causes constant striving until at last desire drowns in sublime love. Desire is too lofty to be at rest in insignificant things. Love itself is its object, and in this life, love is always just out of reach.

The danger, then, is that we amplify our superficial and incidental desires so much that we can't hear our deeper longings. Then we become like addicts going from one fix to the next, unwilling to face the fatal artificiality of our cravings. Renouncing our cravings will not make us apathetic; rather, it will give us wings to fly above the stars. One taste of God, and we will thirst for nothing else.

The one thing necessary is the good we can serve. Even if that good is identical to God himself, we must not promote it with evil means. Evil means bring us to evil ends, not to God. Evil means are infallible signs of disordered desires or of a lack of trust in the power of God to bring about the good he desires.

⟶⟨⟩⟵

A man who finds himself in the cold and deep frost runs somehow until he reaches the heat of the fire; then he is delighted and revives. So also was it with us then; the more we sought God, the more his goodness manifested itself, bringing sweetness to our souls. But how are we now? Let us, however, all return; we do believe that God will renew us in his mercy.

LIFE OF PACHOMIUS

Entrust your hope to God.

RULE OF BENEDICT

Never despair of the mercy of God.

RULE OF BENEDICT

With a ready heart and a happy face, he was tasting before-hand the joys of heaven. He was anticipating in hope the fountain of heavenly happiness from which he now drinks everlastingly.

LIFE OF WULFSTAN

Hope and rejoice, rejoice and love, my soul. The one whom you hesitatingly desired to listen to you prepares an interces-sor for you. As a beggar, you made your request through an-other, because you did not have confidence enough to go to him directly. Behold, he came to you and prayed for you where you failed. What goodness, kindness, love. Behold, he showed you how much he loved you, and how much he enkindled in you a love of him. Insist, then, and hope, not in yourself but in him. He will hear your desire who concludes your prayer: " 'Exult in him, my heart and my flesh' [Ps 84.2], love him, and let 'everything within me' [Ps 103.1] bless him. Amen."

ANSELM OF CANTERBURY, *PRAYERS*

O most kind lover of the human race, . . . manifest your presence and I will have what I desire. Reveal your glory, and my joy will be perfect. "My soul thirsts for you, and my flesh is yours in many ways" [Ps 63.2]. "My soul thirsts for God, the living fountain. When will I come and appear be-fore the face of my God?" [Ps 42.2] When will you come, my consoler, whom I seek? Oh for the time when I will see my joy that I desire! Oh that "I will be satisfied when your

glory has appeared" [Ps 17.15], the glory that I crave. Oh
that I might be made drunk "with the richness of your
house" for which I sigh! If you will only give me to drink
from the "torrent of your delight" [Ps 36.8] for which I
thirst!

ANSELM OF CANTERBURY, *PRAYERS*

[Hope] understands that hard discipline has an end and that
everlasting glory will follow it. After a foretaste of the
earnest money, patience will grow sweet; without hope, patience would have been bitter. Boredom will turn into desire, irritation into delight, delay into longing forbearance.
[His seven years of labor] seemed like just a few days to
Jacob because of his love for Rachel [cf. Gen 29.20].

PETER OF CELLE,
THE SCHOOL OF THE CLOISTER

[Hope says:] I sit on the throne of God desiring good, and in
faith I embrace all his works. By doing good works, I draw
all the earth to myself.

HILDEGARD OF BINGEN,
BOOK OF LIFE'S MERITS

God . . . will receive me then into the highest bliss; and set
me on his lap.

HILDEGARD OF BINGEN,
BOOK OF LIFE'S MERITS

[Heavenly desire declared:] I am the life and greenness in all
good works, and a necklace of all the virtues. I am the delight and understanding of the love of God and the upbuilding of his every desire, because whatever God wishes, I do,
and with the wings of goodwill I fly above the stars of
heaven, so that I bring to perfection the will of God in
every just event. . . . I want nothing except what is holy.

HILDEGARD OF BINGEN,
BOOK OF LIFE'S MERITS

Finally, the blessed father [Benedict] affirms all these things;
the kingdom of heaven will lie open to those who do them
[cf. *Rule of Benedict* 72]. All the things that are described in
this rule are neither too slack nor too restrictive; they look
neither to the right nor to the left, so that they lead the one
who keeps them straight to heaven.

> HILDEGARD OF BINGEN,
> *EXPLANATION OF THE RULE OF BENEDICT*

Let me taste the sweetness of your Spirit; make me thirst
that your will be done; make me know your good pleasure
so that my service may always be acceptable to you.
Amen. . . . Ah, Jesus, fountain of life, make me drink a cup
of the living water from you so that, having tasted you, I will
thirst eternally for nothing but you.

> GERTRUDE THE GREAT,
> *SPIRITUAL EXERCISES*

Ah! O beloved of my vows, understand my cry. Direct your
attention to my prayer and heed me; for the longing of my
heart and the desire of my soul, O my king and my God, call
you, want you, and need you. Because of you my eyes are
dewed with tears, and my gaze is intent on you. You, my
God, my gentleness and love, my hope from my youth: you
are all that I want, hope, and desire.

> GERTRUDE THE GREAT,
> *SPIRITUAL EXERCISES*

God seeks us with grace and mercy; we seek him with
devout feelings, entreating him to heal our misery.

> JOHN TRITHEMIUS, *RULE*

The rational spirit is so noble that no perishable good can
satisfy it. For the things that are inferior to it cannot satisfy it
and make it happy. Inferior to the human spirit are heaven,
earth, the sea, and all that is visible or within the range of
the senses. Only God, its creator, who is incomparably bet-

ter and more worthy than it, can make the human spirit
content and happy. He wanders like a homeless person with
no place to rest, like a starving person without food, as long
as he does not embrace with the arms of love him whose
greatness he cannot resist desiring.

LOUIS DE BLOIS, *SPIRITUAL DOCTRINE*

First of all, I warn you to think often and carefully about
why you entered the monastery—namely, that, dead to the
world and to yourself, you might live for God alone.

LOUIS DE BLOIS, *MIRROR FOR MONKS*

God is going to give us an eternal reward for our holy desires, even if in this life we never attained what we desired.
So act boldly, keep asking, knock, wait patiently; remember
the trustworthy promises of the Lord Jesus, who says:
"Everyone who asks, receives, and whoever seeks, finds; to
the one knocking the entrance will be opened at a suitable
time" [Lk 11.10].

LOUIS DE BLOIS, *SPIRITUAL DOCTRINE*

The worst temptation, and that to which many monks suc-
cumb early in their lives, and by which they remained defeated, is simply to give up asking and seeking. To leave
everything to the superiors in this life and to God in the
next—a hope which may in fact be nothing but a veiled despair, a refusal to live.

THOMAS MERTON,
CONJECTURES OF A GUILTY BYSTANDER

Benedict made it clear that the desire for good is no excuse
for the exercise of evil in its behalf. . . . To become what we
hate—as mean as the killers, as obsessed as the haters—is
neither the goal nor the greatness of the spiritual life.

SR. JOAN CHITTISTER,
THE RULE OF BENEDICT

CHAPTER 18

Love

Near the end of his *Rule*, Benedict recapitulates his teaching:

> Monks should act zealously with a most fervent love—that is, take the initiative in showing each other honor, bear patiently weaknesses of body and character, vie in obeying one another. Let no one follow what he thinks useful for himself, but rather what is to the others' advantage. Let them love the brothers chastely; let them fear God out of love; let them love their abbot with a sincere and humble love. Let them prefer nothing to Christ.

In this brief paragraph Benedict mentions love five times. The objects of this love are God, Christ, the abbot, and the other members of the community. The qualities of this love are zeal, fervor, disinterestedness, sincerity, and humility. It leads to reverence, patience, and obedience.

The love that Benedict has in mind consists of selfless, active care and concern for the good of the rest of creation and a grateful surrender of oneself into the hands and purposes of God. Following the Gospels, the monastic tradition affirms that the commands to love God above all things and to love one's neighbor as oneself (Mk 12.30–31) are really a single command.

The ordering of time, the virtues that form human character—these are so many tin soldiers waiting to be brought to life so they can dance to the music of love. Love is why monasteries are not maintained to produce paragons of Stoic virtue or still life portraits of imagined Christs. People who love as the Gospels require aim to be alive, passionate, joyful, and totally given to doing God's will. God wants people fully alive, wise lovers. Such people want others to become what God wants for them, not carbon copies of themselves. The number of monastic virtues may be finite, but the variety of monastic saints has been quasi–infinite. The discipline of the Lord's school aims to produce discerning and passionate individuals who can represent life for others and be responsible for themselves.

〜

[After struggling with the devil's temptations, Antony] was too feeble to stand, so he prayed lying down. His prayer finished, he called out with a shout: "Here am I, Antony. I am not cowed by your blows. Even though you should give me more, nothing shall separate me from the love of Christ." Then he began to sing: "If armies shall stand against me, my heart shall not fear" [Ps 26.3].

LIFE OF ANTONY

I want you to know this, that Jesus Christ our Lord is himself the true Mind of the Father. By him all the fullness of every rational nature is made in the image of His image. Therefore, we should love one another very much. For he who loves his neighbor, loves God, while whoever loves God, loves his own soul.

LIFE OF ANTONY

[The devils] attack first those who have attained a very great measure. They seek by means of pride and vainglory to turn them against one another. They know that in this way they can cut us off from God, for they know that those who love their neighbors, love God. For this reason, the enemies of virtue sow division in our hearts, that we may be filled with great enmity against each other and not hold any converse with our neighbor, even from a distance.

ANTONY, *LETTERS*

Abba Antony said, "I no longer fear God, but I love him. For love chases out fear" [Jn 4.18].

ANTONY, *SAYINGS*

My children, all of us—male and female—know about being saved, but through our own negligences we stray from the path of salvation. First of all we must observe the precepts known through the grace of the Lord, and these are: "You shall love the Lord your God with your whole soul, and your neighbor as yourself" [Mt 22.37]. In these precepts the first principle of the Law is preserved, and it is on this Law that the fullness of grace depends. The expression of the principle is brief indeed, but its importance in this matter is great and unlimited, for all advice to help the soul depends on these precepts. Paul also bears witness to this when he says that "the end of law is love" [cf. Rom 13.10; 1 Tm 1.5]. Whatever people say by the grace of the Spirit, therefore, that is useful, springs from love and ends in it. Salvation, then, is exactly this—the two-fold love of God and of our neighbor.

LIFE OF SYNCLETICA

Love, then, is a great treasure; and about this virtue the Apostle spoke strongly: "If you distribute all your goods, and if you discipline your body, but have not love, you are sounding brass and clanging symbol" [1 Cor 13.1–3]. And so, among the virtues love is paramount.

LIFE OF SYNCLETICA

Just as dreadful qualities are attached to one another (for example, envy follows upon avarice, as do treachery, perjury, anger, and remembrance of wrongs), so the opposite qualities of these vices are dependent upon love. I mean, of course, gentleness and patience, as well as endurance, and the ultimate good—holy poverty. It is not possible for anyone to acquire this virtue (I mean, to be sure, love) apart from holy poverty, for the Lord did not enjoin love on one person, but on all. Those, therefore, who have resources must not overlook those who have needs. The workings of love, in fact, are concealed, for it is impossible for a human being to supply the needs of all, but this is the task of God.

LIFE OF SYNCLETICA

From this day forward look to the greater virtue—love, for you have taken up the cross.

LIFE OF SYNCLETICA

Above all, love the Lord God with all your heart, all your soul, all your strength; then, your neighbor as yourself.

RULE OF BENEDICT

Prefer nothing to the love of Christ.

RULE OF BENEDICT

His sister, Scholastica, had been dedicated to the almighty Lord from her infancy. She made it a point to visit her brother once a year. The man of God came down to her at a place not far from the monastery and owned by it. One day she came as usual. Her venerable brother came as well with some disciples. They spent the entire day in praising God and in holy conversation. As night fell they had something to eat. While they were still at table engaged in holy conversation the hour grew late. The holy woman asked him: "I beg you not to leave me tonight, so that we can talk of the joys of heavenly life until dawn." Benedict answered her: "What are you saying, sister? I cannot remain outside my monk's cell."

The weather was so mild that no cloud appeared in the sky.

When the holy nun had heard her brother's refusal, she placed her hands on the table with her fingers intertwined and put her head in her hands and prayed to the Lord. When she raised her head from the table, there was such thunder and lightning and rain that neither Benedict nor the brothers with him could go a step beyond the shelter where they were. For the nun, putting her head in her hands, had poured forth tears, which turned the quiet sky into a flood. The downpour did not follow her tears by much. It was as though prayer, downpour, and the lifting of her head coincided with the thunder, so that at the same moment she lifted her head the downpour occurred. The man of God, seeing that he could not return to the monastery amid lightning, thunder, and downpours, began to be upset and said: "May almighty God save you, sister. What have you done?" She answered him: "I asked you and you did not listen to me. I asked my Lord, and he heard me. Go now if you can, and return to your monastery, leaving me behind." However, he could not leave the roofed-in place, so he who was unwilling to stay stayed unwillingly. They spent the night talking and delighting each other in holy conversations about the spiritual life. . . . It was completely just that she could accomplish more who loved more.

LIFE OF BENEDICT

The love of God made Wulfstan unaware of how hard he was working.

LIFE OF WULFSTAN

The servant is afraid to look his lord in the eye. The hireling hopes to receive from the hand of the lord. The disciple eagerly listens to the master. The son honors his father. But she who seeks a kiss, loves. Among the gifts of nature, this affection of love has the highest place, especially when it returns to its source, which is God.

BERNARD OF CLAIRVAUX,
ON THE SONG OF SONGS

[Wisdom said:] I arranged all things in order, when I made the circuit of the heaven. In the *[Song of] Songs,* I spoke of the love of the creator for the creature and of the creature for the creator, how the creator adorned the creature when he made her because he loved her very much, and how the creature sought a kiss from the creator when she obeyed him and was obedient to him in all things. The creature received a kiss from the creator when God gave her everything she needed. I joined the love of the creator for the creature and of the creature for the creator to the love and faith by which God joins man and woman.

HILDEGARD OF BINGEN,
BOOK OF LIFE'S MERITS

Ah, that my soul may choose to know nothing apart from you, and that, tutored by your grace and instructed by your anointing, I may progress well, passionately, and powerfully in the school of your love.

GERTRUDE THE GREAT,
SPIRITUAL EXERCISES

This is our God, who cherishes us with unconquerable love, with unfathomable charity, with inseparable affection, who, because of this, took on himself the bodily substance of our earth to become a spouse and have it as his spouse. He cherished us with his entire being. To love him is to have wed him.

GERTRUDE THE GREAT,
SPIRITUAL EXERCISES

Let the depth of your charity absorb me. Let me be sub-merged into the abyss of the ocean of your most indulgent devotion. Let me perish in the deluge of your living love just as a drop perishes in the depth of the ocean's fullness. Let me die, let me die in the torrent of your immense mercy, just as the spark of fire dies in the stream's strongest current. Let the raindrops of your love envelop me. Let the cup of your love carry away my life. Let the secret counsel of your most wise love effect and perfect my glorious death in

life-sustaining love. There, there, I will lose my life in you
where you live eternally, O my love, God of my life. Amen.

> GERTRUDE THE GREAT,
> *SPIRITUAL EXERCISES*

As iron plunged into fire becomes totally fire, so [Gertrude]
enkindled by divine love became wholly love, which desired the salvation of all.

> GERTRUDE THE GREAT,
> *THE HERALD OF DIVINE LOVE*

On Christmas, Christ told Gertrude: "Just as I am the image
of the substance of God the Father [Heb 1.3] in regard to
divinity, so you will be the image of my substance in regard
to human nature, for you shall receive in your deified soul
the rays of my divinity, just as the air receives the sun's rays.
Penetrated to the depths of your heart by this unifying light,
you will become capable of more intimate union with me."

> GERTRUDE THE GREAT,
> *THE HERALD OF DIVINE LOVE*

Love is the first virtue. Love is required of each believer;
whatever is not done in love merits nothing. Next comes
joy, so that we may serve the Lord, not in bitterness, but
happily.

> JOHN TRITHEMIUS, *RULE*

Happy is that soul which strives constantly to purify its heart
and to turn within itself, and entirely renounces all self-love,
self-will, and self-seeking. Such a one deserves to come
closer and closer to God. Finally, when its highest powers
have been elevated, illumined, and adorned with divine
grace, it will attain unity and simplicity of spirit and will
reach love without pictures and a simple knowledge without
thinking. Now, when it is capable of receiving a wondrous
and ineffable grace of God, it is led to that living font which

flows eternally and is more than adequate to completely refresh the minds of the saints. . . . When, with the power of
love, the intellect rises above all images and is led above itself
(something that only God can grant), it flows from itself
into God. Then God is its peace and enjoyment. . . . Completely enkindled with the fire of divine love, and completely liquefied, it passes into God and, united to him
without a medium, is made one spirit with him, just as gold
and brass are fused into one lump of metal.

LOUIS DE BLOIS, *SPIRITUAL DOCTRINE*

In the course of monastic living and believing, your heart is
enlarged with the inexpressible delight of love and you run
along the way of God's commandments [*Rule of Benedict*
prologue 49]—surely one of the most incomparable phrases
of all time.

ESTHER DE WAAL, *A LIFE-GIVING WAY*

Biographical Sketches

ANSELM OF CANTERBURY (CA. 1033–1109)

Saint Anselm was born in Aosta in northern Italy. A poor relationship with his father troubled his youth. Eventually he went to France, where his mother had relatives. He studied at the monastery of Bec in Normandy, where Lanfranc, another Italian, was the chief teacher. Anselm entered that monastery in 1059. In 1063 he succeeded Lanfranc as head of the school and prior. His was the most brilliant intellect since Augustine, and he was soon a renowned teacher. He was dedicated to the monastic ideal, so much so that he could scarcely imagine any other path to salvation. His writings cover many genres: closely reasoned theological monographs on specific philosophical and theological topics, letters, and prayers. He was elected abbot of Bec in 1078. Fifteen years later Anselm reluctantly agreed to succeed Lanfranc as archbishop of Canterbury. Anselm was not a supple diplomat, and his relations with the Anglo-Norman kings of England were often strained. As a result he spent much of the next fifteen years in exile. In part because exile provided him with leisure, he was able to continue his theological writing. In 1098 he completed *Cur Deus Homo? (Why Did God Become Man?)*, which has rivaled his *Proslogium* (1078–1079) in popularity and influence.

Anselm is represented here by excerpts from his *Prayers and Meditations,* among the most beautiful writings in Christian Latin. In particular, his prayers are suffused with the spirit of the psalms, especially those psalms that express a longing of the human heart for the vision and peace of God. The emotion Anselm expresses in his prayers makes him a significant figure in the transition from the stately and rather detached prayer forms of the first millennium to the more emotional forms of prayer that came after him and were cultivated in Cistercian and Franciscan circles.

ANTONY (CA. A.D. 251–356)

Antony died in A.D. 356. If he lived to the age of 105, as several ancient authors claim, he was born in 251. We know him through three basic sources: a collection of sayings, seven letters, and an influential biography written by the patriarch of Alexandria, Athanasius, who was a very important figure in the struggle against the heresy of Arianism. Athanasius wrote his *Life of Antony* in Greek, but it was soon translated into Latin and became widely known throughout the Christian world. Because of the popularity of this work, Antony is traditionally regarded as the first monk, whereas it is clear from the *Life* itself that there were monks and nuns before him.

Antony was a pious boy who lost his parents when he was still a youth. When he was twenty, he was moved by the New Testament's call to leave all and follow Christ. He divested himself of his property and sent his younger sister to live with some nuns. He put himself under the tutelage of an experienced monk. To find solitude, in 285 he entered a deserted fortress, where he stayed for twenty years. After going to Alexandria during a persecution in 311–313, he retreated deeper into the Egyptian desert. His surviving letters to various monasteries date from 340 or slightly before.

Antony and Athanasius lived during a time of crisis in Egyptian civilization. The distinction between city and countryside was blurring. There was migration to the cities and efforts to flee taxes and other civic obligations. The early monks seem to have come from among elites who had lost their positions or from the new middle classes. Greeks and Copts were intermingling and intermarrying. Traditional Egyptian religion, now mixed with many foreign elements, was challenged by Christianity and gnosticism. It is possible that monks from Christian and gnostic traditions lived peacefully in close proximity, concerned more about ascetic practice than doctrinal clarity. However, Athanasius's Antony will have no truck with heretics.

Athanasius's *Life of Antony* presents the author's ideal monk, an ascetic—that is, someone who led an austere life of self-denial. Antony supported the lawful bishops, avoided or actively opposed heretics, and willingly left doctrinal arguments to the bishops and theologians. Athanasius says Antony's memory, full of Scripture passages, served him in place of books. Nevertheless, the seven letters attributed to Antony suggest that he was an educated man who was strongly influenced by the theology stemming from the brilliant third-century theologian Origen, some of whose speculative ideas were rejected by later theological orthodoxy.

The sayings of Antony included in the collections of sayings by the desert monks and nuns corroborate Athanasius's picture of a wise ascetic who learned his wisdom experientially in struggling against the obstacles presented by the world, the flesh, and the devil. On the basis of this experience, he became a person of great discernment, someone who could detect the work of the devil in the human soul and devise ways of resisting it. His discretion also took the form of moderating his asceticism. Although Athanasius's descriptions of his privations are scarcely conceivable to a modern reader, Athanasius insists that Antony was a specimen of good health, as indeed he must have been if he lived to be 105.

Antony, like many monks celebrated in later saints' lives, was said to have the virtues of the just of the Old Testament—for example, the purity of heart of Elijah. When he emerged from his twenty years in the abandoned fort, he was totally self-controlled—an ideal that some of the monks adopted from Hellenistic philosophy. At times, this domination of the "passions" bordered on disdain of the body.

Athanasius says that Antony was ashamed to give attention to the body or to be seen undressed or eating. Yet he makes clear the Christological basis of Antony's monasticism: all should prefer nothing to the love of Christ.

According to Athanasius, one day Antony addressed the monks at length. He recommended following the Scriptures, consulting a spiritual guide, and perseverance. He urged them not to hesitate to give up temporal goods, however great, for the prospect of eternal goods. To this end he urged them to practice four cardinal virtues (prudence, justice, temperance, and fortitude), as well as understanding, charity, love of the poor, faith in Christ, meekness, and hospitality. Monks should live as men about to die. They should pray to receive through the Holy Spirit the ability to discern spirits. At the end of Antony's discourse, he and the rest of the monks returned to their cells. Theirs was a land apart, inhabited by ascetics seeking virtue, singing psalms, studying, fasting, praying, working, loving each other, and rejoicing in the life to come—and there were no tax collectors.

Later, when Antony moved to his inner mountain, he made friends with the wild animals who were destroying his garden. In later hagiography, monks will always be friends with animals—lambs who lie down peacefully with wolves in the paradise that they create in the desert.

Athanasius's portrait of Antony became a kind of narrative rule for monks. His story of Antony loomed large over subsequent monastic hagiography and provided guidelines for monastic rules. That Antony's virtues and struggles, his admonitions and observances, continue to serve as paradigms is a tribute to Athanasius's vivid recital of Antony's life and teaching.

LUDOVICO BARBO (1381–1443)

The later Middle Ages were not a golden era for monasticism. Few new monasteries were founded, and many of those that existed had difficulties with recruiting, observance, and finances. At the dawning of the modern world the monasteries were not well positioned to come to terms with the new order of emerging nation-states and increasing secular autonomy in economics and learning. However, during the fifteenth century a number of reform-minded Christians struggled to bring new life to monasteries as part of a renewal of the church in leadership and members. Louis (Ludovico) Barbo was one of these reform-minded Christians whose efforts led to the Protestant and Catholic Reformations.

Barbo was born in Venice. At the age of sixteen he was a cleric and commendatory prior (lay overseer) of the Augustinian monastery of Saint Giorgio in Alga, near Venice. His income from this monastery helped pay for his studies in law school. He had a religious conversion in 1403, which moved him to give the monastery of Saint Giorgio to a group of devout clerics. That group included two cousins who were nephews of the pope, both of whom became cardinals and one of whom became Pope Eugene IV. Also associated with the group was Lawrence Giustiniani, who became patriarch of Venice.

In 1408, with papal approval, Barbo was entrusted with the Benedictine abbey of Saint Justina in Padua. The newly appointed abbot first secured from the pope a guarantee that the abbey would be free of all lay interference or control (thus putting an end to the commendatory lay overseers, for whom monasteries were often nothing more than a source of income for themselves). He made his profession as a Benedictine before a bishop and was blessed as abbot in 1409. His first steps were difficult; few men entered the community. Little by little recruitment improved as men were drawn by the serene and stable life of the revived community and Barbo's kindness and discretion. Other monasteries adopted his reforming ideas and practices, and gradually there emerged a congregation of monasteries. In 1419, Pope Martin V approved the new congregation. It was distinguished by the fact that the authority of the congregation was emphasized more than the autonomy of the individual monasteries. Supreme authority lay with the four visitators, who executed the decrees of the annual general chapter. In 1425 Pope Eugene IV approved the practice of electing abbots at the general chapter. Both of these measures were radical departures from the earlier Benedictine tradition of autonomous monastic communities led by abbots of their own choosing. Moreover, the time in office of abbots and other officials was limited by statute.

In making these innovations, Barbo was trying to give greater stability to his precarious work of reform. He was probably also inspired by some then-current ideas about the superiority of a general council over the pope. On papal orders, Barbo wrote a letter about his reforms to the Spanish Benedictine Congregation of Valladolid.

Barbo was named bishop of Treviso in 1437. There he founded a school for poor clerics that anticipated the Tridentine institution of seminaries. He died at the monastery of Saint Giorgio Maggiore in Venice in 1443, and was buried at Saint Justina.

In 1440, Barbo wrote a history of the beginnings of the Congregation of Saint Justina. About the same time he wrote *The Form of Prayer and Meditation of the Congregation of the Monks of Saint Justina* to help implement a decree of the congregation requiring its members to practice mental prayer each day. The work distinguishes three steps of prayer. The first consists of vocal prayers directed to twelve specific saints, asking their help in acquiring particular virtues. The second step consists of affective mental prayer—that is, spontaneous acts of devotion. Barbo specifies for each day some stage or event in the life of Christ that is to stimulate proper devotion. These are assigned for each day of the week; for example, Christ's sufferings are the topic for Friday. Barbo does not elaborate on the third step, contemplative prayer, which he says is ineffable.

In drawing up this work, Barbo was influenced in particular by a work of a Franciscan, Ubertino da Casale. Certainly Barbo's work also has much in common with the Flemish *devotio moderna,* represented by the *Imitation of Christ,* although the lines that connect him with the movement are not clear. In adopting this methodical form of prayer, Barbo was drawing on the most successful spiritual movement of his times, even if later centuries of Benedictines chafed at the idea of the introduction of this alien form of meditation, which seemed to distance prayer too much from the liturgical life of the monks.

Barbo, then, was not afraid to adopt some fairly drastic innovations in polity and piety in order to breathe new life into monasteries, where the fire of divine love and Christian service was burning very low.

BEDE (CA. 673–735)

Saint Bede, who is also called Bede the Venerable, was a teacher, historian, and biblical interpreter. He was born on lands belonging to the monks of the Northumbrian abbey of Wearmouth, to whom he was confided when he was seven. Soon he moved to the monastic foundation at Jarrow, where he spent almost all of the rest of his life. He was ordained a deacon when he was nineteen and a priest when he was thirty. He wrote a much-used manual on calculating the time for Easter, commentaries on many books of the Bible, and several saints' lives. Perhaps he is best known today as the author of the *Ecclesiastical History of the English Nation*.

Bede lived during a period when monasteries often drew on several different written rules for their observances. Bede knew the *Rule of Benedict,* though his life was not governed by it exclusively. Bede was on friendly terms with bishops and monks elsewhere, some of whom helped him with his historical research. Largely through the efforts of his first abbot, Benet Biscop, Bede's own Northumbrian monastery had a fine library for those days. Bede had a solid knowledge of the teachings of the church, which he tried to pass on to the English clergy of his time. When he died, he was working on an English translation of the Gospel of John.

Bede's *Homilies on the Gospels,* which is quoted here, emphasizes exegesis and doctrine, not morality. Sometimes his sermons have two parts, one explaining the Gospel reading for a certain day, and the other explaining the feast being celebrated that day. They are lucid and not particularly long. Christ is the focus of Bede's expositions.

In 796 the twin abbeys of Wearmouth and Jarrow were destroyed by marauding Vikings. Vikings would continue to devastate England for more than a century. Then, in the tenth century, there was a strong rebirth of Benedictine monasticism in England under Dunstan (abbot of Glastonbury, then bishop of Worcester [957–959] and archbishop of Canterbury), Oswald (bishop of Worcester [961–992]), and Ethelwold (bishop of Winchester [963–984]). The customs inculcated by the reform were contained in the *Regularis concordia.* In the course of the reform, monastic influence in the English church increased significantly. King Edgar supported the reform—in part, perhaps, because he shared the reformers' belief that only such a reform would save England from divine punishment. Wulfstan of Worcester was the spiritual heir of these three restorers of English Christianity and English monasticism.

BENEDICT OF NURSIA (CA. 480–CA. 550)

What is known about Saint Benedict comes either from his *Rule* or from the second book of the *Dialogues* (593–594) of Pope Saint Gregory I (d. 604), which is primarily a collection of miracle stories. Gregory does give us a credible picture of Benedict as a monastic guide who combined austerity with gentleness in the same paradoxical mixture one finds in his *Rule.*

Benedict was born in Nursia, seventy miles north of Rome. His parents were probably provincial landowners. He was sent to be educated at Rome, but left the city because of the sinful atmosphere he found there. Around A.D. 500, he began to live as a hermit in a cave at Subiaco, fifty miles east of Rome. He was given provisions by the monk Romanus, who lived in a nearby monastery. After three years of solitude, Benedict was persuaded to become abbot of a monastery in the area. His tenure ended in failure when the monks tried to poison him. Gradually, a community formed around him at Subiaco, and he established a group of monasteries, perhaps on the Pachomian model. The jealousy of a local priest persuaded him to move on. With several disciples, he went next to Monte Cassino, a tall, sun-baked hill eighty miles south of Rome on a main highway—the Via Latina, between Rome and Naples. There he worked to convert the local people to the Christian faith and oversaw the growth of a single large monastery, for which he wrote his *Rule*. He was buried at Monte Cassino sometime around 550. Gregory tells us that Benedict sorrowfully foresaw the sacking of his monastery. The monastery was sacked and destroyed by the Lombards in 581, the surviving monks fleeing to Rome.

Benedict had experienced firsthand various forms of monastic life: solitary (also called eremitic), Pachomian (groupings of small, geographically proximate communities under a chain of command leading to an abbot in chief), and cenobitic (a single community under a single abbot). It was for the latter sort of independent community that he wrote what he called his "little rule" for beginners. His *Rule* drew on the monastic tradition as handed down by the desert fathers, whose sayings and lives were available in Latin. Benedict's *Rule* was also very indebted to Cassian, who traveled extensively in Egypt before bringing his reports on the teaching and practices of the Eastern monks to France. Finally, Benedict made use of the *Rule of the Master,* evidently the work of an Italian monk whose life overlapped with Benedict's. Benedict drew most of the prologue and first seven chapters of his *Rule* from this eccentric document, though he modified it profoundly, shortening it and making it seem much more reasonable, as least to most modern readers. Because we can compare the *Rule of the Master* with the *Rule of Benedict,* we have been able to learn much about Benedict's intentions—even in the unlikely event that Benedict himself wrote the *Rule of the Master* and later revised it to what we know as the *Rule of Benedict.*

Benedict's *Rule* summarizes the written records of more than two hundred years of monastic experience, as well as a lifetime of monastic searching on Benedict's part. The *Rule* is a very practical document. Apart from the prologue and parts of the first few chapters, Benedict's goal was to lay out a framework within which monks could live and pray and be schooled in the Lord's service. Theology and theory are never far below the surface, but the *Rule* looks primarily to conduct.

The usual day of Benedict's monks began at about 2 A.M. with the night office, or vigils. During the rest of the day there were seven additional offices, the most important of which were lauds and vespers, which the monasteries had adopted from the church at large. These eight offices (referred to in their entirety as the liturgy of the hours) were carefully constructed of traditional elements: psalms, biblical readings, antiphons, and some readings from Christian writers. The entire Psalter was recited once a week. On the average, Benedict's monks probably prayed the liturgy three and a half hours a day.

Work required some six and a half hours. For Benedict, to turn from prayer to work was not to turn from the supernatural to the mundane; work, too, was a holy service, not merely a hedge against idleness or a means of support. A third component of each day was holy reading *(lectio divina),* to which some four hours were devoted. This reading was more studious or theological than what has been known in recent times as spiritual reading, and more devout and religious than ordinary study. It was meant to form the monk's mind, imagination, and affectivity in the image of Christ. It was serious work: one was to read entire works, from beginning to end, in order, thoughtfully. It was also prayerful: one was to make the truth one's own, to savor it and learn it by heart.

The ordering of the day was not to be so rigidly construed that monks could not take time to help one another with tasks or problems when the occasion arose. Nor were the monks to be so preoccupied with their own concerns that they could not take time to welcome guests and travelers—who, Benedict said matter-of-factly, are never lacking in a monastery.

The whole of this monastic life was conducted in an atmosphere of quiet and reverence. Absolute silence and sign language were not part of Benedict's regime, though they were adopted later in some monasteries. Similarly, although Benedict liked order, the *Dialogues,* even if the picture Gregory presents there is not particularly accurate, reminds us that in Benedict's time, when rival popes and rival armies and races vied for ecclesiastical and political power, good order was not that of an eighteenth-century garden. Something similar can be said about enclosure. Benedict wanted monasteries to be self-sufficient, and he didn't want his monks wandering outside the monastery or gossiping about secular matters. However, he did build his monastery on a main highway and made provision for monks being sent out of the cloister on journeys both short and long.

Benedict's *Rule* provides for three promises: obedience, stability, and *conversatio morum.* Obedience is to the *Rule,* abbot, and community; stability is life in community under a rule and an abbot; and *conversatio morum* seems to mean something like "monastic lifestyle." In other words, the three promises seem to boil down to one: to embrace the monastic life in a particular community. Whatever community that might be, it would require dispossession of material goods (poverty) and chastity as part of monastic life. Even the monk's attachment to his community through the threefold promise was not absolute. A monk could grow in community in such a way that he was then called to live on his own as a hermit. He might also, it turned out, be sent to missions and other places that, ironically, were not necessarily more solitary than life in community. One thinks, for example, of the monk-missionaries and monk-bishops of the "Benedictine centuries" of the early Middle Ages, men and women like Boniface and Walburga, missionaries to Germany, and Wulfstan of Worcester.

BERNARD OF CLAIRVAUX (1090–1153)

By the end of the eleventh century, the Benedictine rule and tradition no longer enjoyed the same monopoly they had hitherto held among celibate Christian communities in Europe. A first step toward this multiplicity of rules was represented by the Cistercians. The first Cistercian abbey, Cîteaux, was founded in France in 1098 by Saint Robert of Molesme, Saint Stephen Harding, and others who wished to live a secluded life more literally patterned on the *Rule of Benedict*, yet went on to create their own distinct order. Born of noble family, Bernard entered Cîteaux in 1112. In 1115 he was sent to be founding abbot of Clairvaux. Bernard soon became one of the most powerful people in Europe. He helped the Knights Templar receive ecclesiastical approbation; he championed Innocent II against an antipope; he wrote a treatise, *On Consideration*, for Pope Eugene III, who had been a monk at Clairvaux; he preached against heretics and on behalf of the Second Crusade. He was instrumental in the condemnation of some of the teachings of Peter Abelard and Bishop Gilbert de la Porré.

Bernard was a brilliant writer. His liturgical sermons are moving still. His eighty-six sermons on the Song of Songs are one of the masterpieces of European literature. In these allegorical readings of the Song of Songs, he ranges from the most pedestrian concerns of monastic life to the heights of contemplation. His book *On the Love of God* argues that God should be loved simply because God is God. His treatise *On the Stages of Humility and Pride* is a masterpiece of psychological analysis and irony. In this work Bernard avoids discussing the stages of humility outlined in the *Rule of Benedict*, purportedly because he knows more about pride than humility, and devotes himself instead to a penetrating study of pride.

LOUIS DE BLOIS (1506–1566)

In 1520, at the age of fourteen, Louis de Blois (Blosius) entered the Benedictine monastery of Liessies in Hainaut. The abbot at that time was eager to improve the life of the community. He confided Louis's training to a novice master who shared his desire for monastic restoration. Louis was sent to Ghent (1522–1524) and then to the University of Louvain, where he studied Latin, Greek, and Hebrew and earned his licentiate in arts in 1527. That same year, at the age of twenty-two, Louis was elected coadjutor abbot. He continued his studies in theology at Louvain until he succeeded to the abbacy in 1530.

Louis immediately began to teach his monks by word and example. He wrote his *Speculum monachorum* (*Mirror for Monks*, 1538) to teach his monks the love of prayer and religious virtues. When war threatened between Francis I and Charles V, Louis and three other religious took refuge on some monastery property in a small village. There they lived an exemplary religious life, which drew others to join them. At the urging of the community at Liessies, he returned there. He wrote up a set of *statuta* or customs (*Statuta monastica*, 1539). Blosius was instrumental in the installation of the recently founded Jesuits at Louvain. He himself made the retreat prescribed in the *Exercises of Saint Ignatius* and later required all postulants to the monastery to have made the same retreat.

In a series of treatises Blosius spelled out his spiritual doctrine: *Rule of Spiritual Life (Canon vitae spiritualis), Collection of Devout Prayers (Piarum precularum cimeliarchion), Manual for the Humble (Enchiridion parvulorum), Recreation for the Soul (Psychagogia)*. He began a second series of works with the *Spiritual Doctrine* (1551). This series he concluded with a four-part book, the most important part of which was the *Spiritual*

Mirror (Speculum spirituale). Blosius's works were translated many times into most European languages and exercised a considerable influence on Catholic spirituality.

Much of this voluminous spiritual writing consists of extracts from other authors, the fruit of Louis's reading and meditation. Although he was open to many influences, his spirituality is thoroughly Benedictine. His sources are the Bible, the early Christian writers, the monastic authors, and the liturgy. He frequently cites the works of the Rhineland mystics: Suso, Tauler, and Ruusbroeck, as well as Gertrude, Mechthild, Birgitta, and Catherine of Siena. In his writings, the twin currents of Rhineland mysticism and *Devotio moderna* flow together into a synthesis rooted in the Benedictine tradition.

Blosius's goal is practical, his style simple and direct. He is psychologically astute, kind, and positive. The love of Christ is the motive and the goal. He is particularly devoted to Christ in his sufferings, which he regards as the royal road to human beings' union with the divinity. He describes this union in traditional terms: the believer is joined to God without an intermediary and becomes one spirit with God; the believer is plunged into God like iron into fire. Blosius lived to see the beginnings of the Reformation and even wrote a book directed at heretics *(Collyre hereticorum)*.

SR. JOAN CHITTISTER (B. 1936)

A vigorous social activist, writer, and Benedictine monastic who believes that monastics, like all Christians, should be involved in the struggle for social justice, Sr. Joan Chittister, O.S.B., is a member and former prioress of Mount Saint Benedict Monastery in Erie, Pennsylvania. She holds a graduate degree from the University of Notre Dame and a Ph.D. in speech communication theory from Pennsylvania State University. She has served as president of the Congregation of Saint Scholastica, president of the Conference of American Benedictine Prioresses, and a U.S. delegate to the International Union of Superiors General, and she is a past president of the Leadership Conference of Women Religious, where she has also served as chairperson of the LCWR National Task Force on Peacemaking. She is a columnist for the *National Catholic Reporter*. She received an award from *U.S. Catholic* magazine in 1992 for her work for justice, peace, and equality in church and society. In addition to her studies of Benedictine spirituality, she has written many other books and articles. Some of her recent titles include *A Passion for Life: The Face of God* (with Robert Lenz; 1996), *The Fire in These: A Spirituality of Contemporary Religious Life* (1995), and *There Is a Season* (with John August Swanson; 1996). She has frequent speaking engagements throughout North America.

THE DESERT FATHERS AND MOTHERS

In addition to Pachomius and Antony, there were thousands of monks in Egypt and Palestine, most of whose names have not survived. Particularly among the monks of Egypt there developed a body of proverbial sayings and stories. These were passed on by word of mouth and then by writing. Through these written sayings collections, through the lives of monks like Antony and Pachomius, and through reports of those who went out to the desert to visit the monks, the teachings of these men and women who sought obscurity in the desert continue to fascinate and teach today. Helen Waddell, Thomas Merton, and Benedicta Ward have all taken a hand at translating these sayings.

Like Mother Teresa or Dorothy Day, the desert *abbas* and *ammas* embraced a radical sort of Christianity, which sought to strip individuals of anything that would stand between them and their God. Saint Jerome (ca. 345–420), who was the associate and propagandist of the desert monks, summed up their goal: "naked to follow the naked Christ." Like the Cynics, they wanted to be free. Unlike the Cynics, they found their freedom in a society of their own making. They built up the forms of that society by trial and error. What they learned from their successes and failures on their quest for freedom to be with God they handed on in stories and sayings, which, like Jesus' parables and the Zen masters' koans, are meant to tease the mind of the hearers to see truths long overlooked. Through them we can glimpse the lives of the desert monks, but the primary purpose of these sayings is to teach practical wisdom, not record historical fact. The sayings of the desert monks seldom touch on mystical experiences.

When these sayings and stories were written down, they were arranged either alphabetically under the names of well-known monks, or by themes in what are called *systematic collections*. Some sayings never found their way into either sort of arrangement. The sayings do not provide techniques for self-control or ecstasy or union with God. There was no single theory or method of spirituality in the desert, only the haphazardly accumulated wisdom of thousands of devout Christians following a difficult calling in which they waited humbly, longingly, and contritely for the transforming grace of God.

ESTHER DE WAAL (B. 1930)

Esther de Waal is an Anglican woman who, though not herself a nun, has become an articulate spokesperson of monastic tradition and values. She spent her childhood in a country vicarage on the Welsh border. She studied history at Cambridge University, did research as an associate of the Department of Local History at Leicester University, and became research fellow and college lecturer at Newnham. She married Victor de Waal in 1960. She then taught in Cambridge and Nottingham before moving to Lincoln, where her husband was chancellor of Lincoln Cathedral and she a member of the staff of Lincoln Theological College. She also taught for the Open University. Later the family moved to Canterbury and she found herself, as the wife of the Anglican dean of Canterbury, living in the prior's house of the former monastery. There she raised her four sons while continuing to teach.

She began exploring Benedictine tradition and spirituality. In 1982 she launched a program called "Benedictine Experience," in which a group of Americans lived at Canterbury for ten days and followed a modified Benedictine regime. In 1984 she published *Seeking God: The Way of Saint Benedict* (1985). She followed this with *Living with Contradiction: Further Reflections on the Rule of Saint Benedict* (1989). Esther de Waal also has lectured widely on Benedictine spirituality.

Returning to live in the country, she published *A Life-Giving Way: A Commentary on the Rule of Saint Benedict* (1995), which is a chapter-by-chapter commentary on the *Rule of Benedict*. Her commentary is informed by the latest scholarship, but it is also the product of years of practice in Benedictine spirituality. Her gentle wisdom is everywhere evident in her interpretations and applications of Benedict's words. In 1993 she published *A Seven Day Journey with Thomas Merton*. More recently, stimulated by worshiping in the former church of Dore Abbey, a Cistercian monastery near her home, she has produced a study of Cistercian spirituality: *The Way of Simplicity: The Cistercian Tradition* (1998). Another, related interest of de Waal's is Celtic spirituality. She edited *God under My Roof: Celtic Songs and Blessings* (1984) and *The Celtic Vision* (1990), and she wrote *The Celtic Way of Prayer* (1997).

GERTRUDE THE GREAT (1256–CA. 1302)

In 1220, a group of seven nuns set out from Halberstadt to found a new monastery. They had to move twice, in 1234 and 1258, before they found, at Helfta, the site they were looking for. Even after this last move, to a quiet valley in Saxony, the new foundation had a stormy history. It was pillaged in 1285, placed under interdict around 1295, destroyed in 1342, and restored in 1346. In its first hundred years, the community was home to a remarkable group of women who were contemporaries of Dante, Meister Eckhart, and Duns Scotus.

The first of these was Abbess Gertrude of Hackeborn, who began her forty-year term of office in 1251. Ten years later she received into the community a four-year-old namesake, later to be known as Gertrude the Great. This younger Gertrude received an excellent education in the convent. When she was twenty-five she had a profound conversion experience. From then on her intellectual activity centered on theology. Although she was never physically strong, she wrote two works in Latin, *The Herald of Divine Love* and *The Spiritual Exercises*. *The Herald of Divine Love* has five parts: the first is her biography, written by some else; the second is directly from her hand; the third, fourth, and fifth were composed by one of her fellow sisters from her teachings. Other outstanding members of the monastery at Helfta included the abbess's blood sister, Mechthild of Hackeborn (1241/42–1298/99), and Mechthild of Magdeburg (1207–1282/94).

The life of Gertrude the Great and the lives of the rest of the community at Helfta centered on the liturgy. Most of Gertrude's two works are closely connected with the feasts of the liturgical year and the hours of the liturgical office. In this, of course, Gertrude is representative of medieval monastics, for whom the rhythms of the liturgical seasons and the succession of the hours divided time into sacred seasons and hours. As one might expect of someone who drew the sustenance of her spiritual life from the liturgy, Gertrude's writings are saturated with scriptural words and ideas. Christ is at the center of her spirituality. She and her collaborators were good Latin stylists. Nevertheless, her writings can be off-putting to modern readers, but once one becomes familiar with her style, one can be inspired by reading the thoughts of someone who drew from the Bible and the liturgy direction and zeal to devote every ounce of her strength to praising God and finding ways to effectively love her fellow human beings.

HILDEGARD OF BINGEN (1098–1179)

Hildegard of Bingen was born in 1098, the tenth child of a noble family. In 1106 or 1108 she was sent to be raised by the noble lady Jutta, who was an *inclusa* (a hermit who lived in a cell attached to a church). Jutta was attached to the monastery of Benedictine men at Disibodenberg in the Rhineland. Gradually her hermit's cell grew to be a small community of women. Jutta was evidently teacher and guide to these women. Hildegard later declared that from the time she was a little girl she experienced visions but for many years was afraid to tell anyone about them. Hildegard seems to have pronounced vows as a Benedictine in this community about 1112–1115. During her years under Jutta, she must have learned a great deal, from Jutta herself, from participation in the liturgy, and perhaps from personal study. However, Hildegard always maintained that her own learning was negligible and her wisdom divinely given.

In 1136 Hildegard became abbess of the nuns' community. In 1141 she had a vision commanding her to write down the theological teaching of her visions. She reluctantly undertook this task with the help of the monk Volmar, who remained her secretary until a year before she died. She was also assisted by a younger nun named Richardis, who later became an abbess elsewhere, much to Hildegard's dismay. For ten years (1141–1151) Hildegard worked on her comprehensive presentation of Christian faith and practice called the *Scivias*. She felt God wanted her to write it, but just to be sure, in 1148 she also consulted Bernard of Clairvaux and Pope Eugene III for their advice and approval. The *Scivias* (the title means "know the ways [of the Lord]") describes twenty-six visions, and ends with a version of her musical morality play, the *Ordo virtutum*.

In 1150 Hildegard and about twenty nuns moved to the Rupertsberg, near Bingen, to establish an independent monastery. This caused considerable conflict with the monks of Disibodenberg, who did not want to lose their sisters, in part because of the fame that Hildegard was attracting, and in part because of the financial losses to the men's community the departure of the women would involve. Today there are few traces of the Rupertsberg monastery. However, a second foundation at Eibingen (ca. 1165) is thriving, not far from the place where Hildegard built her second monastery. Hildegard wrote the lives of two seventh-century saints: Disibod, an Irishman who was the patron of Disibodenberg; and Rupert, the patron of the monastery she founded.

Amid the poverty and struggles of her new monastic home, Hildegard began her second major work: the *Book of Life's Merits* (1158–1163), which focuses on the conflict between virtue and vice in human history and human life. Meanwhile, she received many visitors who came to her for advice or healing. She wrote music, primarily for the liturgy, containing haunting monophonic melodies with highly compressed poetic texts. She carried on a voluminous correspondence with people who sought her advice, and with others, mainly prelates, for whom she volunteered advice and correction. She also became expert in natural history. She completed a final major work, the *Book of Divine Works,* which like the *Scivias* contains explanations of her visions.

Around 1158–1161, Hildegard made the first of four preaching tours that took her to Mainz, Würzburg, Bamberg, Trier, Metz, Andernach, Cologne, Maulbron, and Hirsau. The last years of her life were embroiled in a fight with the church officials of Mainz regarding the burial of an excommunicated man. Eventually, Hildegard and her community were exonerated.

Before her death in 1179, her *Vita* was begun by a monk named Gottfried; it was finished after her death by another monk, Theoderich. The process for her canonization was never finished, but she is venerated as a saint locally and in the Benedictine order. She was one of most remarkable women of the Middle Ages, a genius in many fields, and a saintly Benedictine.

HUGH OF CLUNY (1024–1109)

Hugh was born of a noble Burgundian family and entered the monastery of Cluny when he was fourteen, after overcoming his father's opposition. He was appointed prior (second in command) before he was twenty-one, and in 1049 he succeeded Abbot Odilo. During his sixty years as abbot, Hugh was the advisor to nine popes and had great influence in affairs of church and state. He supported the reform efforts of Pope Gregory VII and sought to reconcile him with Emperor Henry IV. In 1095 he witnessed the consecration of a new church at Cluny; it was then the largest church in Christendom.

Hugh was noteworthy for his ability to combine deep piety with administrative effectiveness. An early biography of Hugh says that his physical bearing and appearance displayed outwardly his inner harmony. His presence was inspiring to those who knew him. He was very devoted to prayer and reading. It seemed that when he was reading, God spoke to him in a palpable way, and that when he prayed he spoke face-to-face with God. He practiced stern asceticism, but was not so demanding of others. He was a monk through and through.

JEAN MABILLON (1632–1707)

Jean Mabillon received his early education from his uncle, a priest, then studied at the university and the seminary at Reims. In 1653 he entered the monastery of Saint Remi in Reims. Saint Remi belonged to the Benedictine Congregation of Saint Maur, or Maurists, which had a centralized organization and emphasized scholarship. Shortly after making his monastic vows in 1654, he began to suffer from acute headaches brought on by his intense studies. He was sent to the monastery of Corbie and ordained a priest in 1660. He was cured of his headaches through the intercession of Saint Adalard, the founder of Corbie. In 1663 he went to Saint Denis, where he worked on a revision of the edition of the works of Bernard of Clairvaux. In 1664 he became assistant to Dom Luc d'Achéry, the librarian at Saint-Germain-des-Prés, who was working on the *Acta Sanctorum OSB (Acts of Benedictine Saints)*. There Mabillon spent the rest of his life completing the two works mentioned and producing an important study of paleography and manuscript studies entitled *De re diplomatica* (1691) and other learned works. He trained a generation of young scholars and traveled throughout Europe studying manuscripts.

Mabillon found a worthy adversary in Armand-Jean le Bouthillier de Rancé (1626–1700), a distinguished classical scholar, a graduate of the Sorbonne, and the abbot of the Cistercian abbey of La Trappe. In 1683 Abbot de Rancé wrote a work entitled *On the Holiness and Duties of the Monastic Life*. With reference to this work, Mabillon wrote a book explaining the Maurist commitment to study. His work provoked an impassioned reply from de Rancé. Mabillon did not reply immediately, but let his thoughts on the subject mature. Then in 1691 he published his *Traité des études monastiques (Treatise on the Studies of Monks)*. The work is divided into three parts. In the first, Mabillon argues that monastic discipline cannot flourish in monasteries where study is neglected; in the second, Mabillon discusses which studies are most suited to monks; in the third, he focuses on the purpose of monastic studies. After a further written exchange, Mabillon and de Rancé met and agreed to end the controversy.

Mabillon held that the most important studies for monks are those that form in them the new man, of which Christ was the model. He cautioned against vanity and pride—which, he said, will be avoided if monks' studies help them to know themselves in order to become more humble and to know, love, and serve God more perfectly. A few days before his own death, Mabillon advised a young priest: "Be true in everything. Be scrupulously sincere."

Mabillon was brilliant but modest. He was a humble servant of truth. His example, as much as his writings, shows the compatibility of the monastic vocation with scholarship. He was the embodiment of the ideals of the Maurist Congregation, to which belonged many French monasteries in the seventeenth and eighteenth centuries.

THOMAS MERTON (1915–1968)

Thomas Merton is the most important monastic writer of the twentieth century. He was not a great speculative theologian or biblical scholar; he may never be canonized; he may have written too much. Nevertheless, he was a brilliant writer with an incisive mind, a courageous man whose words lodged in the hearts of millions of readers.

Thomas Merton's father was born in New Zealand, his mother in Ohio. They were artists and lived in London, France, and New York. Merton's mother died when he was six, and his father spent much of the next decade in France. Thomas Merton attended a boarding school in England (his father died when he was sixteen), then enrolled at Cambridge. After a disastrous year there, he transferred to Columbia University, where he converted to Catholicism in 1938. At Columbia he deepened his knowledge of English literature and became friends with exponents of neoscholastic philosophy; he received his M.A. in 1939. In December 1941 he entered the Trappist Abbey of Gethsemani in Kentucky. He was to remain a member of the abbey until the day he died, though in his later years he had voiced many questions about the Trappists' way of life.

Early in his life at Gethsemani, he was very happy. His enthusiastic embrace of Trappist life is evident in his autobiography, *The Seven Storey Mountain* (1948). He was ordained a priest in 1949. In the next few years he published *The Waters of Siloe* (1950), *Ascent to Truth* (1952), and *Bread in the Wilderness* (1953). In a telling and true statement, Merton told Mark Van Doren, who had remarked that he hadn't changed much, "Why should I? Here our duty is to become more our-selves, not less." His growing longing for solitude was expressed in some notes, published five years after he wrote them, called *Thoughts in Solitude* (1958).

He was appointed novice master in the same year that saw the publication of *No Man Is an Island* (1955). With this book Merton seems to have become more open to the intellectual world around him, more willing to bring contemporary experience and living tradition into dialogue. No longer so inclined to teach as to question, he recorded his thinking during this time in *Conjectures of a Guilty By-stander,* which, though not published until 1966, contains writings from 1956 on-ward. Merton in effect accuses himself of having been a bystander. From now on he will grapple with the issues of his contemporaries. As he said in *Thoughts in Soli-tude,* genuine solitude brings not separation but solidarity. Merton already was ex-changing letters with many people, but from about 1958 onward he initiated new contacts. In his writings he began to deal with issues like the Vietnam War, racial discrimination, and poverty. He was finally allowed his hermitage on the grounds of the Abbey of Gethsemani. Tragically, Merton was accidentally killed while at-tending an international meeting in Bangkok in 1968.

PACHOMIUS (CA. A.D. 292–346)

Pachomius was one of the greatest monastic leaders of all time, a skilled organizer and a skilled reader of the human heart. We know of him through several versions of his life and through sermons and legislation attributed to him. The best source about him seems to be a document called *The First Greek Life.* According to this document, Pachomius, born about A.D. 292, probably in upper Egypt, was im-pressed into the army about 312. He and his fellow conscripts were taken to Thebes, where some Christians, taking pity on their distress, brought them some-thing to eat and drink. Pachomius prayed to God that if God would deliver him, he would serve God all his life, loving all men and helping them according to God's command. When he was discharged, Pachomius went to the Upper Thebaid, ac-cepted baptism at Chenoboskion, and began serving the poor.

Pachomius became an anchorite under the guidance of a monk named Palamon, who at first put him off. Together they practiced asceticism and prayed. They spun and wove hair sacks to support themselves and to provide for the poor. Pachomius sought to guard his heart from evil influences. He learned the Scrip-tures by heart. One day a voice reminded him of his promise to "reconcile hu-mankind with God." Some time later he was traveling through the desert and came to a deserted village called Tabennesi. A voice told him to build a monastery there, for many were going to come there to become monks. Pachomius discerned the will of God in what the voice told him. He and his brother John set about building a monastery. Others began to arrive. Pachomius taught them by his example of serving others, but many took advantage of him. Eventually, he was forced to insist on obedience to his commands and to expel those who wouldn't listen. Whatever rules he did establish were secondary; the Scriptures were the primary rule.

Pachomius organized the community quite carefully, appointing officials and distributing tasks. The *koinonia* (community as a whole) was headed by Pachomius and his successors; the local communities were guided by a "senior" or "father," each of whom had a second-in-command; the houses into which the local community was divided were governed by a housemaster and his second. Pachomius incorporated other monasteries into his network. There was a general meeting twice annually.

Pachomius built a monastery for his sister and other women who might join her. He appointed the monk Peter to guide them and sent brothers to help the nuns with buildings, burials, and other tasks. Pachomius worked many miracles in imitation of the Lord, but he was not dismayed when his prayers were not answered.

All his life, he preferred to teach by example rather than by rules. Whatever rules he laid down he lived himself. In 328 a teenager named Theodore arrived at the monastery, whom Pachomius groomed to exercise authority as he himself exercised it. Theodore was charming and proved an able assistant to Pachomius, but Pachomius had to work hard to soften Theodore's tendency to be too strict and austere. His relationship with Theodore was fairly stormy.

In grooming Theodore to be his successor, Pachomius sought to provide for a smooth transition after his death. In the event, however, Pachomius was succeeded first by Petronius, who died almost immediately; then by Horsiesios (346–350); only then by Theodore (350–368); and finally once again by Horsiesios.

PETER OF CELLE (CA. 1115–1183)

Peter was born at Aunoy-les-Minimes near Provins. His family was of the lesser nobility of Champagne. He evidently studied in Paris, perhaps while living at the monastery of Saint Martin des Champs. We find him next at the abbey of Montier-la-Celle, where he became abbot. He was evidently an energetic abbot. He supported Alexander III against an antipope and wrote letters of friendship or admonition to various monasteries. In 1161 Peter became abbot of the great abbey of Saint Remi at Reims. In that capacity he served as vicar general to his friend Archbishop Henry. This involved him in many legal matters, both civil and ecclesiastical. He corresponded with Alexander III and even admonished him. The pope in turn entrusted Peter with mandates to settle disputes and effect reforms.

Peter was a close friend of the brothers John and Richard of Salisbury. John had visited with Peter at Montier-la-Celle and dedicated the *Policraticus* to him. When John went into exile in 1163, he accepted Peter's invitation to stay at Saint Remi. His brother Richard also was sent into exile and stayed at Reims. Richard later became a canon regular at Merton in England. In 1179, Peter dedicated *The School of the Cloister* to Richard. In his last days as abbot, Peter oversaw the remodeling of the abbey church.

In 1178 Peter was on a list of possible cardinals, but the honor was not given him. In 1181, when John of Salisbury died as bishop of Chartres, Peter was appointed to succeed him. Peter died after only a few weeks as bishop.

Peter was a devout monk. He was devoted to Christ, especially in his sufferings and in the Eucharist. He was a excellent letter writer who corresponded widely. His letters are models of the mystique of friendship that flourished in the twelfth century. His correspondents are mainly ecclesiastics. Peter was friendly to members of all the emerging religious orders. He loved the church and was particularly concerned that the clergy be above reproach.

Peter's surviving writings include 175 letters and 96 sermons. Peter's sermons are centered on the liturgy; almost all of them deal with liturgical feasts. The sermon format seems to bring out the best in Peter. Amid his exuberant imagery, his sincerity and intelligence are evident and effective.

Peter also wrote five biblical works: two commentaries on Exodus 25–28, two treatises on the tabernacle, and a treatise on the various kinds of bread mentioned in the Bible. He also composed four treatises touching on the monastic life: *On the Purity of the Soul, On Affliction and Reading, On Conscience,* and, most important, *The School of the Cloister,* which is a thorough discussion of the disciplines of life in the cloister.

In *The School of the Cloister,* Peter gives several lists of the essential elements of cloistered (monastic) life. These lists include all the topics identified in this book except work and hospitality. It is interesting to ponder why Peter left these two out, since he was clearly a hard-working and hospitable man. It may also be that he regarded both activities as intruding on the austere ideas of withdrawal and contemplative prayer, which he seemed somewhat more eager to promulgate than to live.

SYNCLETICA (FL. CA. A.D. 400)

Among the sayings of the deserts fathers *(abbas)* are a few sayings of the desert mothers *(ammas)*. Several dozen sayings survive from Amma Syncletica, all of them found also in the *Life of Syncletica,* which provides some basic information about Syncletica's life, though it is mainly about her teaching. We are told that Syncletica was a Macedonian whose ancestors had moved to Alexandria. Her family was well off and pious. She was beautiful and chaste, and, like one of her brothers, resistant to any family plans for her to marry. She was espoused to her beloved, Christ. While she was struggling to avoid being forced to marry, she became very thin. After her parents' death she was able to establish herself and her blind sister in the solitude of a relative's tomb. She gave all she had to the poor and had her hair cut off by priests. Then she devoted herself to a life of solitude, prayer, and fasting. She intensified her regimen when she was struggling against temptation, but moderated it at other times and so preserved her health.

Subsequently, like Saint Antony, she went further into solitude, but like him she was visited by those seeking advice and teaching. She would beg off, saying, "Why do you fantasize in this way about a sinner like me as if I were doing or saying something worthwhile? We have a common teacher—the Lord; we draw spiritual water from the same well and we suck our milk from the same breasts—the Old and the New Testaments." However, they persuaded her by their tears and arguments that it was her duty to instruct them. The majority of the *Life* is then devoted to her teaching. In the last years of her life she seems to have suffered from a hideous disease, probably cancer, which attacked first her lungs and then her mouth.

The Life of Syncletica tells us something of the monastic context of Syncletica's life, but gives us no information as to just when she lived. If indeed the teaching contained in that book is hers, then she must have lived during or after the lifetime of Evagrios of Pontus (346–399), whose teaching pervades the *Life*. Scholars believe the *Life* was written in the fifth century. It seems to come from a time before Evagrios's teaching had been condemned. In the introduction to her excellent translation, Elizabeth Bongie indicates that the *Life* itself had little influence. However, it seems to be a trustworthy witness to the monastic life of Syncletica's time.

Syncletica begins her teaching with a reference to the twofold law of love; this love is salvation. She then refers to the hundredfold, sixtyfold, and thirtyfold yield at harvest time, reserving the highest reward for consecrated virginity. However, she also reminds her audience of female monastics that women in the world may well "struggle more than we do." She distinguishes between those with a taste for contemplation and spiritual enlightenment, those inclined to asceticism, and those in the world who do good works.

The *Life* includes a treatise on chastity, which urges those committed to chastity not to run around unnecessarily, and to be careful in their speech and in their fantasies, and even in their relationships with other religious women. Evil fantasies should be driven out by other fantasies.

Next, she turns to poverty. Her doctrine is that radical divestment of ownership is good for those who have already practiced doing without. The devil is vanquished by poverty, because most sins have some relationship to possessions and their loss. Saying we must keep our "gain" hidden, Syncletica discusses humility at some length.

Then, turning to the Evagrian schema of "thoughts," Syncletica (or the author) warns first against feeling superior, which leads her to offer advice about how to deal with those who seem to be doing well and those who have fallen or are discouraged, which is elaborated in a teaching on pride and humility. There follows a very fine discussion of anger, which is explained to be an outward symptom of the very serious problem of remembering wrongs, from which flow envy, malicious talk, and sadness. There follows a very interesting and unusual section urging those who have been particularly gifted by grace to spend time in the company of abject sinners in order to help them.

The author spends a number of chapters warning against philosophical denials of free will. Origen was a vigorous defender of free will also, but one has the impression that this passage was prompted by a current controversy or danger. Then the author introduces some allegories that have the tone of pep talks, urging readers to stay the course. There follow some final exhortations regarding stability in community, the suitability of different persons for cenobitic or eremitic life, and the need for moderation and discretion.

Although the influence of Evagrios of Pontus is evident in the *Life,* the advice the book gives (and that is mostly what the *Life* does—give advice) seems rooted in experience and common sense. At crucial points the teaching invokes Christ as an example: his humility; his eating and spending time with sinners, which models the devout Christian's call to service of the abjectly wicked.

JOHN TRITHEMIUS (1462–1516)

John Trithemius was born at Trittenheim on the Moselle near Trier; hence the surname Trithemius. He studied at Trier, in the Low Countries, and at Heidelberg, but never earned a degree. In January 1482 he entered the monastery of Sponheim in the diocese of Mainz. He made profession as a Benedictine in November of the same year. Sponheim belonged to the reformed congregation of Bursfeld. In July 1483 Trithemius was elected abbot there, and was consecrated the following November. Both monastic reformer and humanist, he insisted on strict discipline while at the same time building up a renowned library of over two thousand manuscripts and books. Trithemius was in contact with many renowned scholars. He was forced to resign as abbot in 1506, whereupon he became abbot of the ancient Irish monastery of Saint Jakob in Würzburg. He died on December 13, 1516.

Although he did not have the benefit of a rigorous formal education, Trithemius had very broad interests and was an extremely learned man. He read widely in philosophy, studied Greek and Hebrew, and did reading and research in history and theology.

Trithemius was a prolific author. In 1513 he listed fifty-two works he had written; he composed another eight before he died. His works on church history include chronicles of Hirsau, Sponheim, and Saint Jakob of Würzburg. He also wrote a *De scriptoribus ecclesiasticis.* In several of these works, Trithemius seems to have padded his references with invented sources, but they have considerable value nevertheless. Trithemius also wrote many letters, a genre in which he excelled.

Of particular interest here are his ascetic works. He wrote a commentary on the prologue and first seven chapters of the *Rule of Benedict* entitled *On a Rule for the Those Living the Cloistered Life (De regimine claustralium).* His other works include *On the Ruin of the Monastic Order (De ruina monastici ordinis), On the Temptations of Religious (De religiosorum tentationibus), On the Property of Monks (De proprietate monachorum), On the Threefold Territory of Claustrals (De triplici regione claustralium).* Among Trithemius's works are also versions of exhortations he gave to general chapters of the Bursfeld congregation and to his monks.

Summarizing a venerable idea of the Middle Ages as well as his own spiritual teaching, Trithemius declared in one of his letters: "Holy reading arouses the mind, meditation moves it to compunction; prayer seeks, contemplation finds." For Trithemius, study and monastic life lived for God were inseparable. The goal of study was to reach God himself. Study required asceticism, freedom from worldly cares. It was supposed to nourish the heart and draw it toward contemplation. Medieval monks had warned against *curiositas,* a craving for news and knowledge, which distracted one from seeking God. Trithemius used the same term, but with a different meaning: genuine study *(studiositas)* led to deeper knowledge and love of divine truth; vain learning *(curiositas)* sought to penetrate what is beyond the reach of the human mind. Like most monastic theorists before him, Trithemius felt that secular knowledge was not an end in itself, but only a means to help the monk study the Scriptures, which were the primary object of monastic study. Next in importance was the study of the early Christian writers. Trithemius distinguished intellectual or scholastic theology from affective or mystical theology, wherein love is primary and where the final point of arrival is the dark summit where divine truth dwells in inaccessible light.

WULFSTAN OF WORCESTER (CA. 1008–1095)

Saint Wulfstan's life was divided almost in half by the Norman invasion of England in 1066. He spent most of his life in the west Midlands of England, in the territory of the Severn River, which originates in Wales, flows east through Shrewsbury, then south to Worcester and the Bristol Channel. As bishop, Wulfstan came to know the area very well.

He was born at Itchington, near Warwick. His parents—Athelstan, a priest, and Wulfgiva—were fairly affluent. Wulfstan grew up during the Danish invasions. He was sent to Evesham Abbey for initial schooling, and soon afterward enrolled at the more distant abbey of Peterborough. Wulfstan returned home about 1024. In the next few years, his parents joined monasteries. We do not know what Wulfstan did between 1024 and 1034, when he entered the service of Bishop Briththeah (1033–1038), who may have been his half-brother. Ordained a priest, Wulfstan performed his duties while devoting himself to fasting. After several years he asked permission to become a monk. Not long after his entry into the monastic community, Wulfstan was appointed successively novice-master and cantor. He increased his ascetic discipline by spending nights in prayer. Meanwhile, the see of Worcester passed to Bishop Lyfing, and then to Bishop Ealdred. Both were former abbots and busy men of affairs. By 1055 the latter had appointed Wulfstan prior. One of Wulfstan's main tasks was to recover those properties of the cathedral priory that had been unlawfully occupied by others. Wulfstan also sought to enhance the observance of the monks within the priory. In addition, he performed many pastoral functions on behalf of the bishop. He was particularly concerned that the laity know the tenets and obligations of their Christian faith. He earned the esteem of many, in particular Earl Harold Godwinson. In 1062, Wulfstan reluctantly agreed to become bishop of Worcester.

This position brought with it many new responsibilities both secular and ecclesiastical. However, throughout his years as bishop, Wulfstan tried to follow the monastic round of prayer. He devoted himself very zealously to his pastoral duties, preaching, consecrating churches, hearing confessions, and making visitations. When Edward died in January 1066, Wulfstan found himself confessor to the new king, Harold II. Within a year, William the Conqueror succeeded to the throne. Wulfstan advised people to submit to the new order.

His spiritual outlook was shaped by the monastic reform carried out in the mid–tenth century under Dunstan. Although Wulfstan remained loyal to this older English monastic reform movement, he was open to the monastic customs that Lanfranc, the first Norman archbishop of Canterbury and former teacher of Saint Anselm, brought from Normandy. Hence, politically and monastically he adapted to the new order. He remained in office under the Normans longer than any of the English bishops. He was humble and ready to serve wherever he was called. He gradually acquired a reputation as a holy man who could on occasion work miracles, especially on behalf of the sick. He was even-tempered and cheerful, but he insisted on a high level of religious observance among those of his household. He strongly opposed slavery and clerical marriage, while personally seeing to the care of the poor. He always remained an embodiment of the monastic ideals of his time, simplicity and purity of heart, which remained the foundation of his long pastoral career as a bishop.

The primary source for Wulfstan's life and character is William of Malmesbury's Latin *Life,* a reworking of a no longer extant English work by Wulfstan's close associate Coleman. All the stories about Wulfstan included in this book are from the Latin *Life*. There survives a book of prayers, the *Portifolium,* which the saint seems to have taken with him on his pastoral travels throughout his diocese.

Bibliographical Notes

ANSELM OF CANTERBURY

The works of Anselm of Canterbury are available in a six-volume critical Latin edition edited by F. S. Schmitt (Edinburgh: Nelson, 1946–1961). The *Memorials of St. Anselm,* ed. R. W. Southern and F. S. Schmitt, Auctores Britannici Medii Aevi, no. 1 (London: Oxford Univ. Press, 1969), shows his more familiar side.

An excellent study is R. W. Southern, *Saint Anselm: Portrait in a Landscape* (Cambridge: Cambridge Univ. Press, 1990). Benedicta Ward has published a convenient translation of Anselm's prayers, *The Prayers and Meditations of Saint Anselm* (New York: Penguin, 1973). The translations here are mine, from the critical edition.

ANTONY

The excerpts from Athanasius's *Life of Antony* are reworked from the annotated translation by Robert T. Meyer (Athanasius, *The Life of Saint Antony,* Ancient Christian Writers, no. 10 [Westminster, MD: Newman, 1950]). The translations of the letters are based on D. J. Chitty's translation (Oxford: Fairacres, 1975). A more recent edition of the letters can be found in Samuel Rubenson, *The Letters of St. Antony: Monasticism and the Making of a Saint* (Minneapolis: Fortress, 1995), from which work I derive some of my ideas about the relationship of Antony's very theologically informed letters to the picture of Antony presented in the *Life*. The *Sayings* of Antony I have translated primarily from *Les sentences des pères du désert: Collection alphabétique,* trans. Lucien Regnault (Sablé-sur-Sarthe: Abbaye Saint-Pierre de Solesmes, 1981). A more recent translation of the *Life* is Athanasius, *The Life of Antony and the Letter to Marcellinus,* trans. and ed. Robert C. Gregg, Classics of Western Spirituality (New York: Paulist Press, 1980).

LUDOVICO BARBO

The basics of Ludovico Barbo's life, reform, and writings, together with a bibliography, can be found in M. Mähler, "Barbo, Louis," in *Dictionnaire de spiritualité* (Paris: Beauchesne, 1937), 1:1244–1245; and in A. Pantoni, "Barbo, Ludovico," in *Dizionario degli Istituti di Perfezione* (Rome: Edizioni Paoline, 1974), 1:1044–1047. The most thorough study available to me was Ildefonso Tassi, *Ludovico Barbo (1381–1443),* Uomini e dottrine, no. 1 (Rome: Edizioni di Storia e Letteratura,

1952). Evidently wrong in its main contention about the Italian origin of the *Imitation of Christ,* but useful for its bibliography, is Riccardo Pitigliani, *Il Ven. Ludovico Barbo et la diffusione dell' Imitazione di Cristo per opera della Congregazione di S. Giustina* (Padua: Badia S. Giustina, 1943). Here selections from Barbo are translated from the Latin version of his directions for methodical prayer and meditation printed in Tassi, 141–152. Quotations from his letters are also translated from the Latin originals (Tassi, 152–155).

BEDE

Readers can find a first introduction to Saint Bede's life and works and the scholarship about him in the *Oxford Dictionary of the Christian Church,* 3rd ed., ed. F. L. Cross and E. A. Livingstone (New York: Oxford Univ. Press, 1997), 177–178; and Alberic Stacpole, "St. Bede," in *Benedict's Disciples,* ed. David Hugh Farmer (Leominster, England: Gracewing, 1997). Bede's homilies, edited by David Hurst, are to be found in *Bedae opera,* vol. 3/4, Corpus Christianorum, Series Latina, no. 122 (Turnhout, Belgium: Brepols, 1955). These were translated by Lawrence T. Martin and David Hurst as Bede the Venerable, *Homilies on the Gospels,* 2 vols., Cistercian Studies, nos. 110–111 (Kalamazoo, MI: Cistercian Publications, 1991). The translations here are my own.

BENEDICT OF NURSIA

The selections from the *Rule of Benedict* are translated from the Latin text prepared by Jean Neufville for the Sources chrétiennes series and reprinted in what is by far the best English-language commentary on the *Rule of Benedict:* Terrence G. Kardong, *Benedict's Rule: A Translation and Commentary* (Collegeville, MN: Liturgical Press, 1996). Still very useful is *RB 80: The Rule of St. Benedict in Latin and English with Notes* (Collegeville, MN: Liturgical Press, 1981). For Gregory's life of Benedict in the *Dialogues,* the best translation and commentary is Gregory the Great, *The Life of Saint Benedict,* commentary by Adalbert de Vogüé, trans. Hilary Costello and Eoin de Bhaldraithe (Petersham, MA: St. Bede's, 1993). The translation of passages from the *Dialogues* are my own. *The Rule of the Master* is available in an English translation by Luke Eberle (Kalamazoo, MI: Cistercian Publications, 1977).

BERNARD OF CLAIRVAUX

The works of Bernard of Clairvaux were published in a critical edition by Jean Leclercq, C. H. Talbot, and H. Rochais (Rome: Editiones Cistercienses, 1957–1977). They have been published in English translation by Cistercian Publications. I have translated from the Latin. English translations of the two works I have cited are Bernard of Clairvaux, *On the Song of Songs,* trans. Kilian Walsh and Irene Edmonds, 4 vols., Cistercian Fathers, nos. 4, 7, 31, and 40 (Kalamazoo, MI: Cistercian Publications, 1979–1983); and *On Consideration,* trans. Elizabeth Kennan and John D. Anderson, Cistercian Fathers, no. 37 (Kalamazoo, MI: Cistercian Publications, 1976). I have studied the latter in "The Spirituality of St. Bernard for Managers," *Cistercian Studies* 25 (1990): 267–276. There is an enormous amount of literature about Saint Bernard, much of it available from Cistercian Publications.

Various modern students of Saint Bernard, such as Brian Patrick McGuire, Jean Leclercq, Adriaan Bredero, and Michael Casey, have written studies and biographical sketches of Bernard, but there is really no standard or definitive work.

LOUIS DE BLOIS

Two years after Louis de Blois (Blosius) died, Jacques Froye edited his writings as *Ludovici Blosii opera* (Louvain, 1568); this collection went through eight editions. The monks of Liessies, under Abbot Antoine de Winghe, prepared a new edition (Anvers: Plantin, 1632), which was listed by Jean Mabillon in his *Traité des études monastiques* (1691). A good introduction to Louis de Blois can be found in P. de Puniet, "Blois, Louis de," in the *Dictionnaire de spiritualité* 1 (1937): 1730–1738. English versions of many of his works are to be found in *The Works of Louis de Blois*, ed. B. Wilberforce and D. R. Huddleston (London: Burns Oates and Washbourne, 1925–26). Up-to-date bibliography can be found in Lambert Vos, *Louis de Blois, Abbé de Liessies (1506–1566): Recherches bibliographiques sur son oeuvre*, Publications de l'Encyclopédie bénédictine, no. 1 (Turnhout, Belgium: Brepols, 1992). I have translated the quotations from the *Mirror for Monks (Speculum monachorum)*, *Spiritual Doctrine (Institutionis spiritualis)*, and the *Spiritual Mirror (Speculum spirituale)* from the *Opera omnia* of 1672 (Kempten: Rudolphe Dreber), which reprints the 1632 edition, and the quotations from his *Statuta monastica (Monatic Statutes)* from the edition that constituted the tenth volume in the series Scripta Monastica, ed. Ursmarus Berlière (Padua: Antoniana, 1929). I was unable to consult George de Blois, *A Benedictine of the Sixteenth Century* (London: Burns and Oates, 1878; translated from the original French edition [Paris, 1875]).

SR. JOAN CHITTISTER

Passages quoted from Joan Chittister are from *The Rule of Benedict: Insights for the Ages* (New York: Crossroad, 1996). A related book by Chittister is *Wisdom Distilled from the Daily: Living the Rule of St. Benedict Today* (San Francisco: HarperSanFrancisco, 1991).

THE DESERT FATHERS AND MOTHERS

The quotations from *Sayings of the Desert Fathers and Mothers* are my translations, taken primarily from *Les sentences des Pères du Désert: Série des anonymes,* Spiritualité Orientale, no. 43 (Bégrolles-en-Mauges: Abbaye de Bellefontaine, 1985), although I made use of other versions as well. For the English reader there are a number of translations available: Benedicta Ward, trans., *The Wisdom of the Desert Fathers: Systematic Sayings from the Anonymous Series of the Apophthegmata Patrum* (Oxford: SGL Press, 1986) and *The Sayings of the Desert Fathers: The Alphabetical Collection* (Kalamazoo, MI: Cistercian Publications, 1984); Thomas Merton, *The Wisdom of the Desert* (New York: New Directions, 1970); Helen Waddell, *The Desert Fathers* (1936; reprint, Ann Arbor: Univ. of Michigan Press, 1971).

ESTHER DE WAAL

Selections from Esther de Waal are taken from *A Life-Giving Way: A Commentary on the Rule of St. Benedict* (Collegeville, MN: Liturgical Press, 1995). De Waal also wrote two outstanding books on Benedictine spirituality: *Seeking God: The Way of*

St. Benedict (Collegeville, MN: Liturgical Press, 1984) and *Living with Contradiction* (Harrisburg, PA: Morehouse, 1998).

GERTRUDE THE GREAT

Passages from the first two books of *The Herald of Divine Love* are here translated from the critical edition of the Latin text, in Gertrude d'Helfta, *Oeuvres spirituelles,* vol. 2, *Le héraut,* books 1–2, ed. and trans. Pierre Doyère, Sources chrétiennes, no. 139 (Paris: Cerf, 1968). There is also a useful French version of the *Herald* by the nuns of Notre-Dame of Wisques, *Le héraut de l'amour divin: Révélations de Sainte Gertrude,* new ed., 2 vols. (Tours: Mame, 1952), from which a citation from book 5 is translated. There are two recent, though partial, English translations of this work: *The Herald of God's Loving-Kindness, Books One and Two,* trans. Alexandra Barrat (Kalamazoo, MI: Cistercian Publications, 1991); and *The Herald of Divine Love,* trans. Margaret Winkworth (New York: Paulist Press, 1993). Included here also are some passages from Gertrude's *Spiritual Exercises,* translated from the Latin text in *Oeuvres spirituelles,* vol. 1, *Les exercices,* ed. and trans. Jacques Hourlier and Albert Schmitt, Sources chrétiennes, no. 127 (Paris: Cerf, 1967). For an English translation, see *Spiritual Exercises,* ed. Gertrud Lewis and Jack Lewis (Kalamazoo, MI: Cistercian Publications, 1989). Sister Mary Jeremy, O.P., *Scholars and Mystics* (Chicago: Regnery, 1962), tells about the mystics of Helfta, and Cipriano Vagaggini, *Theological Dimensions of the Liturgy* (Collegeville, MN: Liturgical Press, 1977), 740–803, examines Gertrude's spirituality.

HILDEGARD OF BINGEN

Most of the passages from Hildegard of Bingen included here are from her *Liber vitae meritorum,* ed. Angela Carlevaris, O.S.B., Corpus Christianorum, Continuatio Mediaevalis, no. 90 (Turnhout, Belgium: Brepols, 1995). There is a complete English version: *The Book of the Rewards of Life,* trans. Bruce Hozeski (1994; reprint, New York: Oxford Univ. Press, 1997). A few passages are taken from her *Explanation of the Rule of Benedict,* ed. and trans. Hugh Feiss (Toronto: Peregrina, 1990). Texts cited from Hildegard's musical morality play the *Ordo virtutum* are translated from the edition by Audrey Davidson (Kalamazoo, MI: Western Michigan Univ., 1985). The text of the *Ordo virtutum* is also available in both Latin and English on the liner notes to the recording made by Sequentia for Deutsche Harmonia Mundi (1982). Hildegard's life and works are presented in Sabina Flanagan, *Hildegard of Bingen, 1098–1179: A Visionary Life* (New York: Routledge, 1990). There is an excellent translation of the *Scivias* by Columba Hart and Jane Bishop (New York: Paulist Press, 1990). There are many audio recordings of her musical works; particularly noteworthy are those by Sequentia. A reliable version of her *Vita* is *The Life of Holy Hildegard,* trans. Hugh Feiss (Toronto: Peregrina, 1995). Most of the other English translations of her works are based on imperfect Latin editions or German translations, and should be used with caution.

HUGH OF CLUNY

The essential facts and bibliography regarding Hugh of Cluny can be found in F. L. Cross and E. A. Livingstone, eds., *Oxford Dictionary of the Christian Church,* 3d ed.

(New York: Oxford Univ. Press, 1997), p. 799. Further information is available in Noreen Hunt, *Cluny under Saint Hugh* (Notre Dame, IN: Univ. of Notre Dame Press, 1968). The biographical passages included here are my translations from materials contained in H. E. H. Cowdrey, "Memorials of Abbot Hugh of Cluny (1049–1109)," *Studii Gregoriani,* vol. 11 (Rome: Libreria Ateneo Salesiano, 1978), 13–175.

JEAN MABILLON

Basic information on Jean Mabillon's life and works can be found in the article by J.-P. Müller in *Dizionario degli Istituti di Perfezione* 5 (1978): 793–796, and in the entry by G.-M. Oury in *Dictionnaire de spiritualité* 10 (1977): 1–4. Selections from Mabillon's *Traité des études monastiques (Treatise on the Studies of Monks)* are translated from the Gregg Press reprint (Farnborough, England: Gregg Press, 1967) of the original 1691 edition. Regarding the Maurists, see the article by J. Houlier in *Dizionario degli Istituti di Perfezione* 5 (1978): 1082–1089.

THOMAS MERTON

Thomas Merton's writings on monasticism were collected in *Contemplation in a World of Action* (New York: Doubleday, 1971), which contains an excellent introduction by Merton's friend Jean Leclercq, O.S.B. I make use of material from this anthology, but Merton's overtly monastic writings are of limited use here. The rest of his writings—the vast majority—were designed to present what he had learned in the monastery to readers in other ways of life. Hence these other writings are more congruent with the aims of this book. In his earlier writings, Merton tended to emphasize the differences between monastics in their cloisters and the rest of humanity out in the world. In late 1950s he became more and more aware of the solidarity that united the monk with the rest of humanity. This new attitude is reflected both in his reworking of *Seeds of Contemplation* (1949) in *New Seeds of Contemplation* (1962; reprint, New York: New Directions, 1972), and in his *Conjectures of a Guilty Bystander* (1966; reprint, New York: Doubleday-Image, 1968), the latter containing reworked journal entries from 1956 onward. Merton was by then more certain about the questions than the answers and ready to enter into dialogue about his conjectures with all people of goodwill.

PACHOMIUS

The passages from *Life of Pachomius* are from "Pachomius: The First Greek Life," trans. Armand Veilleux, in *Pachomian Koinonia,* vol. 1, *The Life of Saint Pachomius* (Kalamazoo, MI: Cistercian Publications, 1980), 297–423. There is another version of this same *Life,* giving the critical Greek text: *The Life of Pachomius,* trans. Apostolos N. Athanassakis (Missoula, MT: Scholars Press, 1975). Most of the biography of Pachomius in the historical section is derived from this life. I also profited from some unpublished notes of Terrence Kardong, O.S.B., who followed another ancient version of Pachomius's life but drew from it substantially the same picture of Pachomius that I do. Fr. Kardong also discussed many of the same episodes quoted in the thematic section. For recent scholarly work, see Philip Rousseau, *Pachomius: The Making of a Community in Fourth-Century Egypt* (Berkeley: Univ. of California

Press, 1985); and Vincent Desprez, "Pachomian Cenobitism," *American Benedictine Review* 43 (1992): 233–249, 358–394.

PETER OF CELLE

The Latin texts of most of Peter of Celle's works are printed in volume 202 of J. P. Migne's *Patrologia latina.* Several works were edited by Jean Leclercq in his study *La spiritualité de Pierre de Celle,* Etudes de théologie et d'histoire de la spiritualité, no. 7 (Paris: J. Vrin, 1946). Gérard de Martel edited Peter's two commentaries on Ruth and Peter's treatise *De tabernaculo,* Corpus Christianorum, Continuatio Mediaevalis, no. 54 (Turnhout, Belgium: Brepols, 1983). English translations of *On Affliction and Reading, On Conscience, The School of the Cloister,* and sermons 29, 33, 39, and 44 appear in Peter of Celle, *Selected Works,* trans. Hugh Feiss, Cistercian Studies, no. 100 (Kalamazoo, MI: Cistercian Publications, 1987). All the passages included here are new translations from the Latin text in *L'école du cloître,* ed. and trans. Gérard de Martel, Sources chrétiennes, no. 240 (Paris: Cerf, 1977); or from the Latin text of *De afflictione et lectione* edited by Leclercq.

SYNCLETICA

The quotations from the *Life of Syncletica* were all transcribed (with minor alterations) from the translation by Elizabeth Bryson Bongie (Toronto: Peregrina, 1996). Other literature includes Elizabeth Castelli, "Pseudo-Athanasius: The Life and Activity of the Holy and Blessed Teacher Syncletica," in *Ascetic Behavior in Greco-Roman Antiquity: A Sourcebook,* ed. Vincent L. Wimbush (Minneapolis: Fortress, 1990), 265–311; Kevin Corrigan, "Syncletica and Macrina: Two Early Lives of Women Saints," *Vox Benedictina* 6, no. 3 (July 1989): 241–257; and Mary Forman, "Amma Syncletica: A Spirituality of Experience," *Vox Benedictina* 10, no. 2 (winter 1993): 199–237.

JOHN TRITHEMIUS

Sources of information about John Trithemius include the article on him by P. Séjourné in *Dictionnaire de théologie catholique* 15 (1950): 1862–1867; the article by Klaus Ganzer in *Dictionnaire de spiritualité* 15 (1991): 1325–1328; and N. L. Brann, *The Abbot Trithemius: The Renaissance of Monastic Humanism,* Studies in the History of Christian Thought, no. 24 (Leiden: Brill, 1981). Selections included in this book are translated from *Ioannis Trithemii Spanheimensis . . . Abbatis eruditissimi opera pia et spiritualia,* ed. Ioanne Busaeo (Mainz: J. Albini, 1610). Selections from *De regimine claustralium,* his commentary on the *Rule of Benedict,* are identified by the short title *Rule.* The monks of Assumption Abbey were kind enough to let me work from their copy of the *Opera* of Trithemius as well as from their copy of a 1672 version of the works of Louis de Blois.

WULFSTAN OF WORCESTER

All the selections about Wulfstan of Worcester are taken from *The Vita Wulfstani of William of Malmesbury,* ed. Reginald R. Darlington (London: Royal Historical Society, 1928). The translations are my own, but I have consulted J. H. F. Peile, *William of Malmesbury's Life of Saint Wulstan, Bishop of Worcester* (1934; reprint, Felinfact, Great Britain: Llanerch, 1996). The biographical sketch is based on Emma Mason, *St. Wulfstan of Worcester, c. 1008–1095* (Oxford: Basil Blackwell, 1990); my thanks to Ellen Martin for calling this book to my attention and locating a copy for me. I have also translated a prayer for guests from Wulfstan's prayer book, *The Portifolium of Saint Wul[f]stan,* ed. Anselm Hughes, Henry Bradshaw Society, nos. 89 and 90 (Leighton Buzzard, England: Henry Bradshaw Society, 1958–1960).

Permission Acknowledgments

Grateful acknowledgment is made to the following for permission to reprint previously published material:

Cistercian Publications for permission to quote from *The Life of Saint Pachomius and His Disciples,* translated by Armand Veilleux, O.C.S.O., *Pachomian Koinonia,* vol. 1, Cistercian Studies Series, no. 45. Copyright ©1980 by Cistercian Publications, Kalamazoo, MI, and Spencer, MS.

Doubleday, a division of Random House, Inc., for permission to quote from *Conjectures of a Guilty Bystander,* by Thomas Merton. Copyright ©1966 by The Abbey of Gethsemani.

Liturgical Press and Esther de Waal for permission to quote from *A Life-Giving Way: A Commentary on the Rule of St. Benedict,* by Esther de Waal. Copyright ©1995 by Liturgical Press, Collegeville, MN.

The Merton Legacy Trust for permission to quote from *Contemplation in a World of Action,* by Thomas Merton.

New Directions Publishing Corp. and Laurence Pollinger, Ltd., for permission to quote from *New Seeds of Contemplation,* by Thomas Merton. Copyright ©1961 by The Abbey of Gethsemani, Inc.

Paulist Press for permission to quote from *St. Athanasius,* translated and annotated by Robert T. Meyer, Ph.D. ©1950 by Rev. Johannes Quasten, Rev. Joseph C. Plumpe and Copyright ©1978 by Rev. Johannes Quasten and Rose Mary L. Plumpe.

Peregrina Press, Toronto, Ontario, Canada, for permission to quote from *The Life and Regimen of Blessed Syncletica* by Pseudo-Athanasius, translated by Elizabeth Bryson Bongie, Peregrina Translations Series, no. 1. Copyright ©1996.

SLG Press, Convent of the Incarnation, Fairacres, Oxford OX4 1TB, for permission to quote from *The Letters of Saint Antony the Great,* translated with an introduction by Derwas J. Chitty. Copyright ©1975 by The Community of the Sisters of the Love of God.

The Crossroad Publishing Company for permission to quote from *The Rule of Benedict,* by Sr. Joan Chittister. Copyright ©1992 by The Crossroad Publishing Company.

Other Essential Series Books
Available from Harper San Francisco:

SIFTED
—BUT—
SAVED

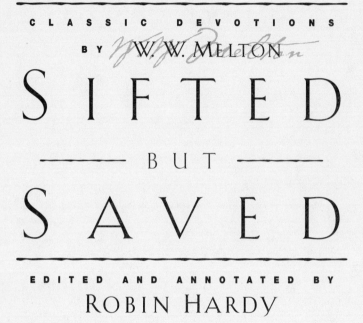

CLASSIC DEVOTIONS
BY *W. W. Melton*

SIFTED

BUT

SAVED

EDITED AND ANNOTATED BY
ROBIN HARDY

BROADMAN
&HOLMAN
PUBLISHERS

Nashville, Tennessee

0-8054-2425-3

Published by Broadman & Holman Publishers,
Nashville, Tennessee

Dewey Decimal Classification: 252
Subject Heading: DEVOTIONAL
Library of Congress Card Catalog Number: 2001035521

Unless otherwise stated all Scripture citation is from the King James Version of the Bible. The other version cited is RSV, Revised Standard Version of the Bible, © 1946, 1952, © 1971, 1973 by the Division of Christian Education of the National Council of the Churches of Christ in the United States of America.

Library of Congress Cataloging-in-Publication Data
Melton, W. W. (William Walter), 1879–1967.
   Sifted but saved / by W. W. Melton ; edited and annotated by Robin Hardy.
      p.   cm.
   Includes bibliographical references.
   ISBN 0-8054-2425-3
   1. Baptists—Sermons. 2. Sermons, American—20th century.
   I. Hardy, Robin, 1955–   II. Title.

BX6333.M39 S5   2001
252'.061—dc21

                                          2001035521
                                          CIP
         1 2 3 4 5 6 7 8 9 10 05 04 03 02 01

This volume is
affectionately dedicated
to my wife

ORAH MELTON
who has been sympathetic
in all my labors
and who has made possible
whatever good has been
accomplished

CONTENTS

FOREWORD

Old books intrigue me—the musty smell, the fragile brown pages, the quaint old typeset. But most interesting are the words: How well have they traversed the years between their conception and my reading? How enduring is the thought they express?

I found this book of sermons—little talks, really—in a dusty stack at a Goodwill store. When I took it home and opened it up, the words leaped out with such aliveness that I kept checking the publication date to make sure it really said 1925. The personal tone of the messages, their relevance to what I was experiencing, and their biblical common sense spoke to me as few contemporary sermons ever had. After reading this little book through in one hungry sitting, I kept it within reach on my bookshelf for the next twenty years, referring back to it time and again, until it occurred to me that I was being selfish. There is a whole new generation of Christians who desperately need Dr. Melton's words of grace and encouragement.

In concession to the changing times, I have modernized certain expressions and edited for clarity. I have added scriptural references and footnotes with historical information, literary references, and, in the few instances it seemed appropriate, my own five cents' worth (adjusted for inflation). I have not tampered with the format of these little talks. As they stand, it is too easy to hear Dr. Melton's voice expounding the One who was, and is, and is to come.

Robin Hardy
Richardson, Texas, 2001

PREFACE

No apology is offered for the publication of this volume; if it cannot live on its merit, let it die as thousands before it have died. But if in its short life it can bear some message of hope and blessing, if it can give encouragement and inspiration to some struggling soul, the author will not regret the labor, time, and expense of sending it out.

The sermons have been selected for their practical helpfulness to the needs and conditions of the average Christian. It is our prayer that the reader will find food for his soul, light for his feet, strength for his battles, comfort for his troubled heart, and refreshment for his weary spirit.

W. W. Melton
Waco, Texas, 1925

1

TROUBLES

*And when the disciples saw him walking
on the sea, they were troubled.*
MATTHEW 14:26

The incident recorded here is a midnight scene. It was in the night following the miraculous feeding of the five thousand with the loaves and fishes. The day had been a busy one for Christ; the crowds had pressed him, and he had taught them, comforted them, and fed them, then late in the afternoon had sent them to their homes for the night.

Then the disciples had boarded a small boat and started across the lake while the Master had turned his steps up the mountain slopes to spend the night in communion with his Father. It was a stormy night: billows rose like mountains on the sea, and the disciples found themselves outmatched by the fury of the storm. All night they rowed their little skiff in the face of the wind and waves but were unable to hold out.

Toward the breaking of day, they began to yield to their seemingly inevitable fate, and one by one they gave up the fight and were ready to die.

In the account of this incident recorded by Mark, he tells us that Christ "saw them toiling in rowing" (Mark 6:48). Through the storm he watched them. He saw their strength fail them, their fears overcome them, and their hearts fill with distress. He watched them until he saw their last hope give way; then he came to them, walking on the water. He had waited for them to come to the limit of their own strength before he saved them, because only then would they fully realize how much he meant to them.

For days they had been in his company, watching him perform miracles, hearing his wonderful teachings, and feeling the thrill of his holy presence; but they missed the real lessons he had given them. They had been so attracted to him personally that they had not seen beyond the physical life. They had failed to learn that he was also a spirit—that he was omnipresent and that he was accessible to them even in the storm, or in any condition. Their admiration of him had been stimulated by the fact that he was a wonder-worker, a teacher of strange things, and a reformer of wonderful ability, but when they were separated from him, they felt they were entirely out of the range of his knowledge and power. His miracles had been exciting and intoxicating, but when they were in the grip of a fierce, terrible storm, they felt its physical force must be matched by their physical strength, and in this they met their defeat. Some lessons cannot be written in books but must be written in human experience;

they cannot be taught by miracle nor precept as clearly as by adversity and disaster.

There are four indications in the lesson that the disciples were in trouble. The first one is the plain statement: they "were troubled." They were not being entertained by the storm; they were being distressed nearly to death. Their situation had become desperate. Their fears were not mere hallucinations but as real as life and as stubborn as death. They had not worked themselves into a frenzy over a frivolous matter. Little by little they had been forced to recognize the growing dangers around them, moment by moment the storm had been bearing down upon them, and bit by bit their spirits had been breaking under the strain.

If someone had come to them in such an hour and such an experience and told them that it was all a hoax, that there were no such things as storms and waves and death, the disciples would have been moved either to anger for the insult or to pity for the maniac who had lost his mind. So the first fact to be learned from the experience is that there are . . .

REAL TROUBLES

Many do not believe it, and try to convince the rest of us that life and the world are made up of shadows rather than substance, of fancies rather than facts, of errors rather than terrors. This group would laugh in the face of the storm and say, "There is no such thing!" They would wave their hand over the storm-swept lake and insist, "This is a fake, for there is no lake," or they would say to the disciples, "Do not cry, you will not die, for it is all a lie!"

But for the benefit of such optimists let me say that *the realities of life are not so easily dismissed.* True, many of us create more troubles than are necessary, and we could dismiss many that come on us as trivial things. But after we have brushed aside all that will go so easily and have joked away all that will be settled so quickly and have denied all that can be denied, there still remains a great host of problems that will not be scared off. They are inescapable facts that demand consideration. This storm could not be joked away. The disciples' fears would not be allayed by a magic wave of the hand. They could not work up a positive attitude when the sea was so deep beneath them, the wind so strong around them, and the boat so frail a vessel.

But the question becomes more complex when one takes into account that Christ watched the struggle but kept himself away from them and allowed disaster to befall his closest friends, his own disciples. This uncovers another important matter: If troubles are to come, why do they come to good people? This has been an unsettled question in all ages. The tormentors of Job asked, "'Who ever perished, being innocent?'" and "'Where [or when] were the righteous cut off?'" (Job 4:7). These questions express the silent thoughts of many who cannot see why a good person should suffer or the righteous should have sorrows and trouble.

In answer, let me point out at least two things. First, Christianity is not offered as an insurance policy against such things. Nowhere in the Bible is the promise made that Christians will not suffer. The reverse is true; we are plainly told that we may expect all such things, but the promise is given that the grace of the Lord will be a support upon which we can safely lean (see John 16:33). The good as well as the bad have suffered in all ages. Believers have been sick, have had losses and reversals, have had misfortunes and sorrows, and have even experienced death just as nonbelievers have.

The second answer I would make is that such experiences may be the greatest opportunities to demonstrate the value of the Christian hope. I knew two blind men. One was mad at the world, out of harmony with everything and everybody because of his misfortune. He cursed God and men because he had to live his life in darkness. The other made his misfortune a blessing. He saw God better through sightless eyes; he felt the warmth and glow of the divine love a little better because of his disability. He seemed to have new occasions for joy and gladness.

The first man turned his day into night; the second turned his night into day by the same misfortune. Both were blind; one made his blindness a stumbling block while the other made it a stepping-stone. For one, it was a door shut and locked in his face, excluding him from all that was good; for the other, it was a door flung wide open, admitting him into new friendships, new senses, and new achievements. The greatest misfortune in life is not the visitation of sorrow, calamity, or disappointment, but it is to misunderstand, misinterpret, and misuse this visitation.

So, summing up the first thought: when real troubles develop and appear on the horizon of life, do not be too stubborn to admit them, nor too foolish to give them serious consideration, nor too blind to interpret them properly and use them.

IMAGINARY TROUBLES

But the fears of the disciples were augmented by a new appearance. When they saw Christ coming to help them, they thought he was an evil spirit. They supposed he was some evil thing because *they were looking for trouble.* If they had been looking for help or deliverance, they would have been quick to cry out for joy when they saw him approaching them.

It only shows that we usually see what we are looking for. Our fears, prejudices, desires, and passions color almost every scene in life. If we look for slights and insults, any little meaningless thing will be misinterpreted to reflect what we are looking for. The opposite is likewise true. If we consider someone a friend, he may be ever so rude but we take no offense because we are not looking for offenses. When we are scared, everything scares us; when we are expecting trouble, everything frightens us.

When I was a child, I had to go to a neighbor's house after nightfall one evening. I was afraid of the dark and soon found myself walking very fast; then I broke into a run, and the farther I went, the faster I ran—I knew something was going to get me. Just when I got to the darkest place in the path, a low spot hedged in by tall weeds, a hog jumped out of the way, grunting, "Oink! Oink!" This was almost more than I could stand. I had been expecting trouble, and of course, it came. In all my childhood experiences, I do not recall ever being as badly frightened, and it was over an imaginary ghost.

It can be said without fear of successful contradiction that most of our troubles are imaginary. This does not deny the existence of the real ones, but it does mean that there are enough real ones without our having to create a lot of fanciful ones. We have entirely too many battles fought out in our minds only and never get further than our imaginations. The same is true of the illusory difficulties that would block our way to success. We can easily see how the drought may ruin our crops, and the insects destroy our fields, and the floods, in time, lay waste our land. How easy it becomes to fret about things that have not happened, and may never happen.

I was on a train one night. The few passengers were beginning to recline in their seats for a little sleep. Across the aisle from me was a mother with a son about twelve years old. She had gone to the end of the car for a drink of water, leaving the son on the seat. While she was away the child moved forward two or three seats where he could have more room to sleep.

When the mother returned and did not see the child, she threw her hands into the air and screamed frantically, "My little child fell off the train!" Of course, this brought the rest of us to her side, and when the commotion was at its height, the boy raised his head, saw his mother, and came back to her, crying.

For thirty miles she made life miserable for that boy. She blamed him for things he had not done and had him weeping over dangers that might come to them. She was going to a new place where her brother lived, and suddenly she became afraid he might fail to meet the train. What would they do? Where could they go? She talked about all of these things to the child until it seemed they were on the most dangerous venture ever made.

I happened to be going to the same city, so I was interested to know whether her brother would be there. Of course, he was, for she had written him of her coming. After she had left the train, going into the station, she stopped and said excitedly, "I have lost my purse!" I stopped to see the outcome of this matter. After looking carefully through an armful of things, she said, "No, here it is." I went to the hotel very much amused at the imaginary troubles the woman had endured. They were as ghosts in the dark.

How interesting to trace this vein running through the human family. Cain thought God was partial to Abel, and he became so enraged over the imaginary thing that he rose up in his anger and killed his brother (Gen. 4:8). Abraham was afraid the king of Egypt would kill him to get his wife, so he lied and said she was his sister (Gen. 12:10–20). Elijah was sure all the good people of his day had been killed but himself and that he would not be alive much longer, but God told him of an army of worshipers hiding in the mountains. What was more, Elijah was in no danger of death since God took him to heaven without dying (1 Kings 19:18; 2 Kings 2:11).

I heard a very interesting story some time ago. A woman awoke in the night and excitedly told her husband she was sure she heard someone in the house. The man had heard that so many times he was not at all afraid. To satisfy the wife, he quietly slipped downstairs and turned the lights on, whereupon he found himself face to face with a burglar.

The intruder pointed his gun at the homeowner and told him to be quiet, that he had already got all he wanted—he had the money, jewels, and silverware in a sack and was ready to go. If the man behaved, nothing would be done, but if he made any noise, the burglar would kill him on the spot. The man, wide awake now, assured the burglar that he had no intention of raising an alarm, but he said, "I have a favor to ask of you."

"What is it?" replied the burglar.

"I wish you would wait here until I could bring my wife down. I want you to meet her, because she has been looking for you every night for twenty years." Some of us live in such dread of bad things that might happen we cannot enjoy the good things that do happen.

SATANIC TROUBLES

The sacred writer leads us on from trouble to trouble. Immediately after the imaginary trouble, he raises a new question. Christ has assured his disciples no harm was about to come, that he was their friend come to help them in their distress. To prove it, Peter demanded that he be permitted to walk on the water to meet the Master. The request was granted, but he had not gone far before he began to sink. Christ rescued him and asked him a leading question: "'Why did you doubt?'" (Matt. 14:31 RSV). He did not ask why Peter sank, nor why he was afraid; he asked why he doubted. This was the core of all his trouble. Who had caused it? The answer to this will solve nine-tenths of our troubles.

Who always causes doubt? The devil. He had made the disciples forget the power of Christ and had filled their minds with fear and dismay. Doubt is one of the chief weapons of the devil. By this means he crushed Adam and Eve in the garden when he made them doubt God. By this he sank the whole world in the days of Noah because everyone doubted, except Noah and his family. Doubt is a seed the devil drops into the hearts of people, from which will spring a harvest of evils. It sprouts weakness, fears, suspicion, cowardice, false accusations, slander, baseless criticism, and a list of evils too long to be named here.

Doubt will destroy the reputation of the most innocent person. The question raised by a malicious tongue could take a lifetime to live down. A baseless rumor that questions the honesty of the chief of police, the morality of the school principal, or the fidelity of the minister may not only ruin careers, but lives too. They may be able to account for every private moment and answer every accusation, but the manufactured doubt will hang over them like a dark cloud. Yet nothing will break one's spirit faster than casting aspersions on God. It does not damage his character but ours.

Let that question be asked in all seriousness: "Why did you doubt?" Can you really tell the reason? Peter had the background of three years of wonderful miracles to brace him and encourage him, and not one single failure had occurred to shake his confidence. The world is full of the evidences of God, but Satan blinds our eyes to them all and makes us wonder whether there is a God. Or, if there is a

God, does he care for us individually? Often when the Christian doubts that he has really been saved, he doubts not only in the face of his conversion experience but in the face of the many promises and guaranties of God.

Why does he doubt? There is but one answer: Satan. It is he who blinds the eyes to all the evidences, makes one forget all the assurances, and constructs a line of false reasoning that will lead one away from the real facts. In order to shake one's confidence, he will magnify the difficulties, point out the weaknesses, remind one of one's faults, and hold up as many contradictions as possible. When you doubt, ask who caused it, why it came, and whether it is well founded. These questions, honestly considered, will dispel most of our doubts.

DIVINE TROUBLES

It will be noted that *as soon as Christ came to them* the storm ceased. The disciples' troubles were at an end. This same condition existed with the sisters of Lazarus. They each cried out, "'Lord, if you had been here, my brother would not have died'" (John 11:21, 32 RSV). All of their troubles were occasioned by the absence of Christ.

And this will account for most of our troubles today. The World Wars sprang out of a militarism that knew no God. When nations forget God, they are soon at each other's throats. Churches also go to pieces when Christ is crowded out. We have yet to find the first example of a minister, preaching to empty pews, who magnified a crucified, buried, and risen Lord. But when he begins to leave Christ out of his message and fills it with all phrases of modernism, it will not be long until there will be space to rent in that church.

Christ is the bond that holds the home together also. We are facing a most alarming divorce rate as a nation. Why so many loveless marriages? Because they are godless marriages. They have not taken Christ into the new home and have not made him the guest of honor. Instead of settling domestic problems on bended knees, we are too prone to settle them in a battle of words. The same reason can be given for the downfall of so many individuals: the absence of Christ in the life.

If life is filled with storms, by all means call the Master in. He can settle every doubt, quiet every fear, conquer every difficulty, overcome every obstacle, and drive back every cloud. We try to preach without him, sing without him, and carry on our mission work without him, thinking to offset his absence with physical effort and material organization. But there is no substitute for Christ. What blunders we make when we rely on grit for grace and schemes for power and tricks for Christ! Enthusiasm will not take the place of the Holy Spirit, and moral improvement will never be accepted instead of regeneration. Our great need is for Christ.

2

DOING GOOD

*[Jesus] went about doing good, and healing all
that were oppressed of the devil.*

ACTS 10:38

The tenth chapter of Acts tells the story of the conversion of
Cornelius, who was a good moral man doing his best to live
right and being religious as best he knew. He formed the habit
of praying to God, though he was an unsaved man, and it
happened to him, as will always happen, that when a person
honestly seeks after God, he will find him. So God moved him
to send a message to Joppa, where there was a preacher who
could come tell him how to be saved. When Peter came, he
found the man very much in earnest and ripe for the gospel.
So he gathered the neighbors into the man's house and
preached a good, warm sermon about Jesus Christ.

It was a remarkable sermon for its brevity, encompassing
so much great truth in so short a space. He went at once to

the heart of the matter and told them that Christ was the Son
of God, come from heaven. His life among the people had
been spotless and filled with good deeds, but the people
killed him and buried him. On the third day God raised him
up again, and after forty days on the earth, he had gone back
to the Father in heaven. Then Peter concluded by showing
them that this was all done so those who were lost might
have their sins forgiven and be saved to a better life—and
finally to heaven.

The sermon Peter preached that day to the friends gathered in the home of Cornelius was interesting in that every
line set out some new aspect of the life of Christ. It was like
the canvas of an artist whose brush puts new meaning and
beauty into the picture with every stroke. Peter stated that
God anointed Jesus, the Holy Spirit filled him, the devils
feared him, the sick were healed by him, and his whole life
was taken up by doing good deeds for the people. Peter had
seen these things for himself and had come there to tell them
this so that they, too, might have Jesus as a Savior. The salvation he provided was not confined to any one race but was
extended to everybody.

AN UNANSWERABLE LIFE

There is one little sentence in the account of that day's
happenings that is most interesting. It is the thought
expressed in that brief line that I desire to emphasize: "[He]
went about doing good." The chief purpose of Christ's coming into the world was to die so that people might be saved.
But since his death did not occur until he was past thirty-

three years of age, how did he occupy his time, and what impression did his life make on the world while he was waiting for the time of sacrifice? He could not have kept himself in seclusion until that day, then walked out and surrendered to the Romans to be put to death. Such a death would have had no meaning to the people, and the world would have been robbed of the lessons and blessings of his life.

So he took advantage of the intervening years and spent them helping humanity to a better plane of living—lifting their burdens, carrying their sorrows in his own heart, healing their diseases, rebuking their sins, setting them an example, and giving life a new interpretation. It became necessary for him to set aside many of their traditions and give them new and better standards. Quite naturally he stirred up the ringleaders of various sects because he taught the people to discard some of the useless things that had been imposed on them. These leaders never lost an opportunity to criticize him, often laid traps to try to catch him, and many times tried to kill him. They circulated unfounded rumors and tried to smear his name, hoping to shake the people's confidence in him, but all of these things only gave him the opportunity to teach the world some of his best lessons.

The real beauty of a masterpiece or the glory of a perfect gem is often brought out by comparing it with false or worthless things. In like manner, let the light of the text be made more luminous by placing it beside some inferior things. First, *Jesus did not go about defending himself.* This would have been the natural thing to do, the human thing. When lies are circulated about us, we feel called at once to set about establishing our innocence. But Jesus felt no need to defend his character; he lost no time by trying to take care of his good name. Instead, he filled the days with helping those in distress, in the grip of disease, or in the power of evil spirits.

In pursuing such a course, Christ gave the world one of its most valuable lessons: a life such as he lived does not need defenders. Without doubt, it will stir up critics and set evil tongues wagging, but do not be disturbed. Such little ripples lashing against the side of a large ship will beat themselves into spray but will not make a quiver in the vessel. The sunshine, the darkness, and the cold wind need no one to point them out or emphasize them; they speak for themselves. Even so, such a life is its own answer to the critics and puts to shame the vultures who hunt for carcasses along the trail of good people. The silence of such a life is more eloquent than any words of defense.

The time was when infidels centered their bitter attacks upon the Bible and tried to level it to the low grade of novels and other books. Good men came to the support of the holy book with a feeling that it must be defended at the cost of life. But we have long since learned that the Bible does not need defenders. It has stood the test of the laboratory, the questioning of the scientist, and the assault of the skeptic. It is as true today as ever, is more widely read than ever, and still holds aloft the highest moral standard the world has ever seen. It is well able to stand against any of the villainous onslaughts that the future may bring.[1]

What it needs is a race of men and women who are willing to believe its teachings and live up to its standards. And just as the Word of God is able to defend itself, even so the Son of God is well able to stand against the attacks of the skulking faultfinders. For this reason he did not go about defending himself when he was on earth, but rather he devoted his days to doing good where sin had brought so much ruin.

Neither did Christ go about boasting of the good he did, but often when he had healed someone, he said, "See that you tell no one" (as in Luke 5:14). How scant are the records of his good deeds! The recounting of only thirty-five miracles—the healing of fifteen sick people and of fifteen lepers, and the raising of three dead people—largely sums up the good works recorded. The writers seem to have preserved only samples of the many things done, with an added statement that if all had been told, the world could hardly contain the resulting books (John 21:25). This partial silence was not an accident; it was eloquent with meaning. And its message is that it is better to do good than to talk about it.

We are in danger of reversing that. Some spend more time tabulating their good deeds than doing them. I am not opposed to keeping records nor against making reports of the things done. But I am against padding the reports by calling attention to the number of kind words spoken, the little courtesies done, and the little so-called self-denials, such as doing without the desired chewing gum or cold drink for the cause of Christ. It is difficult to think of Christ going around keeping count of the things he did. He was too busy helping the sick, comforting the brokenhearted, and lifting the fallen to give time to record keeping.

When the battle is at the hottest, when men are falling on every side, and the air is ablaze with bursting shells, it is no time to write the story of the war. People are making history, but they are too busy to tabulate it. And when the story is finally told, many of the details will never be written. In like manner the biographers of Christ could not tell the whole story.

Neither can the life story of anyone who goes about doing good be told in full. He does not want it all told. Many experiences are too holy to tell. There are many more that words could not describe and still others that are never noted by anyone other than the recording angels and that will never be known until they are read at the bar of eternal justice.

THE ORTHODOXY OF LIFE

When Christ went about doing good, he put the emphasis on *the orthodoxy of life* rather than on the orthodoxy of creed. Again, we are prone to reverse matters. Our hobby is being sound in doctrine; but his hobby, if he should have a hobby, is being sound in life. One may be sound in doctrine and corrupt in life, but it is hardly possible for one to be sound in life and go far astray in doctrine. True, one may be wrong in one's beliefs, but it will be at points that will not impoverish the world. There will be multitudes in hell who were sound in their theology but were sadly lacking in life. There will doubtless be many in heaven who were mixed on their theology but were sound in their moral life.

The Pharisee was a type of the orthodoxy of creed without the orthodoxy of life, and Christ said, "'Unless your righteousness exceeds that of the scribes and Pharisees, you will never enter the kingdom of heaven'" (Matt. 5:20 RSV). They knew enough, but they did too little. I am in no sense decrying the importance of good doctrine, but I am trying to magnify good morals. Far better to be a good man than to be a great preacher.

This was the passion of Christ's life. Just as the financier rises early and stays up late in order to make more money— just as the scientist spends a lifetime in search of hidden facts that he may increase the knowledge of the world—the driving force of the life of Christ was to find more people in need that he might help them. And in so doing, he marked out the field of greatest usefulness for those who would follow him. He set the standard so high that all who try to reach it will find that they are benefactors of the world. A life spent helping others will be the best investment possible for anyone.

The story is told of a young physician who went to the city and opened an office. As his practice was slow in building, he offered his services free to the poor of the city for certain hours each day. In the course of time, his father went to visit him and asked the son how he was getting on. The son answered that he was not doing any good. The first night passed, and the next morning the young physician got up early and went to the office as usual, before the father arose. Later in the morning, the father went to the office and found it crowded with patients. When they had all gone, the father said to the son, "I thought you said you weren't doing any good."

The son replied, "I'm not; these are free patients. I don't make anything off them."

The father's reply was, "But you are doing them good, and that's the main thing. Continue your free work with these people. I'll go back to my business and make the living for both of us."

THE EFFECTIVE ARGUMENT

Going about doing good is an effective argument for Christianity. The skeptic may meet every line of reasoning, but he cannot explain such a life. He may outwit all your theology and outmatch all the theologians, but he cannot stand before the humblest man or woman who has had an experience with Christ and goes about to live as he lived. Such living will turn more people to Christ than all the great sermons.

Some workers on the foreign field were once examining natives who had applied for membership in the church. At last they asked one native what he thought it meant to be a Christian. He could not tell them for a while; then, as if new light had come on the question, he replied, "It is to live like Mr. Ray." Mr. Ray was one of the workers whose life had strongly impressed the native, and his life was so much like Christ's that it was a fitting illustration of the question asked. No greater compliment could be paid that worker.

Such was the high honor paid Peter and John when they healed a cripple. The people were unable to explain it, but then recognized these two as having been with Jesus (Acts 4:13). They had associated with him so much and so long that they caught his spirit and were living like him, and the people saw the likeness.

A CHALLENGE AND A WARNING

This phase of the life of Christ identifies him with the social life of the world. He is spirit and primarily came to save the souls of mankind, but he could not fail to acknowledge the material conditions of the people and be moved by them. The church has in this a great challenge and a great warning. The challenge is to meet and relieve the physical sufferings of humanity. The warning is that this should not be made the chief business, nor should it be a substitute for believers' salvation.

The church is not a commissary for dispensing food and clothing to the poor; it is an institution whose charter is filed in heaven and whose business it is to represent the Lord, both in saving souls and in relieving sorrows as far as possible. It is not to run a soup kitchen. But if by running a soup kitchen it can reach people, then feeding the hungry is a means to an end. The church has not done its full duty when it has built hospitals for the sick and homes for orphans. These are praiseworthy works but are the material side of the gospel only. The other side is saving their souls, encouraging their hopes, building their characters, and helping to shape their destinies for time and eternity.

This is one phase of the Christian life all can engage in. Not all can be preachers or singers or leaders of great movements; but all can go about doing good. Christ had no monopoly on this. He alone brought salvation—there was no competition in this realm—but in service to humanity and in joy and in scattering helpfulness and kindness in the world, all may enter and find no limitations to the opportunities.

The story is told of Captain Scott of England who, when he made his world tour, was seen to scatter seeds of some kind on every shore he touched. Finally, his men asked what he was doing, and he replied, "I am sowing the seeds of the flowers of England, that whoever sees them may know that a Britisher has been here." He had a national pride that is commendable.[2] Suppose that spirit were carried into the church, and each member possessed it. It would turn the church into an irresistible army before which false creeds, false standards, and false prophets would be driven like the shadows before the rising sun.

This is the life that will live the longest. The politician is soon forgotten; the comedian who entertains the people is seldom remembered a week after he is gone; the great musician who sweeps the strings of the heart as well as of his instrument lingers but a little while before another takes his place. Thus the national figures crowd each other off the stage, and the greatness of the first is soon eclipsed by the brilliance of the next.

Such is not the case with the one who goes about doing good. He multiplies his life a thousand times and gives his spirit to all who touch him. Long after his name is forgotten and his story has ceased to be told, the world will be better because he has lived, and new generations will be giving back to the world influences that have come down from him.

During the Great War (World War I), the story was told of a soldier led to accept Christ in a local church. When he returned to his tent and was about to go to bed, he knelt by the side of his cot and prayed. This was a novel thing in that tent, and the other soldiers began to make fun of him, but he refused to be moved from his purpose. The next night he knelt again, and one of the men picked up his boot and threw it at him. The next morning this man found the boot neatly polished beside his cot. The simple deed convicted the soldier, and he was soon led to accept Christ. What the chaplain and his sermons had failed to do, the soldier who had the Christ-spirit accomplished by one wordless act.

The demand for such a life is greater than for any other kind. There are so many to crush, criticize, and ignore those who are struggling under the burdens of life, and so few who are willing to share them. There are many who will love those who love them, but how many are willing to love those who hate them? This is what Christ did. There are many who will make a dinner and invite friends to enjoy it, but who will make a dinner and invite strangers and enemies? Here Christ excelled. Many are good and kind enough to help the afflicted when they come to the door seeking it, but how many are willing to go out into the highways and hedges and find them in order to help them? In this Christ was preeminent. The world is desperate for people who will take time from their businesses, their studies, and their pleasures to go out on a mission of doing good. The public is ready to crown the heads of such persons.

On a beautiful spring evening a father took his five-year-old girl into a London park for a walk. They came to the monument of Mr. Fawcett, the one-time postmaster general of England and a man highly honored by the people. The child stopped her father and asked what the monument meant, and he explained. Then the child asked what was standing just behind the statue, and the father explained that it was an angel putting a wreath on the head of the good man, showing the appreciation of the people for his great life.

After a moment of silence the little one asked the father if the people would make a monument to him after he was gone, but the father told her that they erected such monuments only to unusually good people and that they would not honor him in this way. But the child could not understand that, for to her, that father was the best man in the world. At length she said, "The rest of the people may not know you are good, but I know it, and if they don't put a wreath on your head, I will come and put it there myself."[3]

True, the crowds on the street may forget the good you have done, or they may fail to reward it properly, but those you have helped will not forget it and will crown you in the inner chamber of their affections. And ultimately, God will crown you with the crown of life spoken of in Revelation 2:10.

NOTES

1. Therefore, it is unnecessary to burn heretics, either at the stake or in print.

2. Robert Falcon Scott (1868–1912), the English explorer who reached the South Pole only weeks after Roald Amundsen found it first. All five members of Scott's party died on the return trip, but Scott had kept his journal up to

the day he died. See Diana Preston, *A First Rate Tragedy: Robert Falcon Scott and the Race to the South Pole* (New York: Houghton Mifflin Co., 1998).

3. My gut feeling tells me that this was Dr. Melton and his daughter.

3

REAL WORSHIP

And Ezra blessed the LORD, the great God;
and all the people answered, "Amen, Amen," lifting up
their hands; and they bowed their heads and worshiped
the LORD with their faces to the ground.
NEHEMIAH 8:6 RSV

We are frequently called to look back to the faithful of old to
get our bearings and to catch their spirit. The eighth chapter
of Nehemiah contains some of the richest lessons on divine
worship found in any literature. A little remnant of the scattered race of Jews returned to Jerusalem, the holy city, to find
it in utter ruin and desolation. After a brief period of surveying the ruins, they set about under the leadership of
Nehemiah to rebuild the broken walls. The work was done in
the face of bitter opposition and great dangers.

When the task was finally completed, a great celebration
was announced to be held on the slopes of the hill before the

city gate. The day arrived, and the Jews came from near and far to join in the festivities. It was not a picnic, nor a time for patriotic speech making, nor a time of calling the Jews to arms to defend themselves against the hostile neighboring tribes; but it was a day spent in reading the Scriptures. Whoever heard of such a celebration? They had a copy of the Law, which many of them had never seen and were hearing for the first time, so they spent the day reading it aloud that all the people might hear it.

Many wonderful lessons are crowded into the story of that day's proceedings. We are especially taught the manner of worship. How profitable for us if we are willing to sit quietly and let that congregation teach us the art! We may learn at least six fundamental points from the first few verses of the chapter. The first is . . .

UNITY

"And all the people gathered themselves together as one man" (Neh. 8:1). They put away all their petty differences, their grievances, jealousies, and criticisms of each other and bound themselves together with such cords of fellowship that in the sight of God they seemed as a single person. Their hearts were fixed on one thing; their prayers were united for one thing; their souls were in such harmony that one man could have voiced the cry of them all.

The church will never learn a more valuable lesson than that. Many times the concept is voiced in New Testament language, such as "'Every city or house divided against itself shall not stand'" (Matt. 12:25) and "They were all with one accord in one place" (Acts 2:1; see also 4:31–32). The glory of the kingdom of God is in the unity of its people.

If the allied armies had fought as separate armies in the World Wars, they would have fought a losing battle. But when they came together, selected a common leader, and marched under one command, they quickly drove the enemy forces from the field of conflict. In scriptural terms, "Five of you shall chase a hundred, and a hundred of you shall chase ten thousand" (Lev. 26:8 RSV). How the Christian forces need to learn and to emphasize the value of such unity!

On one occasion, when Paul was on trial for his life before the Sanhedrin, he saved himself by dividing the enemy, aligning Pharisee against Sadducee (Acts 23:6–10). This has been the devil's tactic for ages. He works to divide the Christian forces; once this is done, he can win any victory. Likewise, churches can accomplish almost any worthy aim if they will stand solidly together. But the moment they are divided, they are disarmed and disqualified for even the least conflict. Unity is our password, our badge of honor, and the seal by which we shall be known to the world as the army of God.

The most pathetic scene known to any of us is when Satan divides the people of God into factions—men and women who have been redeemed by the same Savior, who should be joined in inseparable union to accomplish the same cause, and between whom there should exist the most sacred fellowship—split by the tricks of the evil one. What a travesty of Christianity when Christian men shoot from the hip at each other and lie in wait to catch each other in faults in order to pounce on them! This is none other than a burlesque of the most shameful type. Yet, it is a thing too frequently found, and wherever it exists, the cause of Christ is halted, and the devil holds the reins of power until the situation is corrected. The happy expression of our text in describing the gathering of Jews on that occasion is that they had ruled the devil out, had put aside everything that had a tendency to separate them, and were locked in each other's confidence and love.

THE LAITY

The same verse tells us another interesting thing. Ezra, the scribe, was asked to conduct the service. Nehemiah, the great leader, reformer, and prophet, stood by and had the scribe hold the service. It will be remembered that Nehemiah was the public leader and Ezra was the priest. The prophet was the public proclaimer, but the priest was the silent and unobserved mediator between the people and God.

The heart of this great matter might be expressed by the word *laity.* It is the proper recognition and use of the layman in the work of the Lord. We have too long regarded church work as preacher's work. For ages no one was expected to take a leading part in religious matters except preachers. Fortunately, the times and conditions have changed. This is becoming preeminently the layman's day, and rightly so.

Thus it was in the days of the apostles. Those first deacons went everywhere teaching the people about the risen Lord. They even held revival meetings and aroused interest in missions as if they had been preachers. We are certain this is

God's plan and deplore what we have lost during the past years by giving too little recognition to the work of our laypeople. Now they are fast coming into their rightful place. Business leaders are giving their best to the work of the Lord. They are giving their valuable time—time that is worth hundreds of dollars a day in a material way—to the progress and welfare of God's kingdom. They travel hundreds of miles at their own expense and give their sane counsel and wide experience. With their experience they lay on the altar of the Lord hundreds of thousands of dollars each year to build little mission stations, strengthen little struggling churches, and plant the banner of the Lord out on the farthest frontier borders.

Many of them are lending themselves to serve as assistant pastors, Sunday school teachers, leaders of young people, financial advisers, and other roles in which they can reinforce the pastors. Double honor is due this host of business people who put devotion to God above their business and who give him the first place in their hearts and in the plans of their lives.

I am sure it was not a mere coincidence that the civil leader Nehemiah laid this heavy responsibility on the clerk of the council and asked Ezra to have charge of the services that day. It was the will and plan of God written in human experience and in history so all the world may know how God works.

LOYALTY

The third verse of this chapter presents still another lesson worthy of the most careful consideration. It says that

Ezra continued to read the Scriptures from early morning until noon, and that during all this long (and it might be called monotonous) service, the people stood. Here are three things of striking beauty and novelty. The first is the character of the service: it consisted of reading the Bible, occasionally stopping to tell the people what the language meant.

Such a service would not hold the people of the present day very long. The preacher who speaks for an hour loses his audience after the first "offense" or two. The public now demands that a preacher be brief, funny, and popular. His sermon must be in modern phraseology, sandwiched with gripping illustrations, and spoken extemporaneously.

The second characteristic of the service was its length—"from the morning until midday." Only something of unusual interest could hold the people for so long. Paul may have preached until midnight and have only one sleeper fall out of the window (Acts 20:7–12), but it would not be safe for us to try it. Ezra may have held his audience all morning with nothing but reading Scripture, but my audience would not be so faithful, I fear.

The third feature that deserves notice was the fact that the people stood for the entire service. They did not have the accommodations we enjoy but stood out in the scorching sun—bareheaded, mothers holding babies in arms, and on the slopes of a rocky hill. They stood with almost breathless silence while the Word of God was being read to them.

The service might be summed up in three brief words: the people stayed and prayed and paid. Enough funds were contributed for the work and more, enough prayer was made to bind them together in their efforts, and enough faithfulness was demonstrated to keep them in their places until the services were over. Now, all of these fine qualities grew out of a meeting that was void of gimmicks, that made no effort to entertain the people, and that had no thrills except the Word of the Lord. What is the lesson of it all? The answer is clear: *the value of the Word of God.* If the people will listen to it, it will make them loyal and worshipful. These people came from long distances just to hear it read. They did not get tired of it, though the services lasted half the day, and they did not complain about having to stand on the open hill under the burning sun.

Today, complaining people lay the blame on poor preaching and feel justified in going away. I would not excuse the blundering efforts of the men who are to lead the people of God. Each one should do his best. But I would call the people to consider what is infinitely more important than the minister or his sermon: the message from the Book of God. If the minister is not eloquent, the sacred Word itself should be eloquent enough. The gospel will draw people farther, hold them longer, lift them higher, and make them holier than all the philosophies of the world. So this phase of the morning worship could be fittingly expressed by the word *loyalty.*

ATTENTION

The third verse also states that "the ears of all the people were attentive unto the book of the law"; in other words, *they paid attention to what was said* in the service. Again the writer has preserved for us a valuable lesson, and again he has hinted at one of our greatest weaknesses. Attention is the key that unlocks the door of interest.

Isn't it alarming, the number of things we take to church with us when we go to worship? Recently a good woman was complimented on a certain social function she had at her home, and she replied, "I planned it the other morning at church." Another woman told how she had designed a dress for her little girl while the services were going on. Some men build their houses, others plan their business deals, and some plant their crops while the sermon is being preached.

Many come and sit through the service but do not hear one word or carry away one blessing. They are absorbed in their troubles, their pleasures, their work, their enemies, or their friends. Some are buying, others are selling; some are silently recounting recent experiences while others are look-ing into the future. Some are criticizing what is being done and said until, if there should come a word of encourage-ment meant for them, it would be overlooked. Others are busy about things here and there until the sermon is over and not a thought has been lodged in the brain.

The parable of the sower given by Christ clearly illustrates this same truth (Luke 8:5–15). Some do not hear at all. Others hear only the frivolous, amusing, or superficial, and some hear enough to be saved but not enough to be happy, useful, and fruitful. Then there are some who really pay attention to what is said, then go out to translate their feel-ings and resolutions into life and actions.

It is no wonder that the chapter in Nehemiah tells us the people wept when they heard the sacred words. The wonder today is that men and women can hear what God's Book says about our sins and our condemnation and about the Christ who was crucified for us and not weep.

Some time ago I attended a service in which the minister was graphically telling of the crucifixion of Christ—a story which would bring any thoughtful person to his knees in silent worship. I looked out over the audience to see what effect it seemed to be having and was astonished to see a number of people asleep and others showing that they were not interested in the drama recounted to them. Chilled at heart, I asked myself, "If this story will not interest the people, what will?" Still, it is fair to say that as a rule nothing proves more powerful in holding the attention of the congregation than the story of Calvary; the incident cited is an exception.

REVERENCE

The fifth verse tells us that when the speaker opened the book, the people stood up. They felt that they were in the presence of God, so the best way they could show their reverence for him and respect for his Word would be to silently stand with uncovered heads while God spoke to them. What a lesson! Reverence is fast becoming a lost art. There is disregard for the Lord's day, the church, the Bible, the ordinances of God, and all sacred things. This is not a careless statement, nor the cry of a pessimist. You need only look around to see the things mentioned. How is the Christian Sabbath different from any other day of the week? "Remember the Sabbath day, to keep it holy" (Exod. 20:8) seems a thing meant for some far-off time and race. It is not an unusual thing that Sunday is made the big day of fairs, auctions, and similar things. My attention was called one day to circulars advertising a new addition to the city and stating that the coming Sunday would be the first day of sales of lots in that section.

Go down the street and see that many of the stores are open doing even larger business early Sunday morning than they do on a regular weekday. The gas stations are open, as are the convenience stores, the grocery stores, and the real estate offices. What happened to Sunday? And what happened to reverence? The fairs, theaters, hunting and fishing expeditions, excursions, and sports—all such things that call the people away from worship and out into the regular stress and strain of life—seem to know no day of rest.

This same spirit is exhibited in the church house, which is fast becoming the social center of the community—the place of entertainment, games, parties, and sometimes even dances. The papers recently told of a prayer meeting that was turned into a boxing match. After a short prayer service, the meeting was adjourned, and the rest of the evening was devoted to a boxing contest at the church.

What have these things led to? Irreverence is the first fruit from the vine, and it will express itself in many forms. Contempt for all that is holy will soon follow. Poor conduct during the services is another consequence, as are lack of attention and inappropriate regard for serious matters. Disrespect for the Word of God, for prayer, for singing, for the sermon, and for any attempt at worship are some of the expressions of irreverence.

It might be argued that these Jews of old who assembled with such reverence were filled with superstition and did not know enough to cast some of these things aside—that they made themselves slaves to such inconveniences because of their ignorance. Whenever worldly wisdom or scholarship sweeps the simple faith of the people away, it leaves them in worse condition than it found them. Real knowledge, real culture, and real science all lead to God. Only those who get tangled in the bypaths and underbrush swing to infidelity and skepticism. So-called science may analyze the body in search for life and, failing to locate it, will conclude there is no such thing.

A materialistic physician said to me on one occasion, "There is no soul in man. I have cut their bodies into thousands of pieces, and the heart is just a muscle of the body— no more soul in it than there is in the hand or foot." It is such cheap imitations of science that brush God aside; real science will find him in the farthest reaches of the universe with its telescope and in the tiniest particle of matter with its microscope. Learning does not weaken faith in God; it strengthens it. The only kind of education or science that snatches faith from the hearts of people is the superficial kind—the kind that offers theory for fact, shadow for substance, or chance for God.

SINCERITY

Another touching incident is shown in the statement of the ninth verse, "For all the people wept, when they heard the words of the law." *Sincerity* is the word that expresses the thought here. That was quite a moving scene. As Ezra read the warnings from the Book of God, the people all felt that the message was intended specifically for them. They were cut to the heart as they looked into their own ugly pasts and saw the sins that earned them God's judgment. They were so desperately in earnest about the matter that they all wept— the old men and women, proud young people, and little children. It was not considered a weakness for one to weep over his sins on that occasion.

I am fully persuaded that no one has to weep to be saved or to be a Christian, but I am also convinced that the nearer one comes to God, the more easily the tears flow. This is true because one sees the shame of his sins more clearly and, seeing it, cannot restrain the tears. It is also because one feels the warmth of God's love and is melted by his kindness. So the people on this occasion were brokenhearted because of their sins and were overcome with the goodness of God's love in offering them complete forgiveness. It is no wonder they wept.

I raise the question of whether today's tendency to a dry-eyed religion is not cause for some alarm. Have we minimized sin until we no longer feel the shame of it in our hearts? If so, there is reason to be concerned. Have we failed to sound the warning of God's law against sin to the point that the sinner no longer fears sin? Then we are in danger of preaching such a religion of love that the lost will come to feel that God will spare them in any case.

Christianity *is* a religion of love, but let it not be forgotten that the law of God must break the impenitent heart. The real worshiper often finds himself overcome by emotion, either for joy or sorrow, and when the mere reading of the Word of God causes tears to flow, that itself is evidence of attention, interest, sympathy, sincerity, penitence, and praise.

CHARITY

A final lesson is found in the tenth verse, "And send portions unto them for whom nothing is prepared." In other words, the real worshiper will find himself a charitable person. Christianity has always been a charitable religion. It is impossible for one to kneel and pray unless his soul is moved with the deepest and holiest emotions. And likewise it would be impossible for him to go out and see others hungry, cold, or needy and not respond to their needs (James 2:15–16). The fires kindled in his soul by the Spirit of God will make him compassionate toward the misfortunes of others. While the church is not purely a social institution, it cannot fulfill its mission in the world without having regard for social conditions. One's prayers before God send him out to find the needy in order to help them, and he who prays but will not help his suffering neighbor will come to a time when he cannot pray.

4

TWO MEN IN ONE

When I would do good, evil is present with me.
ROMANS 7:21

There has been much discussion about the real meaning and application of the seventh chapter of Romans. Half the world has insisted that it was the experience of the apostle Paul before his conversion and is therefore the experience of all unsaved persons. The other half has contended that it is the true picture of the saved soul, struggling to overcome the evil powers with which one must contend all his life.

Both theories are correct, and yet neither is wholly correct. It is a bit of the experience common to humanity. It is not confined to any one class or age or race, but could be as readily spoken of one as the other. It is true of the saved and of the unsaved; it is true of the old man and of the young child; it is true of the civilized man and of the uncivilized; it is equally true of the educated and of the

ignorant; it is the case with the high-churchman and with
the low-churchman and with the no-churchman.

It was as true of Adam in the garden, fresh from the hand
of his Maker, as it was of Paul, recently converted from his
pet theories and prejudices. And it is just as true of me, living in this far-off age. Scientists tell us that the entire human
body changes every seven years, but this is one part of our
makeup that has never undergone a change. The human
family has passed through many transitions, and the races
have been widely separated by geographical lines, speech,
modes of living, and culture, but we all meet again on this
common plane: "When I would do good, evil is present with
me." I can stretch my hand across the intervening years and
lay hold of Paul, my brother, and say to him, "You have
related my experience exactly." It is one tie that binds
humanity into a brotherhood and makes us all kin.

THE CONFLICT OF IMPULSES

We now set ourselves to the task of discovering as many
points of contact as possible between ourselves and the
writer of this remarkable passage. In so doing, we shall
doubtless find that he was made up of much the same clay as
we are and that there are as many open doors for escape from
our bondage as were open to him. One need not look far to
satisfy himself of the reality and the universal application of
the truth in the verse. It reminds us that there are *two spirits
struggling against each other in the heart of each one of us;* one
of them wants us to do good, and the other one tries to hinder the good we want to do.

I do not need a Bible or a preacher to tell me that. I know it is true in my own life and would have known it if I had never heard the gospel, but the Bible helps me to understand the situation better and how to overcome it. This is, perhaps, the best-known fact in human experience, for the witnesses to it are the number of people who have been born and have reached an age of individual action. The child knows it long before he has completed grade school, and the heathen knows it long before the missionary reaches them with the gospel. It has been found to be a controlling factor in life from the land of the Eskimo to the wave-swept shores of southern Africa.

The two spirits make up the sum total of life. They express themselves in the extremes of emotion and conduct: in love or hate, in joy or sorrow, in righteousness or wickedness, in helpfulness or hurtfulness. One of these spirits makes us love people, while the other one makes us hate them. One of them would have us say words of kindness, but the other would make our words cut like a whip. One spirit would send us out as peacemakers, but the other would throw the whole world into a vortex of war. We find within us something that makes us want to meditate upon the good and holy and long for the companionship of the truest and the best, and then we are swept by a contrary spirit that would fill our minds with thoughts of evil and ugliness. So in this little line, Paul says to us all, "Let me tell you something about yourself." Or rather, "Let us think through this something you have already discovered."

No Soul with Only One Impulse

There is a second lesson to be learned in the text: *no person is left entirely to one impulse.* God does not entirely forsake us, nor does the devil wholly give us up as long as we are on earth. This view, I know, will cross some pet theories, but as it seems true to us, we pass it on to you. It crosses the preaching of many who overemphasize the unpardonable sin, but it is our judgment that most of the illustrations used to prove that God deserts sinners break down and refute themselves.

How often we hear of reprobates who claim that they have committed the unpardonable sin, weep over the fact, and say they would give the world if they had not done so. These very sobs and statements prove that they have not committed that grievous wrong. For as long as anyone wants to be saved, he can be. Revelation 22:17 so declares it: "Let him who is thirsty come, let him who desires take the water of life without price" (RSV). We maintain not that God has forsaken man, but rather that man has forsaken God. We believe that God follows the impenitent to the very gates of death and pities him even after the last hope fades away.

We do not deny that there was, or is, such a thing as an unpardonable sin, but when it does occur, the wretched victim does not pine for God or heaven but scorns them with the last breath. The confidential confessions of wicked men have convinced us that God clings to them, even through their recklessness. They have expressed a wish that things were different, that they might live a better life, and that they could undo the past; these are the admissions of the silent visits of that better Spirit who would make life happier for them.

In addition, this fact crosses the holiness theory—that people become so good they are no longer tempted to do wrong. We cannot speak here out of experience, but we have observed many witnesses who made such a claim and later in life were found to be living very carelessly. According to Scripture (such as 1 John 1:8, 10 and 1 Cor. 10:12) and according to human nature found everywhere, we must conclude that the devil never ceases his attacks on the saints as long as they live. Goodness is no bar to his insinuations; his hot breath would sear the soul of the noblest and the best.

NO OPEN FIELD FOR RIGHTEOUSNESS

Third, *there is no open field for righteousness.* No good cause ever went unhindered to its glorious climax, but it had to fight its way through opposition, criticism, and hindrances to win its case by sheer merit. This is true in the individual life; the devil will never give his consent for us to be good, nor will the critics on the street cease their attacks, nor will it ever be easy for us to live justly and righteously. The evil one will continuously attempt to snatch the good seed away and plant weeds in its place.

This is also true of every worthy movement. It does not matter how worthwhile the undertaking is or what benefit it would bring to society; opposition to it will arise from some unexpected source. Hardly a little schoolhouse is built on the plains to give the rural residents a better education but that somebody will criticize the undertaking and say it is useless.

The same is true of church houses that are erected for the worshipers—they rise in spite of the objectors. While this text in Romans was written about the individual life, it is just as true of the public enterprise. There is only one place where there is no objection to what is being done, and that is in the cemetery. Every community has its objectors who are always against every movement for the betterment of the community. They are against the taxes, against the building of good roads, and against building new public buildings; to them it seems a dreadful waste of the taxpayer's money. This bunch was born "in the objective case and kickative gender."

Let it be remembered that this attitude is not a mark of greatness; it is one realm in which anyone may become an expert without going to school. To be the community critic and objector does not require much brains.

THE COST OF MORAL WORTH

I draw a fourth lesson from the passage: *moral worth is as hard to get as material worth.* Just as honey is housed within a hive guarded by a thousand bees; just as the rose is put on a thorn bush; just as the gold lies deep in the earth, hid away in small particles with tons of rock and dirt; just as pearls are found in deep waters and oil in deep wells, even so are success, character, righteousness, and heaven found along thorny paths. Diamonds would be very cheap, and no one would have any desire to possess them if they could be picked up along the road. But the fact that these stones are so rare and hard to procure makes them very valuable. In like manner, righteousness is more of a gem because it costs much to possess it.

Is it a strange thing that costly things are hardest to come by? It is so much easier to remain poor than to become rich. It is also easier to be ignorant than to have an education. One can be poor without an effort, but he cannot be rich without an effort on someone's part. One can also live in a little hovel without paying much, but he cannot occupy a mansion without this unpleasant burden. A person can drift downstream, but he cannot drift upstream; he must swim. Disease is contagious, but health is not. A person can drift into hell, but not into heaven. He can neglect his soul and lose it, but he cannot neglect it and save it. When anyone wants to do something good, there are many to hinder him, but when he decides to stir up mischief, there are many to help him along the way.

AS HE THINKS IN HIS HEART

A fifth lesson may be found in the principle behind Proverbs 23:7: *The public life is a proclamation of the secret victory or defeat.* "When I would do good, evil is present with me," but which one overcomes, the good or the evil? Life will be its own answer, and no argument will be needed to reinforce it. A person is good or bad just as the good or the evil overcame in the secret struggle of his life. There are hundreds and thousands of little battles fought out in the inner soul that the public knows nothing about, but in time the results will begin to express themselves in the public life. Little by little, attention is drawn to some virtue or some vice. The outside world does not know its history but has come to see and accept the results that have surfaced in the life. In time, they can no longer be kept secret.

Let me ask, "What makes a man a thief?" You answer, "Stealing." But I insist that he was a thief before he stole, or he would not have stolen. Then when did the man begin to be a thief? Many temptations came to him that no one else knew about. He may have suppressed them for a long time, until finally he yielded and got the consent of his mind to steal. That is when he becomes a thief: when he becomes willing to do it. The only factor lacking now is the proper opportunity. He is a thief in spirit and mind, but not in fact. No law could convict him yet, but his conscience and his God have already convicted him as guilty of a deed that he has not yet committed (see Matt. 5:21–22; 27–28). Now the public knows nothing of what has taken place in his mind, but one day an opportunity comes when he can carry out his desires, and the public discovers what he has known for some time.

Let me suppose a case: A woman attends a social function on a rainy afternoon. When she stands her umbrella in the corner where there are many others more or less similar to hers, she decides it will be a good chance to "make a mistake" when she comes out and get a better one than the one she brought. But when she leaves, there are several persons going out with her, so she blindly thrusts her hand into the corner, hoping to get a good one.

Being accompanied by others, she is afraid to examine her prize until she gets home. When she looks, what does she find? It is her own! Was she a thief? The law would say no; her conscience and her God would say yes. She had her consent to steal, but an accident prevented it. The matter was already decided in the secret struggle. The real issues of life are most often fought out behind closed doors, where no eyes can see. Here is where real courage is forged, where real victories are won, and where real character is born, then nurtured, and grows.

There are four persons within each of us: the person our enemies think we are, the person our friends think we are, the person we think ourselves to be, and the real person that God sees within us. If we are dragged into court we may be put on public exhibition as the one our enemies think we are. This will not be a true picture, for all our virtues will be ignored and all our faults will be exposed and magnified. And if we are given some great honor, we shall again show the world one side, but it will be the other side. Our faults will be glossed over, and our virtues will be magnified.

And even when we are alone diligently searching our hearts for our real selves, we shall be unable to discover all the facts, for many of them, both good and bad, remain hidden from our own scrutiny. But when we stand before God the testimony of friend and enemy alike will be irrelevant, for he knows the real facts about us. He has seen the struggle; he has watched the hard, long fight to overcome our tendency to evil and has weighed the results in light of the circumstances.

GOOD CAN BE DONE

A sixth lesson may be pointed out: *Good can be accomplished in spite of the evil.* The history of the church is a fitting illustration of this fact. Think how many hindrances had to be overcome in the early days of Christianity. One of the

Twelve turned traitor, and no more staggering blow can come to a movement than for one of the inner circle to walk out and denounce it as a failure, unworthy of the sympathy and patronage of the people.

A second setback came as another denied even knowing the Lord when Christ was on trial for his life. Then the Lord himself was killed. Surely this will end it for all time! But the group rallied. Still, before they got their scattered numbers together, one of their best deacons was killed, others put in prison, and the little band was soon broken up. How often their hopes must have seemed to fade into darkest night.

How did all this affect Christianity? The apostles went on with their preaching and their healing. The good women, the deacons, and the laymen went everywhere telling about the risen Lord, until the news of him and the spirit of him filled the whole land.

This has been the history of Christianity throughout its life—it has endured in spite of the evil it encountered. Just as those early Jews rebuilt the broken walls around Jerusalem in the face of opposition, criticism, and wicked schemes to hinder them, so the walls of the kingdom of God have always been built. The children of God cannot afford to take counsel of their fears, nor stop to listen to their enemies, nor get the permission of the devil before they go on with their work. All great and good things are accomplished over the head of opposition, without the help of the kickers, and without waiting for the hindrances to get out of the way.

Progress and civilization have had to go forward against the tide of opposition. When Fulton launched his first little steamboat he was called a crank and a fool.[1] Whitney's patent rights to his cotton gin were stolen.[2] And when the first steamer crossed the ocean, it did so in the face of much criticism. Wise men had written long treatises showing how a steamship could not cross the ocean because it could not carry enough fuel to last it all the way. But against the advice of many noble heads, the crew launched its vessel and carried a copy of the learned theories to the other side.[3]

By this indomitable spirit men pushed back the wilds of the frontier and built their homes on the edges of civilization. They pulled the railroads and factories out to them, turned the deserts into blooming gardens, and laced the country with roads and highways. This spirit that refused to be stopped by obstacles and hardships has built our civilization.[4]

And it is this spirit that characterized the early church. The little band of followers of Christ refused to be hushed into silence by the persecutors but spoke out, even at the cost of their lives. This irresistible spirit has sent a thrill through every last worker on the frontiers of civilization to plant courage in his heart, holiness in his life, and power in his hand. It is this spirit that has also fortified the individual at home against the innumerable encroachments of evil and has made him strong in spite of his weaknesses, brave in spite of his fears, holy in spite of his temptations, and consecrated in spite of his bent to do wrong. When one would do good, evil will be with him. But when one would do good, he can do good, for God is also with him, and God is mightier than any evil.

NOTES

1. Robert Fulton's experimental 1803 steamboat, launched from Paris on the Seine River, sank due to the weight of the engine. He used what he learned from this failure to design and build the *Clermont,* the first commercially successful steamboat in history. Its launch was a milestone in modern transportation. See the excellent book for young readers by Ralph Nading Hill, *Robert Fulton and the Steamboat* (New York: Random House, 1954).

2. In 1793, Eli Whitney invented a cotton gin that could clean cotton as rapidly as fifty workers doing it by hand. Demand for the machine outstripped his factory's ability to produce them, so competitors began making and selling "knock-offs." Whitney sued, but it took years for the courts to establish his sole right to the patent. By then the life of the patent had almost expired, and Congress refused to grant him an extension on it. Wilma Pitchford Hays, *Eli Whitney: Founder of Modern Industry* (New York: Franklin Watts, Inc., 1965), 44–47. Another excellent juvenile book.

3. In 1838, the British ship *Sirius,* equipped with steam-driven side-wheels, became the first ship in history to cross the Atlantic using solely steam power. Travel time: 18 days (*World Book*). See also James Dugan, *The Great Iron Ship* (New York: Harper & Brothers, 1953), 21.

4. Pioneer bashing is popular today. But as much as we revere the pristine wilderness, how many of us would actually choose to live in it as our great-grandparents did? We decry our forefathers' actions in taming the wilderness from the safety and comfort of a lifestyle that their actions made possible for us.

5

SIFTED BUT SAVED

*"Simon, Simon, behold, Satan demanded to have you,
that he might sift you like wheat, but I have prayed for
you that your faith may not fail; and when you have
turned again, strengthen your brethren."*
LUKE 22:31–32 RSV

The incident recorded here took place immediately before the
Crucifixion, in the twilight of the most stressful hour the Lord
ever passed through. The lives, principles, and loyalty of everyone close to him were being tried as gold is tried in the fire.
The sneers and ugly thrusts of the Pharisees were taking more
definite shape, expressing themselves in flaming outbursts of
hatred. The followers of Christ were deserting, the disciples
themselves were being sifted, and the enemies of Christ were
exultant over the imminent downfall of Jesus of Nazareth.

His death had already been determined, the mob was
even at the moment forming, and the betrayer had gone to

close the deal. The remaining disciples, trembling under the suspense of the threatening storm, gathered around their Savior as if to protect him.

At last Peter grew bold and boastful, declaring he would cling to Christ and defend him with his very life. (The episode in the garden when he cut off the man's ear indicated that he meant to carry out his word—John 18:10.) This boast followed the statement from Christ recorded in these verses from Luke on the previous page. It proved a rebuke to the zealous disciple and revealed some startling things to them all.

Peter's pledge of loyalty was not the prattle of a child to Christ, even though he knew that it would not be carried out in the way Peter assumed. It did not seem sheer mockery, even coming from such a fickle enthusiast. Instead of rebuking him with bitter denunciations, Christ parted the curtain of the immediate future with a tender hand, revealing three lessons, and with words of deepest sympathy, he sent the disciple into the dark to fight the hardest battle of his life. These words, which must have been spoken privately for Peter's ears only, expressed a warning, a promise, and a directive.

A WARNING

How little Peter knew that all day Satan had been camping close to him, begging Christ for permission to get hold of that disciple! Peter had been the one desire of Satan's heart that day. If he could get Peter for just a little while, how he would torment him, harass his soul, and show him how worthless he was! But this was not an unusual desire. It is always the aim of Satan concerning the children of God, especially when such children show zeal for Christ. If Peter had been a nominal believer in Christ, with little love, zeal, and loyalty, there would have been little care on the part of Satan for him.

The fear of our hearts should be that our lives are not causing Satan any anxiety. Good for the Christian whose life gives Satan lots of trouble, whose influence he fears, and whose consecrated zeal makes him tremble! Satan always wishes to get hold of such a Christian. So it was a high compliment paid that disciple when the devil singled him out of all the followers of Christ and desired most of all to crush him. It was evidence of Peter's strength, proof of his worth, and the declaration of his merit.

This desire of Satan to sift the child of God only expresses what the demon would do to all the works of God if he could. He would crush every Christian and every cause that dares to oppose him. He would pull into the dust every church, mission station, and institution that lifts up Christ and defends his cause. He would hush the mouth of every singer of Christ's gospel, still the notes of every instrument that praises him, and silence even the prattle of little children who worship him. He would recall every missionary from the foreign lands if he could. What wreck and ruin, what mischief and havoc, what destruction and desolation he would cause if he could!

But this raises a most interesting question: Why does he not do as he wants to? Is he hindered? Is he prevented? Is he without power to execute his wishes? Ah, there lies our hope. *Satan can do nothing without the permission of Christ.* This is shown in the story of Job. Satan desired to sift that good saint, also, but could do nothing until God gave him permission to destroy his property. But God prohibited him from touching the body of Job. Later that was granted, but Satan could not take the life of Job. Satan was at the end of his leash, going as far as he could but not as far as he desired.

This fact is also shown in the story of Moses. Satan desired the body of Moses, but the Lord hid it away in some silent spot in the plains of Moab, and the devil could not find it (Deut. 34:5–6; Jude 9). This is so in the life of every Christian in the world. He would sift us all, he would wreck our hopes, he would crush our souls. But he can do nothing without the permission of Christ.

Satan is not equal with God. He cannot create or control the world. He is not an equal competitor with Christ in the spoils of the world. He is a creature ruled and controlled by the Creator, in whose hands are all things. The struggles of life do not exhibit the relative strength of God and Satan. The division of souls for heaven and hell is not a scramble between God and the devil. He sought to be the rival of God in heaven and was thrown out. From that day until this, he has been a beggar at the footstool of God and not a prince on the throne of God.

But to say that Satan cannot operate without the permission of God opens still another question, and that a harder one. It is an undisputed fact that he makes trouble for the children of God. It is also quite evident that such right is granted by the God of the Christians. So why would God grant such permission? This is not a childish question. And the answers to it may be multiplied many times over. Tempting to do evil is all that Satan is permitted to do. He cannot make the Christian yield to it, he cannot force him to commit one sin, he cannot destroy him with the hardest calamities. He can only tempt him. And there is no sin in being tempted; the wrong lies in the yielding to it. Even so, with every temptation the Lord provides a way of escape (1 Cor. 10:13).

Consider this: A world without temptation would be a world without merit. Someone without the right to decide for himself would be a mere machine, deserving no credit nor blame for doing as he did. One without temptation may be innocent, but he cannot be righteous. Innocence is untested and untried goodness, but righteousness is goodness that has been tested and proven. The innocent has had no occasion to be otherwise, but the righteous had a chance to do wrong and would not do it. The untempted person is like a greenhouse plant that is beautiful because it has been shielded from the excessive heat, cold, and wind. But the Christian who overcomes temptation is like the oak on the mountain, which is stronger, greater, and more useful because it has withstood the storms. It has woven the strength of the storm into the fiber of its life.

Temptation is God's school to grow great characters, great lives, and great souls. The sifting of Satan may be as the refiner's fire burning away the dross so that the gold may shine more brilliantly. Or it may be as the machinery to the cotton: stripping, picking, pressing, carding, spinning, weaving, dyeing. When the process is over, the fabric that emerges is fit to be worn in kings' palaces. The process may seem hard, but the ultimate glory warrants it.

The above reasoning will seem to some to justify the father who thrusts his child into pits of depravity that he may learn the ways of sin and therefore be able to combat it. But such a conclusion is absurd. The one who willfully follows temptation will not easily escape because he will not want to. Someone who is not afraid of sin will become a victim and then an ally of it. The strength and courage of a Christian will have ample opportunity to be tried by the sin that overtakes him; he need not put himself in the way of sin to find it. Every exhortation of the Bible is that we should be on guard against sin, run from it, shun the very appearance of it, not yield to it, escape from it as one escapes from a great danger. (For instance, Gen. 4:7; Rom. 6:12–13; 1 Thess. 5:22; James 4:7.) And all along the way of life, we are warned that sin is a pit into which we will fall, that Satan is a deceiver lurking in the path to trap us, that he is a roaring lion looking to devour us. (See Prov. 28:10; John 8:44; 2 Cor. 11:14; 1 Pet. 5:8.)

Nowhere are we instructed to do something wrong in order to accomplish something good. Our concern is not in setting up a fight with the devil for the exercise we would get out of the struggle, nor for the skill we would develop, nor for the glory we would attain in overcoming such a foe. Most of us are weary with the struggle against evil in even the tamest and most uneventful life, without seeking new thrills in larger arenas with a greater number of demons. Only the one who is properly fearful of the devil and tries to escape him can overcome him. No one who engages him in secret combat for the fun of it will conquer him.

Now Christ broke the news to Peter that the devil wanted to pick him to pieces and show him off so the world could see how little good there was in him. Satan hoped that when the struggle was over, the real good in Peter, as compared to the worthlessness, would be as a small grain in a great stack of straw and chaff. The battle was cruel, but the disciple wove the strength of the storm into the fiber of his life. He may have left the field limping, but he became wiser and stronger to face the next battle.

A PROMISE

The text also states a very precious promise: that while Satan is sifting the disciple, the Lord will be with him, upholding him, sustaining him, and encouraging him throughout the conflict. With such a promise as that, a soul could brave anything. Daniel went into the den of lions with just that promise, and he found that God was all he needed (Dan. 6). The Hebrews were thrown into the fiery furnace, where they found One walking with them who was like "the Son of God," and when they came out, there was not even the smell of smoke on their clothes (Dan. 3). The prayer of Christ on one's behalf is more powerful than all earthly wisdom, skill, or armed forces to deliver him from the power of Satan. It is an impregnable fortress in which one can hide with perfect safety.

But what are some of the most valuable lessons drawn from this part of the story? First, there is the fact that *Christ has an interest in our struggles.* At the very time that our hearts are most broken, he "intercedes for us with sighs too deep for words" at the Father's throne (Rom. 8:26 RSV; see also v. 34). When life seems in vain—the battle lost and despair most crushing—then comes a thought sweeping the mind like an electric current—a memory is awakened, the clouds dispelled, the atmosphere cleared, and the soul lighted with holy joy. "My Savior knows all about it and will help me!" He knows each sparrow that falls and even the number of hairs on the head of each child (Matt. 10:29–31). He sees each flower that "is born to blush unseen, and waste its sweetness on the desert air."[1] Not one escapes his eye.

The story has often been told of a young college football player who was the top athlete in his school. A short while before the championship game of the season was to be played, he was suddenly summoned home to the bedside of his blind father. Gloom hung over the school because the game was lost without this brilliant player.

The day before the father passed away he called the son to his side and told him the end was near and that he knew his heart would be heavy, but he wanted his son to return to school and do his best. And the father reminded him that it was just a week before the big game. "You know, I never had the privilege of seeing you play, Son, but for that game, I'll be watching from above. Just do your best."

After the funeral, the son returned to school, but everyone else felt it was useless to ask him if he would play so soon after his father's death. The game was played as scheduled. Not only did the boy play, but never had anyone seen him play so well. At the victory banquet that evening, he was asked how he could concentrate on the game with the memory of his father's death on his heart. He replied, "That is what made me play so hard. Father told me he would be watching me for the first time, so I did my best for him." The story may be fiction, but the lesson is true. Our Father is watching from above, and he sees every struggle, every sorrow, every burden. The very thought of it is enough to give courage, hope, and strength to every struggling one of us.

When I was quite a young child, a neighbor dropped his eyeglasses into a well, where they were floating in the case on the water. He tried to get me to climb on the bucket and go down and get them, but nothing he could say or offer would induce me to do it. After a while my father came along and, seeing the situation, asked me if I would not go down and get them for the man. I expressed my fears, but he assured me that if I would go he would hold the rope and would not let me fall. So I put a stick across the bucket and got on, holding onto the rope. Every foot I went down into the deep, dark well I felt my father's strength at the other end of the rope. I knew I was safe, for he would not let me fall.

Translate that same confidence into life. That is why the missionaries can leave home, family, comfort, and all and go far away to a heathen people and bury their lives, forgotten by the rest of the world. It is because they know *the Father above is holding the rope* while they go down into the well. That confidence sustains the children of God when some great sorrow or affliction comes to them, and they smile through their tears. The well may be deep, dark, and cold, but the Father who holds the rope will not forget his child who hangs on the other end.

I do not ask to be spared temptations, but I do ask that when they come, the Father will not leave me to fight alone. I am sure some day sorrow will come my way, as it is the heritage of us all. I cannot ask that I be spared this blow, but I can ask that the Father will draw close when it comes. That is what Christ promised Peter the night Satan sifted him.

A little girl prepared to retire in a sleeping car one night as the train sped on in the face of a terrific storm. A grown man across the aisle asked the little girl if she were not afraid to go to sleep when such a strong wind was blowing, but she answered in the negative. The man said, "I am afraid we will go into a ditch."

But the child answered back, "I am not afraid, because my father is the engineer." That is the secret of life. As long as our confidence in God is unshaken the world is all right, life is worth living, and there is hope ahead. But when we forget that his hand is on the throttle of the world, then hope goes, and despair comes; faith dies, and doubt springs up. When our relationship to God and our confidence in him are settled, the fears that disturb us soon vanish, and we are at peace (see Isa. 26:3).

A DIRECTIVE

As quickly and surely as day follows night, *great obligations follow great blessings.* At the same time that Christ gave Peter assurance of his presence and help in the hour of conflict, he quickly led that disciple into the doorway of a great future, showing him how the blessings of that night should be passed on to others. "'When thou art converted, strengthen thy brethren'" (Luke 22:32). First, *he needed to be converted.* Not saved from his sins—that had doubtless come to him before—but changed from the former life to a different life. The word *converted* (translated as "turned again" in the RSV) means to face about, to reverse one's opinions or thinking. When more light comes on the subject, the person gives up his previous position and takes a different one.

In Peter's case, he had been a fickle man—unsettled, unstable, and uncertain. The experience with the devil that night took all the fickleness out of him, and he went on to become one of the strongest witnesses of his day. He was no longer the impulsive man of the former years, but a man whose experience had taken the impurities out of his life— one who had been mellowed and ripened into a far better servant. From that night on he had a stronger faith in Christ, a greater fear of the devil, and more sympathy for imperfect humanity. What precept, example, sermon, and miracle had failed to accomplish, a humbling experience did for him.

The Lord might have said, "Peter, the experience tonight will settle you, and when you are firmly fixed, then go out to help others." It is often true that the strongest characters have been shaped by the hardest adversities. Pearls come from the hurts made in the flesh of the oysters by grains of sand or some foreign substance, but nature walls the hurt in with a tissue to protect it. This hurt then becomes glorified and desirable. The value of the oyster is greatly enhanced by the injury. That is the lesson here. The Lord caused the cruel experience to be turned to advantage for the disciple.

A second lesson is that he became *a specially prepared helper of others,* prepared by his own trial to help others in similar troubles. Here was a man who could speak out of bitter experience as he urged a fickle race to cling to God—a man who knew firsthand the sorrow of a shaky faith and careless words. After that night he could speak with more authority.

Some years ago I was called to the hospital to see one who was very ill. The relatives were standing near with their hearts broken over the imminent death of their loved one. Another woman I had not expected to see was there too. She had just passed through some dreadful experiences. Little more than a year before, a child had been burned to death in her yard; within a few months following, a second child died almost exactly the same way. Soon after the second tragedy, her own son was killed in a crash.

I was sure this woman could not help the family in trouble because her own grief was so great. But I had not been in the room two minutes before I saw what a comforter she was, having just passed through the greatest school of life. I sat silent and helpless while this good woman shared comfort out of the deep ordeals of her life and spoke with a certainty of which I was totally ignorant. These events, so fearful and cruel, had made her soul so mellow, her faith so strong, and her words so gentle, that she was able to do what I could not do; for in this woman the Lord had one specially trained and prepared for the task.

The wider interpretation of the passage is that *every experience of life may have two values in it:* one to strengthen and help to fortify ourselves; the other, to help others. The first is the blessing we get for ourselves; the second, the blessing we are to pass on to someone else. The first is a condition of the second, for how can I establish, stabilize, and fortify others unless I myself am settled? The second is an obligation growing out of the first, for surely all who are strong should help those who are weak. The law of life as well as the law of God has bound the burden of the weak upon the shoulder of the strong, to sympathize with, share with, and suffer with the less fortunate of our fellows. Therefore, when you have been saved, help save others. When you have developed a strong faith, help weaker ones to attain that same strength. When you have learned the secret of a happy life, pass that secret on that others may know it and be encouraged.

NOTES

1. Thomas Gray, *Elegy Written in a Country Churchyard* (Boston: The Atheneum Press, reprinted 1909), 55–56.

WALKING WITH GOD

And Enoch walked with God.
GENESIS 5:24

The fifth chapter of Genesis is one of the dullest in the entire Bible. It is a rather monotonous record of the names of men about whom very little is known. All the chronicler seemed to know was that each was born, had a family, and died at a ripe old age. But when he came to the name of Enoch, he could not pass it without adding two interesting bits of information. He tells us how Enoch lived and what became of him. The two thoughts are particularly interesting because of their uniqueness. Saying that Enoch walked with God and disappeared from the earth is a novel way of telling us how good this man was and that he went to heaven. That is the meaning of the statements.

What does it mean to walk with God? It means more than to be a Christian. True, one cannot walk with God without being a Christian, but not every Christian walks with God. It carries the idea of a higher type of Christian life than is exemplified by most people. It certainly expresses in easily understandable language that Enoch was saved, but it tells far more than that. It tells how this saved man conducted himself, the company he kept, the spirit he had, and the things he enjoyed in this world. When these things are known, it is not difficult to settle some other questions about his life. There is no need to warn such a man about his language, about his honesty, about his love for his fellow man, or about the many other things that vex some of us. He settled a handful of negatives with one positive. By walking with God, he forgot the other things that need to be shunned. The Christian life is always best preserved by filling it with good things rather than trying to guard against the ugly things.

GOD'S INTIMATE

The passage suggests the thought of *intimacy*. Two walking together so constantly would be unthinkable unless there had grown between them the warmest friendship and fellowship. They must have become confidential friends, or they would have soon drifted apart. Two who enjoy the same things, whose interests lie along the same line, who share each other's goodwill, cannot be happy when separated. Abraham had the distinction of being the confidential friend of God, the one to whom God would tell his secrets (Gen. 18:17–19). This is the highest distinction one may attain in this world—to become in a sense a private secretary to God.

Such was the honor Enoch had because of his close devotion to the Lord.

The passage also suggests *the constancy of such a life.* He did not associate with God occasionally but regularly. He did not walk with God today and forget him the next day—but daily, hourly, constantly. Such intimacy with God is never accomplished by spasmodic living, nor by an occasional great deed, nor by a sweeping experience, nor by an hour of most holy devotion, but by a life of continuous living in the presence of God.

Walking with God indicates *they went the way God chose.* God did not walk with Enoch, but Enoch walked with God. God chose the way, and Enoch went with him. In such a course lie both the life of obedience and the life of submission. Not only yielding to God's will but following it diligently. Not only consenting to it but gladly accepting it. Not only submitting to the choice and will of God but embracing them and finding joy in pursuing them to the last step of life. This is what makes the Christian life useful and happy. Not that the life is made good by yielding to a set of unpleasant rules regulating its conduct and controlling its desires, but by desiring what God wants for one's life.

PURITY AND PROGRESS

Such a walk conveys the thought of *purity.* One cannot walk with God and the devil; it is either God *or* the devil but not both. They do not go the same direction, and it is impossible to walk with both. The New Testament has a clear teaching on this point: "'No one can serve two masters; for either he will hate the one and love the other, or he will be devoted to the one and despise the other. You cannot serve God and mammon'" (Matt. 6:24 RSV; see also 2 Cor. 6:15). Such a walk forces us into a definite and unequivocal alignment with God or against God. He is a jealous God, not sharing the affections of a single little child with the devil. He wants all the heart or none of it.

This walk with God is *a walk of progress,* not of idleness, nor of indifference, nor of mere opposition, but of forward movement. Many Christians stop right where they were saved; they never grow nor advance one step. They are not walking with God. Many others spend a lifetime criticizing those who are going forward. Such friends may be saved, but they do not walk with God. If one walks with God, he will move toward the accomplishment of God's will, for that is the direction God is going. He will also find himself out helping stricken humanity, for that is where our Lord was most often found. He will discover that he is intensely missionary, doing all he can to save the lost world, for that was the work closest to the heart of our Master. And he will find himself in harmony with the purpose of every movement for good.

These are some of the landmarks that point the way our Savior walked. Let no church member think he is walking with God if he is constantly opposing the work of the church or making it harder for others to carry it on; his Lord loved the church and gave himself for it. All who walk with him will be glad to do the same thing. The things one loves and the things one hates will largely indicate whether one walks with God or not. Also, the things one helps and the things one hinders point with accuracy to the harmony or discord between a soul and God.

WHEN THE INTIMACY BEGAN

When did Enoch begin to walk with God? This is not a foolish question, since he lived at a time when it was not popular to be a follower of God. The world seemed to have gone after other gods, and the worshiper of the true God must have stood almost alone in his day. There are several answers to our question. First, *he began to walk with God when his first child was born.* Genesis 5:22 seems to indicate that before the birth of the child Enoch had not walked with God, but that after this little one was laid in his arms, he was moved to follow God.

This is a striking lesson. The responsibility of parenthood is enough to bring most fathers and mothers to their knees— their own offspring lie helpless, waiting to be trained in the ways of life. Enoch was not only the parent, but the teacher, example, and standard by which the young life would measure itself. What the child was to be in this life and the life to come would be determined largely by the father. The child's relationship to time and eternity, to people and God, to things right and things wrong—all would be influenced, if not wholly fixed, by the father who had given him life.

I think it was not an accident that this story was preserved for us, but that it was given to teach one of the most profound lessons of life. A father who can look into the face of his own innocent child and not want to be a better man is strangely lacking in his makeup. Here is a little life without a habit, without a stain on it, without a mark or a blot on its life or character, and the father is given the first chance to make it or mar it. The child's first lessons may be learned at his knee; he will be the child's first hero and ideal, and the standards of life will be lifted or crushed by the father's example. Such reminders are enough to make honest men try to live better for their children's sake.

But the obligation deepens. The child is born into a world where the race of humans had largely deserted God and gone after other gods, and the child will follow unless some strong influence holds him securely to the right path. It is not enough to be a nominal believer in God. It is imperative that the father's influence for God shall outweigh all the contrary influences. This is doubtless the thing that drove the father to God in much prayer for help to live, wisdom to direct, and courage to withstand the evil influences of the day, so that the son would be drawn to a life of goodness. Many are the parents in the world who have been made better men and women because they have been driven to God on behalf of their children.

There is another answer to the question when Enoch began to walk with God. It was *when he was a young man*, just starting out in life, with the best of his life still ahead of him. How his example shames the frivolous crowd of today who insist that a young man is expected to sow wild oats. Such rot is a doctrine of devils. Hundreds of the finest men of the world never sowed wild oats, and they are better because of it. The noblest thing in the world is a group of consecrated young men, young men as full of ambition, passion, and daring as any to be found, yet with principle enough to master the lower elements of life and live a true, clean life in spite of the demons trying to drag them into the gutter. Here was a young man who did not fill his early life with crimes to be wept over in later years, and the most perceptive youths follow his example.

Among the many tricks of the devil, none is more artful than to delude a young man into wasting the best part of his life, and then offering the last fragment to God when he comes to die, just because young men are expected to do that kind of thing. Such a trick is like the upas tree whose sweet nectar draws the bees from afar, and when they have sipped, they fall dead in the blossom.

The time for a man to begin his religious life is when he is young. He does not wait until he is old to begin his life's vocation, nor to get his education, nor to find his wife. Yet the devil would have us believe religion would interfere with all these things and should be postponed until they have all been settled and are out of the way.

But God's plan is different. "Remember also your Creator in the days of your youth," and " 'Seek first his kingdom and his righteousness' " (Eccles. 12:1; Matt. 6:33 RSV). God wants the life before it is spent in sin, before it is wasted and useless. He wants it with all its ambition, all its zeal, all its possibilities, and all its power. Just as the nation calls young men of certain ages to bear the burdens of war, even so the army of God needs to be filled with strong young men who are able to carry the banners of the Lord and plant them on the parapets of the nations of the earth.

When did Enoch begin to walk with God? *When he lived in the midst of a rebellious nation* (Gen. 6:5–6). He did not wait for all the rest to be religious before he turned and began to live for God. He did it when he was almost alone as a worshiper of the true God. It is easy to be religious when everybody is religious, but it is quite different when you have to be religious alone. One deserves no credit for being good when all around him are good, when all the influences around him help him to be good, when it would be difficult not to be good. But for one to rise up in the midst of an evil and perverted generation and break away from its habits, customs, and influences and stand out as a lone target for the arrows of derision and ugly epithets is an act of unusual courage. Enoch did it because God meant more to him than all the jeering world, and he had a courage to match his convictions.

Far down the years Enoch had a like-minded kinsman in the person of Joshua. When all Israel seemed bent on following idols, Joshua said to the crowd of his fellow travelers, "You can do as you like, but as for me and my house, we will serve the Lord" (Josh. 24:15, paraphrased). How admirable when a young man reared in an un-Christian home in the midst of a bitter anti-Christian community rises above his environment and throws off the yoke of antagonism toward God to love him instead! And how honorable is the young man who refuses to be swept down by the degenerate current of his time but, like Moses, turns away from position, privilege, and praise and chooses instead to identify with the sufferings of God's chosen (Heb. 11:24–26).

GOD, THE SILENT PARTNER

Enoch walked with God while he went about his secular work. He did not turn aside from secular pursuits to be religious but carried his religion into his business with him. This is the ideal way, and such a person is the ideal Christian. Christianity is not a thing to be put on and taken off at will but is to be woven into one's life and character.

There are those Christians who separate themselves from everyone and everything secular and live their lives in seclusion so that they may be religious. They fear that they cannot live righteous lives while they associate with other people and follow secular callings. This is a burlesque on the Christian religion. The principles of the religion of Christ are to be lived in public as well as in private. They are to be carried into the store, the office, the shop, the field, and into every walk of life. They are to be lived out in work and play alike. They are to govern our lives every day of the week, not solely on Sunday.

Although Scripture does not tell us this, we feel that Enoch was a great businessman, *making his God the silent partner* in every transaction. People like this show the world that the business of the material life can be carried on according to the principles of righteousness. They give answer to the quibblers of all ages who say that "religion and business will not mix." They demonstrate that business people can be great Christians.

Some of the most effective Christians of the modern times are not ministers but executives who take time from their busy lives to give God the best of each day. It is their consecrated wealth, business judgment, and skill that God uses to notable results. Such entrepreneurs of the present day are following the example of such illustrious forerunners as Abraham, the stockman; Moses, the courtier; Paul, the tent-maker; and Lydia, the seller of purple. Such persons have lifted the cause of our God above reproach and have sanctified all their professions by making God the principal director of every concern.

RESULTS OF THE PARTNERSHIP

What were the results of a life spent as Enoch lived? It will not be possible to ascertain all the results, but some things are so certain as to be beyond question. First, *the honor that came to his child was no small reward.* Methuselah, this son born into his home in the early years, lived to be the oldest man on record. This long and useful life of the child was a fitting reward for the father's faithfulness. It was this child who served as the connecting link between Adam and Noah. His life overlapped the life of Adam by nearly two hundred and fifty years, and it overlapped the life of Noah about six hundred years, thus making it possible for the story of Creation and God's dealing with Adam to be handed down to Noah practically firsthand, passing through only one other person. Adam told Methuselah of God's wonderful works, and Methuselah told them to Noah and his sons, who carried the accounts beyond the Flood.

While the records do not tell us that this place of honor accorded Methuselah was a reward for Enoch's good life, it seems hardly possible that such a strange coincidence should occur without purpose or plan. To us, it is the recognition God gave to his faithful saint.

A second result is *the glorious translation of God's trusted friend* into the home beyond without passing through the gate of death—an honor that came to but one other and an honor that perhaps will never come to another, except at the coming of our Lord. It was a demonstration that the honor God confers on his confidential friends is limitless.

Even the best of his saints do not hope for such a singular experience as escaping death, but the other more wonderful prospect of being carried to the home of God is the common hope of each of his children, from the greatest to the least. And our walk with him on those streets of gold will be determined by our walk with him on the fields on earth. The friendships of heaven will be made on earth, and those who walk closest to him here will know him best up there.

A PREVAILING GOSPEL

So mightily grew the word of God and prevailed.
ACTS 19:20

The nineteenth chapter of Acts is a wonderful bit of history of the struggles of the young church. It puts us in possession of some facts that are worthy of consideration by the church today. The first of these is that the gospel did not have an open field, but grew up in an age and among a people prepossessed with many bitter, contrary views. To live at all, it had to gain its footing in spite of these. This it did by its own merit and did it so remarkably that the writer declared it "grew" and "prevailed."

A second lesson written into the bit of history is the method by which those early preachers carried on their work of evangelizing. And here again many modern leaders might get some valuable hints from the primitive methods—methods that were so signally blessed of God that it might be well to try them in this far-off day. Their effectiveness is shown by the fact that before them the walls of opposition crumbled and by them the bulwarks of the enemy were battered down.

Paul was a narrow preacher. He saw but one remedy for the ills of mankind. He seemed to have little to do with many of the theories, held in that day and this, to solve the sin problem. The belief in salvation by education and environment is not a new thing; it is as old as civilization. But Paul did not think well of it as a plan of human redemption. He preached that the gospel of Jesus Christ offered the only remedy, that the souls and destinies of individuals were safe when they rested upon Jesus Christ alone, that the gospel we have was of divine origin and not a human production, and further, that it prevailed over its detractors by the power of God and not by tricks and schemes of men.

THE GOSPEL'S METHODS

That we might be more specific, let the question of methods be raised. By what methods did the gospel grow and prevail? And this is a sane question, for when someone or something succeeds in the face of many obstacles, everybody wants to know how it was done. So it is fair to ask how the gospel gained such a hold on the people, seeing how they were cradled in opposition and fed on the milk of hatred for this new doctrine.

I know of no better way to answer the question than to read what the early Christians did and how they did it. *They adopted the prayer route.* They did not lift a hand to advance their cause for ten days and nights after Christ left them.

They shut themselves up to prayer, much prayer, continual prayer, earnest and agonizing prayer. They gained their first victory on their knees, before the real battle was faced. Their courage was born there, their vision came then, their message was given during that time, and—most valuable of all—they learned that while Christ was absent in the flesh he was present in the Spirit and that their work was under his personal direction.

They clung to this prayer method as long as they lived; they followed it in every trial. When they chose a successor to Judas, they did it by the prayer plan, that they might make no mistake (Acts 1:23–26). When they selected their first deacons, they resorted to the prayer method (Acts 6:3–6). They got good men this way, men like Stephen, who died rather than allow the cause of his Lord to suffer defeat in his hands.

When they met impostors, they conquered them by prayer rather than physical force. They healed the sick, cast out evil spirits, and even raised the dead by prayer. They often stirred up the hatred of men until their own lives were in peril, yet they did not defend themselves with physical weapons but by prayer.

These references are sufficient to grasp the lesson. We will not be able to improve on their plan. Our selection of pastors succeeds best when God is called in to make the deciding choice, not when men are selected because of their training or other good qualities. The calling of pastors, the selection of deacons, the choosing of leaders anywhere will have the surest guarantee when it is done under the leadership of God. The importance of prayer in the success of the gospel cannot be overemphasized. Our revivals reach the highest peaks when real prayer has gone up to the throne of God.

A second method cannot be overlooked in the study of the first Christians' work: *the Holy Spirit method.* True, it is closely related to the former, but it is quite a different thing. For he is the one who helped them to pray; he gave their words point and power when they spoke. He made their sermons so irresistible that the hardest cases melted before them. Enemies, governors, and emperors listened to them because of the Holy Spirit. Even demons trembled, not in fear of the men, but in fear of the power that made the men fearless.

Let us come back to the old-time plan of depending exclusively on him for our success. Have we forgotten how they succeeded? Do our sermons seem to fail? Do people hear and go away none the better? There is an emptiness that might be explained, and a weakness that might be strengthened. Our need is for the Holy Spirit. There is no conviction for sin without him. There is no real repentance without him. There is no salvation without him nor any saving faith. Have we tried to preach a better life instead of a Holy Spirit salvation? Have we urged the lost to quit their sins and come into the church instead of to fall on their faces before God in penitence?

It is one thing to stop doing our ugly deeds and another thing to be saved from our sins by the power of Jesus Christ. Sinners are not saved by tricks and schemes any more today than they were in the former days. If these first Christians succeeded in bringing people to their knees in confession of sin by the help of the Holy Spirit, we might find him a wonderful addition to our many plans of saving the world. Not less organization, but more Holy Spirit. Not less tactful planning, but more power from God. He would not have us do away with our common sense or human agencies, but he would have a larger part in our plans. He would be the planner.

A third observation might be made as we study the methods by which the disciples' gospel prevailed. That is *the content of the message.* What did they preach? They often denounced the sins of mankind, but with it they offered the forgiveness of a Savior. They pulled down the idols with a firm hand, but they lifted up a true God in their place. They openly condemned the immoral practices of the day but in the same breath offered the hope of a better life.

Their sermons were shot through and through with the three dominant facts. First, Jesus Christ was crucified, buried, raised, and ascended to heaven as the only hope of the world. Second, Yahweh is the only true God, and all persons are called to recognize him and worship him.[1] Third, eternity will reveal the good and the bad in all our lives, and a just recompense will be meted to each. The apostles may have given illustrations to make the truth clear, but only such stories that would serve the purpose to the glory of God. They gave the gospel the first and highest place. It was the only message they knew. They believed it, lived it, preached it in a fearless way.

Some of us might improve our message by studying their messages. There are many interesting tidbits that might prove helpful to men and women, but will such information serve to point them unerringly to the Savior? There are many branches of science, and who does not enjoy them as an intellectual feast? But when a preacher stands before the lost to tell them how to be saved, let him remember that the destinies of souls are hanging on his words. There is nothing that will meet the need quite as well as the plain gospel of the Lord Jesus Christ. There is no substitute for it. It is not to be compromised. It cannot be improved upon. The Lord gave the message complete in every detail, and he who adds to or takes from it endangers his own head.

Still another word might be said concerning their methods. *They looked more for encouragement to the little inner circle than to the world outside.* Its small beginning became an avalanche of power because they kept the inner circle clean and close to God. As long as they were devoted to the cause, there was hope of success, but if their faith broke, all hope was lost. It matters little that a dozen people are the sole believers in their cause, if that dozen will cling to their leader and keep faith with him.

Martin Luther went out from the Catholic Church and with him a few friends. The Protestant world can testify how well he succeeded in his new undertaking. John Wesley was the founder of the Methodist Church. The little beginning has grown tremendously, but it would have failed the first year of its life had the little inner circle of its advocates broke faith. William Booth gave the world the Salvation Army in the same way.[2]

The lesson is not hard to see. The hope of the church is within the church, not with its friends outside. Likewise, any defeat is not caused by its enemies but emanates from within the inner circle of the church. Just as Christians' vision, faith, and loyalty are, so will their success be. Their foes mean little; they are not to be dreaded. Keep the inner circle clean, keep the faith strong and the vision clear, and difficulties will melt as the snow beneath the springtime sun.

THE GOSPEL'S FOES

But the text raises another question. What were the foes over which the gospel prevailed? The first one was *a series of unexplainable setbacks.* One of the closest friends betrayed Christ. This would naturally give the new cause a great shock. Its repercussions did not fade before another one denied him outright, which added to the seriousness of the situation. Then the worst of all occurred: Christ was put to death. These first three setbacks occurred within one day's time. Later, the first deacon was stoned to death, and the church was scattered to the winds by persecution. These catastrophes were hard to understand, but the gospel grew in spite of them and prevailed.

A second foe was *infidelity in the church.* It will be remembered that many people were caught up with the new movement, but later drifted back to Judaism. They denounced Christ and went back to Moses as their hope of being saved. These people said by their conduct, "We have tried your Christianity, and it has not satisfied us." This is always a serious problem. Foes on the outside are not to be dreaded as much as foes from within. Having come from within, they are far more hurtful than the infidel without.

The enemy within has always been the real problem for the church. He strikes his hardest blow when he gets into the pulpit. When our preachers are infidels, the holy cause seems headed for the rocks. It was an especially great wonder for the gospel to prevail when many of the leaders and teachers were without conviction or genuine experience. Its success in the face of such adversities proves its claims of superiority and guarantees its ultimate victory in the world.

Another foe so prominent in that day, and more so today, was *the imitator of the good.* Simon the magician went into religious work for the material gain he could get out of it (Acts 8:9–24). The seven sons of Sceva, mentioned in Acts 19, were strangers to Christ, but they posed as his devout followers and as intimate friends of Paul. But when they tried to cast out an evil spirit in the name of Jesus, they failed and were exposed.

The church has always had to meet the counterfeit. Many things spring up which sometimes act as rivals of the church for the affections of the people. Religious associations are an example. I am aware that they are not openly acclaimed as a rival, and many of their best friends would not wish them to be thought of as such, but the fact remains that they are in competition with the church for the members' time and energy.

The lodge movement is another example. I am a lodge man and speak from experience. Many of its best members would resent the open statement that the lodge is esteemed more highly than the church, but for many (and for some who are unwilling to admit it), that is the truth. To them, the lodge more nearly meets the needs of the suffering world than the church does. If this is true, it is because the church members who belong to the lodge do their charity work through the lodge rather than through the church. If this is the case, no further proof is needed that they give the lodge a higher priority.

Many such cases might be mentioned, but these are sufficient. These imitators of the good may not be wholly condemned as evil, yet because of their strong qualities, they can be made a substitute for the church and thereby weaken the claims of the church. The early church had such foes to overcome. And we are indebted to the sacred writer for confirming that the gospel prevailed over them all.

Let another foe be mentioned, since it is discussed in this same chapter—*the influence of bad literature.* It is said that under Paul's preaching, the people were induced to bring out their valuable libraries [worth over six million dollars at today's value, according to NIV notes] and burn them in one great bonfire. These were books of sorcery that lured the curious with promises of attaining forbidden, mysterious knowledge until the victims were hopelessly trapped in Satan's grasp.

There is no need more pressing today than a repetition of that sweeping victory for the gospel. The world is sown with the most evil literature. Its poison springs from every kind of press, from the religious to the comic. This flood of degradation is burying the unwary and the innocent. What shall the ultimate harvest of this awful seedtime be? God grant that the gospel will overcome this seed and choke out the noxious growths that may spring from the adversary's cunning planting, as it did then![3]

A last foe will be mentioned: *the business person who runs his business in opposition to the church.* Acts 19:24 tells of one

Demetrius who made his living by making images of his heathen temple and selling them to the ignorant people as things of spiritual value. When the gospel was preached, the people turned from their idols, denounced their heathen temple, and no longer bought wares of this craftsman. Of course, he had a quarrel with Paul and the gospel. But we are told that the gospel prevailed over him and his nefarious business.

It has not been the last bad business the gospel has put down. I am confident it was by this leavening influence that America shook off slavery. I am equally as confident that the great lotteries, of which the Louisiana lottery was chief, went before the same power.[4] The race track, gambling, open saloon, and brothel have gone down under the influence of the gospel, and God hasten the day when other businesses that exploit the souls and bodies of mankind will be forced to close their doors.

THE GOSPEL ASKS NO OPEN FIELD

Let one more word bring this discussion to a close. We do not ask an open field for the gospel. It is not of such flimsy stuff that goes down when a contrary wind blows, but it has always shown itself able to meet any opposition. The Bible was loved most when the whole world was trying to destroy it. The church was purest when it cost people their lives to champion it. The gospel is not for the child only, but for the strongest man as well. It is not for the Sunday school alone, but for the busy street and the crowded marketplace as well. It needs no apology for its existence; it stands on its own merit. It is open for close inspection even in the laboratories.

It challenges the scientific world to use its best wits to investigate its claims and will stand unshaken when they have all moved on. It does not ask you to accept its histories on faith alone. The spade of the archaeologist is bringing to light facts long lost and buried that prove the stories.

Another word to sum up and reinforce our facts: The Bible does not need defenders of the truth; it will take care of itself. It does need devout believers and followers. The best recommendation of the gospel is a good life. The simple life of a person who was redeemed by the power of the gospel is the best testimony to its efficacy. Give us good people whose lives are clean and unquestioned; they may be uneducated and unknown, but they are the best defenders the gospel could have.

NOTES

1. Yahweh (YHWH) is the covenant name of the God of Israel. See Exodus 3:14–15, in which God explains the meaning of his name to Moses.

2. See Edward H. McKinley, *Marching to Glory: The History of the Salvation Army in the United States* (New York: Harper & Row, 1980).

3. As Dr. Melton mentions, the converts in Acts were moved by the Holy Spirit to expose and destroy their *own* possessions of demonic persuasion.

4. "Following a long national tradition, the South turned to lotteries to generate revenue to rebuild the war-ravaged region [after the Civil War]. The Louisiana lottery was the most notable because of its unseemly end. In 1868, the

Louisiana Lottery Company was authorized and granted a twenty-five-year charter. A carpetbagger criminal syndicate from New York bribed the Legislature into passing the lottery law and establishing the syndicate as the sole lottery provider. . . . This lottery was a prolific money maker. Attempts to repeal the twenty-five-year charter were defeated with assistance of bribes to legislators.

"Scandals and antigaming sentiment led to additional state and federal legislation against lotteries. In particular, religious leaders led the move against them. By 1878, Louisiana was the last of the legal lotteries in the country. The Louisiana Lottery survived until Congress enacted a prohibition against moving lottery tickets across state lines by any method. This act led to the abolition of the Louisiana lottery in 1895. When the lottery was disbanded, it was discovered that promoters had made huge sums of ill-gotten gains." Website: Roger Dunstan, *Gambling in California,* Chapter 2: "History of Gambling in the United States." http://www.library.ca.gov/CRB/97/03/Chapt2.html

OUR UNVEILED SELVES

*Then Joseph made haste, for his heart yearned for his brother,
and he sought a place to weep. And he entered his chamber
and wept there. Then he washed his face and came out; and
controlling himself he said, "Let food be served."*
GENESIS 43:30–31 RSV

The story of Joseph and his brothers is one that never grows
old. It grips both the fanciful child and the philosophical
man. Each new thrill in its unfolding seems to surpass the former one until the climax is reached when the brothers bow
down to him, as his prophetic dreams long before indicated
they would. The story is too well known to need repetition
here, but it is necessary for me to refer to a few of the main
points for our discussion to have the proper connection.

Some twenty years before, the sons of Jacob had sold their
brother to a caravan of traders en route to Egypt and had
carried back to their father the sad fabrication that wild

beasts had torn the lad to pieces. They held up Joseph's coat, bloodied by the slaughter of a lamb, to prove their story.

Years passed slowly by and with them came many changes, both to Joseph and to his brothers. In the midst of a great drought, ten strong men went from the hills of upper Palestine to Egypt to buy food for their families. The journey was not without its exciting experiences. They were interviewed by the Egyptian dignitaries, who were first suspicious, then certain that the travelers were spies. The brothers vigorously denied this accusation and with long speeches told the story of the pioneer of Palestine, who was an honorable man and whose sons—themselves—had come in search of food.

After being then allowed to purchase grain, they opened their sacks at the end of the first day of the trip home and found every man's money in the mouth of his sack. How could this mistake have occurred? They were not thieves so were confounded by the presence of the money.

They arrived home. After months of careful economy the supply of food was exhausted, and they were forced to return to Egypt for more grain. This time they took with them Benjamin, the youngest son of the home, whose mother had died soon after his birth. When they stood before the man of Egypt and offered their money for his corn, little did they know they were trying to barter with their brother whom they had sold as a slave years before. But Joseph knew his brothers, and when he looked on the face of Benjamin, his only true brother whom he had not seen since Benjamin was little more than a baby, he was almost overcome with emotion. When he could not hold back the tears any longer, he ran into his private room and wept until he was quiet. Then he washed his face and came out, acting as if nothing had happened.

A Secret Sin

Of the many lessons that might be drawn from the story, none is more clearly seen than the breaking out of a secret sin. Twenty years had passed since they had committed that secret crime against their brother. The real truth had never been told; the awful facts had been smuggled in the hearts of these ten men, and Joseph had dropped out of the family history forever. But all of a sudden, they are led strangely back to relive that fateful day. Joseph asks them about the family, the father, the brothers, and this forces them to tell that one is missing out of their number. That touch awakens the memories that have been sleeping for long years.

Yes, one is missing, and what became of him? They look at each other with guilt on their faces. They whisper to each other, not knowing that Joseph understands their language, saying, "'In truth we are guilty concerning our brother, in that we saw the distress of his soul, when he besought us and we would not listen; therefore is this distress come upon us'" (Gen. 42:21 RSV). They agree among themselves that the long-dead sin is crying out for vengeance. It had never been told, yet somehow it is known and is calling them to justice. The skeleton of that crime had rattled its dry bones and stood upright like a living thing to walk out into the open court of the world and tell the long-buried secrets. They had reassured themselves with the fact that no one knew, but it now appears that it has been told all over Egypt.

We would do well to learn some lessons from secret sins. The first is that *they are not dead because they are secret.* Here is where the world has gone far astray. People think that if sins are not known, they will never amount to anything. David thought that. When he sent Uriah into battle to have him killed so that David might take the man's wife to be his own, no one knew what was on his mind. David had a right to send the man into battle, so he committed, in the name of war, a crime that would have been punished by death if the real facts had been known. David meant it to be a secret that no living person should know. But one day the prophet of God stood before David and uncovered the sin. It was not so much a secret as David thought (2 Sam. 11:1–12:15; see also Pss. 38 and 51).

Even if no one ever discovers the sin, there are two who know it, and these two are unmerciful in their judgments: God and oneself. A noted detective said he could often point out criminals as they walked the street by the way they shunned the police officers. Their crimes had been committed in other parts of the country, and no one was suspicious of them where they were, yet they somehow felt uneasy in the presence of an officer. The conscience of a guilty person will not make friends with an officer of justice. The crimes that are supposed to be dead may speak out. The unconscious muttering of a drunken wretch picked up in the streets of a Texas city led to the solution in another state of a dreadful crime that had baffled all authorities. The deed was secret but not dead.

Another lesson worth learning is that *sin will not go out of date.* A twenty-year-old sin still cried out for justice. The public may forget it, the records may be destroyed, the witnesses may be dead, the hounds of the law may cease their pursuit; yet that secret, silent sin will trail a person as long as he lives, even across the continent or into foreign lands. It will push its ugly face into any crowd, slip into bed when one is asleep and wake him with dreadful nightmares, and it will startle him with weird cries that have been wafted across a half-century.

These brothers of Joseph relived the whole scene. They saw the anguish on his face; they heard him plead for his life as he pleaded twenty years before; they saw the tears in his eyes. That scene they had tried so hard to forget would not be pushed aside. And even if one can forget, it still remains on the books of God. After a thousand years and more, that secret sin will still be clamoring for justice; it will never be silenced.

Still another lesson is that *the least little things arouse the sleeping sin.* Every word of Joseph seemed to pry open that old wound and fasten the guilt on them. Once Herod killed John the Baptist he never got away from the reminders of it. The miraculous works of Jesus later distressed him, for he thought it was John come to life again (Matt. 14:1–12).

When I was a boy, I was working on a farm for a man who had me planting cotton. The seeds were running low, and I was anxious to finish the task; so to make quick work of it I dug a hole at one end of the field and buried a lot of the seed. The sin was hid; the man would never know. But the rains and the sun told the tale, and in a few days the most embarrassing witness I ever faced pushed up through the ground right where I had buried those seeds. I pulled up those young cotton shoots, but they kept coming up for a month. I had a hard time keeping the secret thing hidden.

A SECRET SORROW

The story not only tells the facts about a secret sin, but leads us into the closet, behind a closed door, and shows us a man overcome with emotion. When Joseph hears the self-condemnation of his brothers, sees them relive that scene of long ago, and hears them recite the deep sorrow it caused his father at home, then looks on the face of his little brother Benjamin, he is unable to bear it any longer. He rudely runs from their presence into his private room and breaks violently into tears.

The cold-blooded world is ready to say it is a weakness to give way to one's emotions. If we admit that it was giving way to emotion, at the same time we must admit that if emotion could not be expressed in an instance like this, then there is no place for emotion anywhere in life. And when one rules out of his life all sentiment and all emotion and lives on a plane of purely mercenary principles, he becomes sordid, base, stingy, and heartless.

Sentiment plays a far larger part in the average life than we care to admit. In fact, a life wholly void of it is a dangerous thing. When one loses sympathy for humanity, one becomes an animal. My admiration for Joseph rises when I see his heart break in sympathy for his troubled brothers. If he could laugh at their fears, make fun of their sorrows, and add miseries to their grief, the name *Joseph* would not mean as much to me as it does coming through hidden tears.

But the lesson deepens with his self-control. Giving way to emotions or to sentiments is not the real lesson, but being swept by these without losing one's balance is the amazing thing. Two extremes are in constant conflict in our hearts. Will our sentiment rule out our reason, or will our reason dismiss our sentiment? Either extreme is unhealthy. Fortunate is the one who can give sentiment its just dues and at the same time keep well balanced in all his dealings. Whoever is controlled exclusively by either one will fail somewhere in life, either in the commercial sphere, the social sphere, or the moral sphere. The two extremes may supplement each other or may be brought into sharp conflict.

The story teaches still another lesson. *The public and the private sides of life each have their place.* By weeping in his chamber and showing a calm face to the public, Joseph alternately gave way to his feelings, then controlled them. At one point the heart was in control, but when he left his chamber, he locked his feelings inside.

There are many who live their entire lives before the public. They tell all they know: all their experiences, sorrows, pains, and secrets. They have no private lives. Then there are many others who keep it all to themselves. They may suffer almost death without hardly a groan or may have great sorrows but carry them in their silent meditations. They do not drag their misfortunes before the public, nor unload their grievances on the neighborhood, nor parade their afflictions as if they were assets to be proud of. The face is not always a true index to the heart; a smile does not always mean that one is happy. It may mean, as with Joseph, that they weep behind drawn shades, but when they come out in public, they wash their faces and meet the crowds with a pleasant expression.

If the chance meeting of these long-separated brothers revived the secret sin of one group, it also stirred up the secret sorrows of the other. The old wound in the heart of this missing brother was reopened by familiar voices and faces; it was probed so deeply that it bled as if it were a new wound. How he longed to tell them who he was and what great things God had done for him and to assure them that he had forgiven them. And how much he had to say to his little brother!

He was not restrained by any hatred or ill will, but his judgment told him to hold off for a while. It was a clear illustration of the fact that the forgiveness of a sin does not blot out all its tracks. Long after a crime has been pardoned, its ugly footprints linger in the sands of time. Even if these brothers had truly repented and Joseph had really forgiven them, a long line of sorrow still lay along the trail their sin had made. The last groan of the father when they left home was for that long-lost boy.

How applicable is this lesson! Forgiveness does not erase the effects of sin. A child in his anger may throw a stone through a windowpane. Later, he may become ashamed of his tantrum and truly repent, but the glass is still broken. A nail may be driven into a beautiful piece of furniture, but when it is withdrawn, the gaping hole remains to shame the vandal. A man in hot passion may kill another, and when he has had time to cool down, he may become truly penitent, but that does not make the dead man live again. The tracks of sin are not so easily washed away.

A SECRET SERVICE

The incident we have read not only reveals a secret sin and a secret sorrow, but it also demonstrates *a secret service.* After the first visit to Egypt the sons of Israel found that their money had been put back in their sacks, but they did not know how that happened. They were congratulating themselves that they had escaped with their lives, but, in fact, one of them did not escape, for he was kept a prisoner. But now they found an unexpected kindness had been shown to them. Was it an oversight? Was it a decoy to lead them into a trap? Or was it a real kindness from some unknown friend? They were really distressed by the discovery.

For his part, Joseph was content to do the deed and remain in the background. The Bible is full of the stories of such anonymous helpers. They rendered the service, then dropped out of sight. Such was the lad who furnished the loaves and fishes when Christ fed the multitudes (John 6:8–9). Who was he? Nobody knows. His name will never be repeated, but the story of his gift will be told around the world as long as the world stands. Certain prophets, disciples, and women played a most interesting and important part in the history of the early Christian movement. Their deeds were recorded, but their names were not. After all, it is the deed that counts, not the one who did it. This secret service is more likely to represent real sacrifice and real merit than gifts heralded by loud announcements.

Again we are dealing with a problem fraught with dangers. Some are likely to render service and make gifts for the temporal advantage it brings. Others are likely to swing to the opposite extreme and do everything secretly. This may become as hurtful as the first, for the world needs the example of such lives. Others need to be stimulated to selfless actions by such service, and if it is covered up entirely, the world is robbed of the encouragement it would have spread. The real merit of the deed lies first in the motive behind it; second, in the spirit of it; third, in the measure of it; and fourth, in the results of it. Whoever serves to bless others will himself be blessed, whether the others are or not.

Let it be noted that when Joseph put the money back into the sacks of his brothers, he was returning *good for evil, a blessing for a curse.* They had hated him once, but he loved them and withheld his identity while he did it. They had sold him into slavery to be carried into a strange land, but he received them as guests into the royal palace and had them protected and entertained with all the authority of the nation. And when they took their leave, they carried his tangible blessing with them. This spirit is to be the ruling passion of the worshipers of God until the end of time.

When some philanthropist gives his millions to endow a college, to build a cathedral, or to establish an orphanage, it is right and appropriate that the public should recognize the worthy service. But too often the crowns are reserved for such heads while life is teeming with the common people who have rendered a service far smaller in size but far richer in sacrifice. On a great ship the captain is on dress parade and is lauded for the comfort and safety his passengers have enjoyed, but far down in the engine room is a little group of men covered with dirt and sweat who have long hours and little pay and whose names are never mentioned; yet their faithful service is what ensures the success of the voyage. The public crowns the captain and forgets the man in the hold.

A great preacher sways the crowds with his eloquence; he instructs them, leads them, lifts them, inspires them. And the audiences, in turn, are lavish in their praise of him. But how many have been forgotten? It may be that his wife at home has made a far greater sacrifice than he, but her head goes uncrowned. Or maybe the success of the minister is due to a group of faithful members who have been in the background, doing the drudgery; these have not been seen in public, yet they have made possible all that their leader has achieved.

The world learned a great lesson on this point at the close of the first World War. America brought from the fields of France the body of an unknown soldier and buried it in Arlington National Cemetery, thereby saying to the world, "We owe a debt of gratitude to the common soldier who gave his life. Great Britain, Belgium, France, and Italy did likewise, bringing home a native son to be honored for all."[1]

In England, they bore the body of a nameless boy to a resting place in Westminster Abbey among the kings, queens, poets, reformers, and national figures who had held empires in their palms. This was a fitting tribute to one who had served silently but had served his best. It takes a greater spirit for one to serve unseen than to serve when all the world is applauding. But let it be remembered until death claims us that the quiet, unnoticed servant has won the approval of the all-seeing God, who rewards in full.

NOTES

1. The inscription on the marble sarcophagus in Arlington National Cemetery reads, "Here rests in honored glory an American soldier known but to God." Following World War II, the Korean War, and the Vietnam War, an unidentified soldier from each of those conflicts was laid to rest near the first, and the memorial was renamed The Tomb of the Unknowns.

9

FOUR SERIOUS QUESTIONS

For we must all appear before the judgment seat
of Christ, so that each may receive good or evil,
according to what he has done in the body.
2 CORINTHIANS 5:10 RSV

I wish you would forget that I am a preacher in the professional sense and that what I am saying to you is called a sermon. I wish rather that you would take my words as a personal, private talk with each of you in a quiet place. Let them be the sanest words I am capable of uttering, about the most vital matter you will ever face. I am not especially concerned about your hearing and remembering my sermon as long as you absorb the facts set forth in this little passage.

If we are to deal in perfect candor with the passage above we cannot escape asking four questions. The first: What fact does the text reveal? This must be settled before it is of any value to us. This is the one thing that must be discerned before any passage can be interpreted or made practical. And in our answer to the question, we do not desire to dress it up prettily but to let it stand out in its ruggedness, without frills or trimmings. What does the text say?

THE LIFE TO COME

The writer tells us in no uncertain words that when life is over, there will come a time when *all people who have ever lived will be brought before God to receive the just rewards of life.* The writer does not stand alone is his declaration but is in accord with all those sacred writers who were moved by the Holy Spirit and whose writings have been preserved in our Bible. Matthew voices the same truth many times; a striking instance is the last section of the twenty-fifth chapter. Luke also sounds the same warning, twice in the thirteenth chapter. John in the third chapter reminds us again of the same inescapable fact, though clothed in words a bit different. Most of the writers in both the Old Testament and the New have been careful to include this warning in their bits of revelation.

The text tells us plainly that life does not end with the grave as some have thought, but that the grave is only the doorway of the life that is real. This life is only the background of the real life; it is only the dressing room for that life to come. Here in this brief span we are given the opportunity to choose our characters for the next, to decide our real destinies, and to determine our real state. And finally we will be called into the presence of the great Judge who will give us the destinies we have chosen, the clothes we have woven, and the estates we have purchased for ourselves.

Three facts make this a dreadful certainty. One, there is no escaping it for anyone. It will not be left to our option. We will not be consulted about it. We will be there, and be there just as we have chosen in this life. The second thing that makes it serious is that no deed can be undone, and no life changed then. Regrets, tears, prayers, and promises will be too late. Individuals will not come there to decide their fate; that is already decided. They will come to enjoy or endure the fate they have determined for themselves. The third thing that puts the sting in the text is that there will be no shifting of responsibility. Each decides his own course in life; each chooses his own lot; each lives his own life by which he is to be judged. The blame cannot be shifted to others.

The text also tells us that immortality is not for the just alone but for everyone—for the just and the unjust, the good and the bad. As the good is recognized, so is the evil also remembered; the one is rewarded, and the other is punished. The good and the bad may live close by each other on earth but not in heaven. The bad may clothe themselves with the cloak of the righteous in this world but not in the next. If anyone comforts himself with the delusion that he will never meet his sins again, let him carefully read this text—read it until it burns its way into his deepest soul and stands out in letters of inescapable light on the conscience.

A further fact is expressed here: the judgment will be just and perfect. It will be according to what we have done. In this present life one labors, and another gets the praise for it; one plants, and another reaps, or the good goes unrewarded altogether. God has promised that no deed will go without its just and full reward and that no life will get more or less than it deserves for the labors rendered. This is a great comfort when we look at the injustices so often found in the earth. The courts of heaven will not miscarry; no witness, judge, or jury will be bribed. No one will bear the guilt and punishment of another. These facts are not to be played with; they are firebrands that must be handled with greatest care.

My Duty as a Preacher

The second question I am confronted with is, in view of the facts of the text, *What is my duty as a preacher?* I am God's spokesman to tell you these things. I did not choose this calling as my life's work; in fact, I was slow to yield to what I knew to be my duty. I did not make my message. I am here on business for the King of heaven, and this is my duty. So how shall I discharge it?

Three paths are open to me. I might be silent on this unpleasant matter. I might preach much on God's love, his forgiveness, and his compassion. I might even tell people that God is too nice to condemn them and with these flattering words make many friends for myself. People would like me better if I preached those things rather than the awful fact stated in the text. What shall I do? A second option is to point out the facts as stated, then cover them with apologies until they become a joke. Finally, I can come with all the sincerity of my heart, sound the warnings as they are revealed in this book, and urge you to act on the light given. What shall I do?

Before I answer this question let me remind myself that I must answer to God for my behavior. I must meet the consequences of my labors, whether they are good or bad. Let me further remind myself that people's souls and destinies hang on my words. If I am silent and they lose their souls, I am in a large way responsible for it. If I teach them things that are not true, I am worse than a murderer; I hurt more than the body. Let me also remind myself that a faithful word properly spoken may prove the turning point of many. But my duty embraces more than that; it binds me to my task though everyone should rise up to curse me. It drives me forward even if no one accepts a word spoken.

My place is as the watchman on the wall, who sounds the warning when he sees the enemy coming (Ezek. 3:16–21). He cannot make the people believe him, nor can he make them run for their lives, neither is he responsible for their safety beyond warning them. But this is his duty, and if he fails in this, disaster is inevitable. If I know that a day will come when all persons will meet God and I do not tell them about it, I am worse than a traitor. If I have found that we in our present lives are determining our futures, and I do not urge you to the best possible life, I am worse than the creature who covers poison with sugar and gives it to his friend as candy. In the face of the facts, I must cry out to all, "'Prepare to meet your God!'" (Amos 4:12 RSV).

The ministry is a calling to be feared as well as honored, not only because it is sacred, but because it carries such tremendous responsibilities. Suppose I teach error for truth, and people believe it and lose their souls? How terrible for me, the one misguiding! Or suppose I have learned from the Bible that all sin must be punished by the God of heaven, and I fail to warn my hearers and urge them to give up their sins? How my silence will mock me, and shame me, and curse me in the end! Or suppose I have found a great Savior who can forgive all our sins and rescue us from their awful penalties, and yet I fail to tell you so you can take refuge under his mercy? What a crime is mine for not rescuing the perishing! (see Prov. 24:11–12).

Now the text tells me all these things and sends me into the world to tell others about them. What is my duty? Some will not believe me, some will joke about it, some will criticize me, some will hate me and plan all kinds of mischief for me. But what is my duty?

There is only one answer. Knowing that these things are true whether anyone believes them or not; knowing that I am called of God to attend this business, not to please people or entertain them; knowing that I must answer to him for my actions, I have no choice. I must be faithful to him, to my responsibilities, to myself, and to you. I can only repeat with all the earnestness and seriousness of my heart the words of the text, "We must all appear before the judgment seat of Christ."

YOUR DUTY AS A HEARER

But the text calls me to consider a third question—one, if possible, more important than the others. What is your duty? In the face of the facts presented in this passage and elsewhere; knowing that God has revealed them to us for our benefit; knowing also that this is the only true revelation the world has ever had of God, of sin, of our souls, of eternity, of our rewards, and of punishments, *what should you do with these facts?*

You sat with much satisfaction while I arraigned myself before my duties and chained myself to my task, but now you must look into the same mirror with me. Your face could have been black with dirt and grime, and you would have felt no shame if you had not known it. But when you have looked at your reflection just as it is (for the mirror does not lie), you no longer have any excuse. Since the soul that sins will die (Ezek. 18:20), and you have sinned by your own admission, your case requires your full attention so that the impending danger may be averted. As "the wicked shall be turned into hell, and all the nations that forget God" (Ps. 9:17), and your actions declare that you have forgotten God, yours is a serious situation. Since "we must all appear before the judgment seat of Christ," and since both the good and the bad in our lives will be examined by an eye that cannot be deceived, what is your duty in the light of God's revelation?

There are three options open to you; you may do any one of them. The first is to reject it all—disregard all that has been said on the subject, close your mind to all God's insistent messages, and with life in hand, take your chances. Some have done just that; some are doing it now. Just how they have fared for their decision we cannot know. A few of them have left dying testimonies. Without exception, so far as this writer knows, they have left expressions of regret and disappointment. Not one has gone out of the world with a shout of joy. They have approached the end with great fear and often with a prayer for another chance. Some have warned others to avoid the mistakes they have made and have urged them to make better use of their lives.

I repeat, you may do that. You may regard the Bible as a myth, as a collection of impossible stories, as the fabrications of men. You may ridicule the doctrines of heaven and hell, judgment and eternity, but your opinion does not change immutable facts. If you could tear every passage on hell out of your Bibles, it would not disprove it. If you could convince the whole world of your views, you still could not undo the realities. But such behavior is not a proof of one's ability nor a trait of superior intellect. It is not a mark of greatness in any respect.

The second thing you may do is a thing many have done and are still doing, yet is more dangerous and subtle than all the cunning tricks from hell. That is to accept it intellectually—to admit the facts, believe in the realities as proclaimed in the Bible—but rest the case there. Satan does not care that we acknowledge the Bible and Christianity as long as we do not embrace them. It does not bother him for us to agree with Christianity if we do not accept it and practice it. It is all right with him for us to believe in prayer as long as we do not pray. He will not object when we acknowledge a god, provided we do not make him our own God. Satan's most artful scheme is to have people be in-laws to the church—to have them possess a form of religion without any sense of sin. If

Christianity cannot be entirely laughed out of court, then let it be unanimously accepted, except without the personal element. Let the masses be swept into the church without serious thought—no repentance, no deep conviction, no consecration.

Or on the other hand, when they have made full confession of the facts of Christianity, let action be postponed as long as possible. All the arts and devices from the lower regions are brought into play to blind the eye, block the ear, and soothe the conscience, lest people should realize that their sins are serious realities for which they will be held accountable. But since God has been perfectly frank with us about the future, let me ask again, what is your duty in the light of these facts?

The third thing you might do is to believe his Word; accept his remedy for sin; and face life, death, and the judgment with a sense of preparedness, peace, and satisfaction. This is why the prophet cried, "'Prepare to meet your God,'" and the apostle said, "It is appointed for men to die once, and after that comes the judgment" (Heb. 9:27 RSV).

Six hundred years before Christ came, Ezekiel arose as God's spokesman and said, "As I live, says the Lord God, I have no pleasure in the death of the wicked, but that the wicked turn from his way and live" (Ezek. 33:11 RSV). Then the apostle Peter joined his testimony with that of the prophet and said, "The Lord is not slow about his promise as some count slowness, but is forbearing toward you, not wishing that any should perish, but that all should reach repentance" (2 Pet. 3:9 RSV). What now, in the face of these pleas from God, is your duty? Settle it right, for your decision must stand the test of the judgment. Settle it right, for it cannot be undone in the next world. Settle it right, for heaven, earth, and hell wait to see what your decision will be.

GOD'S DUTY IN THAT DAY

This brings us to the consideration of the fourth question suggested at the beginning. *What will be God's duty on that day?* If he had kept silent and not warned us of that approaching day, there could have been no blame resting on us if we had not made preparation for it, since we did not know about it. But now that God has been faithful to warn us of it, not once nor twice but many times, the responsibility has been shifted from God to us.

Not only has he told the fact of such an examination coming, but he has also revealed the requirements to pass it, those who will be there, what they will be examined on, the rules of the test, and what the rewards will be. These facts are not only written in the Bible, but in our very instincts and consciences. They were not meant to frighten but to inform us. If the text cited proves to be a fable instead of a fact, then no dependence can be put on his pledges of love, his promises of forgiveness, or his assurances of mercy. He cannot ignore his own Word. Ample provision has been made for the salvation of every soul. Enough pleas and warnings have been sent out.

Now that God has purchased redemption for all, now that God has called all and warned all, now that God has diligently endeavored to save all, what must he do when that day comes and some there would not believe him? His duty will be twofold, to the saved and to the unsaved. He has promised salvation and deliverance to all who trust him; this he must guarantee to the last one. Regardless of how imperfect the past life or how feeble and struggling the faith that linked us to him, his first duty toward the saved is full and complete protection. This he will give. Christ has put himself between the Christian and all danger at the judgment, and under his sheltering wing there is perfect safety for every trusting child (Rom. 8:1).

But what of his duty toward the unsaved? He has no option in the matter. His own Word binds him to forsake them and leave them to their destiny, the destiny they chose for themselves while on earth. Yes, he loved them and did all within his power to save them from their end, but they rejected his love and his offers of help; now they are rejected by him. He would even now pity them and help them, but he cannot. They would not have him, even if he pressed his claims hard on them. Justice demands the punishment of their sins, righteousness demands the removal of all evil from the presence of God, and holiness demands the complete separation of good and evil. He will gather the good up to himself, and send the rest away into eternal "outer darkness" (Matt. 25:30).[1]

The text tells me my duty as a minister; I may fail to do it and be the poorer by it. The text tells you your duty; you may refuse to do it and be the loser by it. The text points out God's duty, and he will do it, even if you and I fail utterly in ours.

NOTES

1. To question what will happen to those peoples who never heard the gospel is a red herring. We cannot know but leave them to God's mercy. However, anyone reading this book *has* heard the gospel and cannot claim ignorance for himself.

10

FAITH IN THE LABORATORY

*By faith Noah, being warned by God concerning
events as yet unseen, took heed and constructed
an ark for the saving of his household.*
HEBREWS 11:7 RSV

The eleventh chapter of Hebrews has been called God's gallery of the heroes of faith. The details of their lives are not mentioned here, just their names and the one or two deeds that made them illustrious. It would be difficult to select the greatest from among them because they seem mutually to surpass each other. But for our present study we have decided to direct our attention to Noah, whose faith saved his life and the lives of his family when the world was destroyed by flood.

While it is our purpose to analyze his faith, we recognize the task as a difficult one. No analysis can reveal all the elements in real faith, for each new condition calls out a new quality. But since so many fine attributes have come to the surface in his case, it will be interesting to study what we find.

FAITH AND COMMON SENSE

It is recorded that when God warned Noah of the coming flood, Noah did what any sensible man would do if he believed the warning. He began the construction of an ark to save himself. Judging by common sense, I consider this the most prudent action. Noah was practicing "preparedness" and "safety first." It was the most sensible thing he could have done under the circumstances. Now let it be remembered that faith most often acts along sensible lines. Our conduct is the measure of our credulity. What we do is usually in keeping with what we believe. The fact that Noah began the construction of an ark was sufficient proof that he believed God's warning. Likewise, the fact that he believed God could not be proved by stronger logic than the building of the ark. This fact is made clear by the conduct of people everywhere.

In 1848, it was reported that gold had been found in California in great abundance and that there were big opportunities for one to accumulate wealth. These stories spread through all sections of the country. But how much were they believed? Let that long trail of weary pilgrims who crossed the mountains and deserts be the answer. Men would not have left their homes and families to brave the long months of dangers, hardships, toil, and sacrifice if they had not believed these reports. Their belief found expression in hasty preparations for the journey. They believed the reports and therefore went in search of gold.

This is the thought expressed by James: "Faith apart from works is dead" (2:26 RSV). Noah might have shouted himself hoarse about the coming flood, but all his pleas and exhortations would have been silly chattering were he not building the ark. This is why men invest the last penny they have in foolish speculation; they believe in the venture, therefore risk everything. This is why farmers plow, sow, and toil for months with no reward. They believe in the prospect that has not yet come, and their actions are in keeping with what they believe.

This also explains why the missionaries sacrifice everything that is dear to them at home and bury their lives in some distant field to live and die among people who often misunderstand and oppose them. They believe that the gospel is their hope of salvation, and because they believe it, they pour out their lives in efforts to rescue the perishing. Faith expresses itself in action, and action is the proof of faith.

FAITH AND FEAR

In the King James Version of this text, it says that when Noah heard of the coming flood, he was so "moved with fear" that he began constructing the ark. This has a double meaning. The first is that *Noah had such regard and reverence for God* who had spoken to him that Noah obeyed him at once. The second reading is as forceful as the first: that he *trembled at the thought* of the coming catastrophe. Three things are crowded into Noah's motivation: faith, fear, and common sense.

There is a strong tendency among certain sects to substitute presumption for faith. In the story of David's flights from Saul, it is recorded that David came to a little village to hide. When Saul heard David was there, he set out to capture him. David prayed to the Lord and asked two questions: First, will Saul come to this place? God's answer was in the affirmative. Then David inquired, "Will the people of this place deliver me to Saul?" The Lord said yes. David said, "It is time for me to go" (1 Sam. 23:7–14, paraphrased).

David's belief in God made him run away. Faith does not always take a brave stand in the face of danger, but often makes us run. Faith does not always throw the burden of responsibility back on God to protect one: it most often makes one willing to cooperate with God in doing what plain reason would suggest. David believed and therefore acted. He who believes is expected to act sensibly.

I witnessed a dreadful disaster on one occasion. Two brothers saw a danger approaching. One of them said, "I will not run. I do not believe there is any danger." The other one said, "I see danger, so good-bye," and he ran for his life. The first lost his life; the other survived. The belief of the second made him act sensibly. He might have made loud boasts of his faith in God to take care of him, but such a boast would have been foolish. Running to save one's life does not discount one's faith in God. It might be a clear proof of one's faith, because it leads him to take action based on the reasoning God gave him. The same faith that makes us trust God makes us use our best judgment in all matters. The farmer who plows and sows because he believes in a coming harvest has another reason for plowing and sowing: he is afraid of the certain starvation of his family if he does not do it.

Faith works both ways: it makes us work, run, plan, and use our full powers of reasoning, and at the same time it makes us look to God for help to do our best, leaving the consequences with him. A "faith" that makes a farmer pray and sing instead of cultivate his crops is not faith at all but the rankest presumption. Real faith recognizes God, but it also recognizes the presence of real dangers and handles them in a cautious manner. Faith trusts God as if God were the only hope, yet works as if the task had to be done by work alone. Noah believed God; therefore, he built the ark as God instructed him. He did not sit down and trust God to save him when the flood came; he built the ark and trusted God to use it to save him.

FAITH AND THE USE OF MEANS

Faith does not disregard the use of means to accomplish the will of God. The ark was God's plan. The gospel is God's plan. The physician is most often God's plan for restoring health. God can heal without him but chooses to allow the physician to participate in the miracle of healing.

A few years ago a woman came to my home in a great hurry and called for me. She was a stranger to me but was on a visit to her son whom I knew. Nervous and excited, she practically commanded me to get my hat immediately and go with her to her son's home where the baby was sick. I gladly went, but by the time we reached the house, I had formed some opinions about the case.

She and I entered the room where her son and his wife were with the sick child, and immediately the grandmother took things in hand and told me to pray at once for the baby. I inquired whether they had called a physician and was soon informed that they did not believe in physicians, medicines, or any material remedies but in God only. I asked them why they had the cold cloth on the child's head, why they nursed him so carefully, and several other questions pertaining to the material side. Then I told them I would not consent to pray unless they were willing to use such means as God had already given them to relieve the baby's suffering and counteract the disease.

After some talk, they slowly yielded and said they would get a physician and follow his instructions. Then, with as much earnestness and tenderness as I had in me, I prayed for the sick child, for the family in their care of him, for the physician in his diagnosis and treatment of him, and that above all God would receive glory from the sickness and the healing.

I would not leave the wrong impression with you here. God is not confined to the ways of the physician, nor to the remedies offered; his healing is not dependent on human and material ways and means, but he *does* use them and honor them. Real faith puts a prayer in the heart, a song on the lips, and a labor of love in the hand, sending us out to meet the needs of humanity crushed under sin and disease. It does not stop to pray when people are cold, hungry, and suffering but causes us to work and to pray as we work.

FAITH AND CRITICISM

We are not told what the neighbors thought of Noah in his wild and fanciful venture, but it is easy to draw on our imagination here without fear of going far astray. Beyond doubt, it was an age of unbelief; Noah was quite certainly the only one who had faith enough to listen to God's warning and risk so much to act on it. Our conclusion is that he was the joke of the country. On the one hand, faith leads people to do what is most common-sensical when all is said and done. But before the full tale is told, this same faith leads to actions that seem preposterous to the unbelieving.

Ezra, Nehemiah, and many other reformers were not taken seriously by the people of their times, but their faith led them on in spite of the atmosphere of derision. *Real faith does not waver before criticism.* It sees what the natural eye does not see and is ruled by a higher logic than the mere physical life can attain. It is anchored by a force stronger than human reasoning. It answers back, "I believed, and therefore have I spoken" (2 Cor. 4:13; see also Ps. 116:10). When hope is built on material things, it vanishes when they fail. When hope is built on faith, it will stand when all around it has been swept away. It is easy to be brave as long as the masses are shouting your praise, but when they are attacking you, criticizing you, and lying about you, only a faith that is upheld by an unseen hand can sustain you.

Perhaps this age more than any preceding demands a faith that can stand the test of criticism. Everything sacred is being tried in the furnace. The critics have riddled our Bible in trying to cut its heart out. But we are confident that when they have worn themselves out with the effort, they will find that they have not changed one truth or principle. They have also declared war on the church. They have placed it alongside other organizations, with no authority beyond men, no mission except the social, and no doctrine other than the brotherhood of man. What has escaped them? Our Christ, our ordinances, our faith, have all been made to pass under the critic's stamp of disapproval. But something within us tells us not to worry; these storms will not cause a ripple on the surface of the eternal. Give us a faith that is resting on the Rock of Ages, and it will carry on unshaken by all the scoffing of the times.

FAITH AND CERTAINTY

The note that was heard clearest in Noah's faith, as well as in that of all the worthies of the past, was the note of *certainty*. There was not the least possibility of anything God had told them failing to happen. So strong were they in their belief that they hung their lives on the accurate and literal fulfillment of the promises. This is what moved Noah to immediate action and kept him steadily at his task. The coming danger was as real a fact as if it had already burst on them. This is where so many of us fail; we have one foot on faith and the other on doubt. We believe one minute, only to tremble and worry the next.

A minister told this story: He was holding a revival meeting in a small town, when one day at the close of the service a woman asked him if he believed in prayer and if he had faith in God. Of course, he professed both. Then the woman told how she had spent most of the night before in prayer for her son in a distant city, and that near morning she had felt a perfect assurance that God had answered her prayers. Her son had not only been saved but would come home that day to tell her about it. Then she asked the minister to go to the train station with her to meet her son. No argument could shake her confidence. The minister reluctantly went with her to meet the train. She could hardly wait, but he dreaded to see it come, for he did not believe the son would be on it.

When they saw the train pull into the station, the mother ran down the side of it looking at the face of everyone who came out, but the minister stood back watching with much concern. Finally, he saw the woman throw her arms around the neck of a man. Encouraged, he walked down to where they stood. When she had introduced her son to the minister, she, being almost overcome with joy, turned to the son and said, "I know a secret—God has saved you."

He quickly asked who had told her. She answered, "God did, early this morning." Then he told her how he had been saved at a church in the distant city the evening before and had come home to tell her the news. The certainty in the mother's heart of God's faithfulness is one of the most essential elements of real prayer. The driving force in Noah's faith enabled him to face the taunts of the neighbors and launch out on what seemed to be the silliest venture. There was but one explanation for it all: he trusted God.

FAITH AND PATIENCE

We do not know how long Noah waited for the flood to come. It was doubtless a long period; some have said a hundred twenty years. This is purely a guess, as the Bible does not tell us, but it was no doubt far into the years. The long delay was a severe test of the good man's faith. Every day the flood was delayed, doubts, criticism, and teasing had further opportunity to wear him down. It took a far stronger faith for Noah to act after years of delay than it did immediately after the warning from God. The faith that can span the silent years and be unchanged by the delay will meet any test of life or death, time, or eternity, before men or God. Such a faith held on after the original directions had faded from age, the lesser lights had flickered, and time had grown old. Waiting on God is an art that few of us have mastered.

It is told that Adoniram Judson went to Burma as a missionary and preached for six years without a convert. But the delay did not cool his ardor, nor weaken his faith, nor shake his confidence. Finally, God gave him one convert, and the joy of it almost swept him away.[1] The strong missionary churches of that little land are the fruit of a faith that clung to God in spite of the discouragements that tried to overwhelm it.

FAITH AND SUBMISSION

While Noah's faith made him as bold as a lion, it also made him as submissive as a small child. He entered the ark and allowed God to close the door from the outside, for the text says, "The Lord shut him in" (Gen. 7:16). Never was anyone more helpless and dependent. The ark had no engine, no sail, no rudder—no power to make it go, nor to stop it, nor to guide it. If ever a man was nailed in a box and thrown on the wide ocean with no control over his destination, it was this stalwart man of faith. Yet without fear, but with perfect confidence, he committed his life and that of his entire family to God's keeping.

There were many possible dangers. The receding flood would naturally draw the ark to the limitless ocean. There was not one chance in a million for it to land safely; it might strike on the steep slopes of the mountains or be dashed to pieces by the wind and waves. How many potential dangers were ahead! But none of these things seemed to disturb him; his faith kept him anchored to God. Such a faith recognized God at the helm.

This, in fact, was the real test of the whole matter. There might have been ulterior motives behind all his former conduct, but when he entered the ark and submitted to being locked in until the same hand should unlock the door from the outside, this was the real proof of his unwavering trust in God.

FAITH AND SACRIFICE

It is significant that the animals selected for food were also the ones chosen for sacrifice to God. Of these, Noah took seven of a kind, but of the unclean animals he took only two of each kind (Gen. 7:2). We do not know whether he made daily or weekly sacrifices to God, but since it was his custom before entering the ark and continued after he left the ark, we are led to believe he did not discontinue his sacrifices even while he was shut within. Here we are led again to speculate just a little, but it is a speculation that follows lines of reason. Since he did not know how long they would be adrift, the fearful heart would have left off the sacrifices lest there not be enough for food. *How easy for the unbelieving to see hard times ahead!*

I had an excellent member who began cutting down his giving to religious causes, until finally he quit giving altogether. In conversation with him one day, I asked the cause of it. He very frankly told me that he got to thinking about it, and if he should lose his position he could not support his family. I asked if there were any danger of his losing his position, but he knew of none. Then I reminded him of the new car he had recently bought, of the two thousand dollars he had just spent on his home, and of the usual amount of clothing and food he had purchased for his family. How remarkable that his fears came before him only when he thought of giving to the Lord's cause.

This is strange, but it is natural. When we begin to curtail our expenses, we cut off the Lord's part first; if any debt must go unpaid, the church debt is the first to suffer. Too often the church and God get the remnant or what the people can spare without missing, or what cannot be used in a more selfish way.

FAITH AND PERSEVERANCE

The first act of Noah after leaving the ark was to build an altar, call his family around it, and offer a sacrifice to God. Why should a man pray when the danger is past? It would be natural for him to pray when the flood is raging around him, but why be so zealous in religious matters when everything is all right? *This is a distinguishing mark of real faith.* Fear and dangers will bring a person to his knees quickly, but if they do not elicit real faith, the prayers will cease as soon as the perils cease. Some people become very religious when they lose their health, but when they grow stronger they become as profane as before.

There are many ways of testing faith. Some of us are good Christians as long as everything is favorable: health is fine, business is good, the bank accounts are nice and fat, and life is filled with sunshine, flowers, and music. But suppose everything were reversed: health breaks, business fails, accounts dry up, and friends leave. Then what kind of Christians would we be? If you have plenty, you are willing to do your part, and you can be a happy follower of Christ, but if at one stroke you were to lose it all, what would your attitude be then? The right kind of faith will put within us a courage like that of Job's: "Though he slay me, yet will I trust in him" (Job 13:15). Real faith leaps the barriers, outruns the dangers, scorns the very suggestion of doubt, ignores the scoffs and jeers, and declares its confidence in God in the midst of the howling storms.

NOTES

1. Adoniram Judson (1788–1850) went to Burma as a pioneer Baptist missionary in 1813. His work included a Burmese translation of the Bible, which he completed in 1834. See Courtney Anderson, *To the Golden Shore: The Life of Adoniram Judson* (Valley Forge: Judson Press, 1987).

11

THE CREED
OF THE ATHEIST

The fool hath said in his heart, There is no God.
PSALM 14:1

This address is not intended primarily as a vindication of the Christian religion but as an investigation of the claims of the atheist. Such an investigation will, of necessity, bring Christianity into the limelight. It will not be necessary to point out here the shades of difference between the agnostic, the skeptic, the infidel, and the atheist, but for this discussion let them all be grouped into one class, for they all repudiate the Christ and are therefore anti-Christian.[1]

It would be a far more pleasant task to make an appeal for Christ based solely on reason. This is the ground on which the atheist most often takes his stand to make attacks on the Christian religion, and on this ground we are willing to measure swords with the opponent. Or a still greater pleasure would be to fight the battle on the ground of experience. But this would be unfair, since these skeptics have no experience to fall back on, and they would be compelled to fight in the dark.

But since we are to enter the field of the adversary, we must explore his hiding places and discover his strength. We shall therefore ask three questions: First, what is his program? Second, what has he accomplished with his system? Third, what does his system offer mankind?

THE ATHEIST'S PROGRAM

In answering the first question, it will be observed that the text that we have read from the Fourteenth Psalm shows that the atheist's program is purely negative. He makes no claim, he offers no theory, he solves no problem; he seeks only *to destroy the claims of others without offering anything in their place*. A line of reasoning is started in this negative position that must be followed to its logical conclusion if the theory is worth serious thought. If there is no God, then of course there is no Christ, no heaven, no hell, no judgment, and no punishment for sin nor reward for goodness.

This makes the good and the bad equal for all practical purposes. It says to the unprincipled man, "There is no hereafter and no punishment, so do as you please." It takes all moral restraints off the wicked and tells the altruistic that his life is a useless sacrifice since there will be no reward for the deeds done. It is destructive rather than constructive. It concentrates on pulling down the hopes of others rather than trying to build up the broken and discouraged. Such a system hangs suspicion around the neck of the good, raises a question mark after the names of the noblest, and laughs at the humblest and best among mankind.

A negative program is always the way of least resistance. It is easier to deny than it is to affirm and to prove the affirmation. It is easier to criticize than it is to change. The negative farmer may spend his time killing weeds, but if he does not plant any crops his work is all for nothing. The schoolteacher may spend all day finding errors, but until he gives a positive truth, his students learn little. The religionist may find great satisfaction in denying what others believe, but it is worthless warfare unless he can offer a better doctrine and a better purpose.

A most interesting story is told of Henry Ward Beecher: On one occasion when many of the most prominent men of his city were gathered for a banquet in his honor, the noted infidel Ingersoll was seated near the distinguished minister. Throughout the informal part of the evening, the lawyer repeatedly twitted the minister about his religion, but not a word of reply was made.

Finally, the guests began to call for a speech from Dr. Beecher, who, when he arose, told the friends he was unable to speak as he would like, for on his way to the banquet he had seen something that made him very sad, and he had not been able to shake it off. When pressed for an explanation, he told the guests that he saw a crippled child crossing the street on his crutches when a big burly fellow ran into him, kicking the crutches out from under him and sending him sprawling in the mud. Then he ran off without offering any help to the unfortunate child.

On hearing this, Mr. Ingersoll was the first to his feet, exclaiming, "Whoever did that was a brute and should be punished!"

Then Dr. Beecher turned to Mr. Ingersoll and said, "You are that man! Humanity is the child hobbling to God the best way he knows, and you have kicked his crutches out from under him and offered no help."[2] Until the atheist can offer a better way to mankind, he has no right to kick our best hopes to pieces.

The British government had three hundred of the most skilled men of the empire working three years on that great ocean liner the *Lusitania,* and when it was finished, it was the last word in ocean comfort. But one shot from a little German submarine sent the work of three hundred skilled workmen to the bottom of the sea in a few minutes, along with a thousand lives.[3] A child can spoil the work of the artist with an act that requires no skill nor a special kind of instrument. A hog can ruin a beautiful flower garden that has required years to grow and train. An ignorant criminal can spoil the fortune another has spent his life to earn.

It requires no skill to destroy, to ridicule, to deny. The street gossiper who prides himself on criticizing everything designed to help people needs to learn one thing: it requires no thought, principle, character, nor expertise to follow such a course, for the lowest life form in town can do it as well as he.

To tell me there is no God does not help me. It only takes away my best hopes and leaves me without an anchor to my life. As long as I have my belief in God, I am more concerned about spending my life in a worthy way, but when you sweep that hope away, you leave me adrift without a pilot in the midst of a stormy ocean, with my sails torn to shreds and my ship cracking up. A blind fate is my only prospect.

If you tell me there is no God, then where do I find direction for my life? What motive do I have for doing good, or even knowing what *good* is? Where do I find the strength to wade through unexplainable sorrows? I cannot live on a negative program. If you would have me aspire to the highest, then give me a standard above myself. If you would have me be of real service to the world, show me the value of such service. But the program of the atheist offers no standard and no principles; it simply denies the divinity of the ones I hold.

THE ATHEIST'S WORK

There has never been an age entirely free from the influences of skepticism. A few men have stood in almost every community and tried to sway the thinking of the people away from God. Here and there they have formed their little social bands, and in their meetings they attempt to indoctrinate each other, cheer each other, and encourage each other, but such organizations are usually short-lived.

Let us more carefully study the influence of such men and such organizations. What civilizations have they ever built? The former Soviet Union was perhaps the nation most under their power. What of it today? What of its standard of living, social development, school system, government, economic system? What are the results of its history of closing the door against the gospel of Jesus Christ?

I need not discuss them; it is enough to say that the infidels of the world would not live there. It is a land of boundless wealth and resources, but these valuable possessions are nearly useless to the people without God. What has this same influence done for any other country where God is either ruled out or reduced to an image? All the good found in these lands are things that have been taken from Christian lands and governments.

If you ask me for civilizations that Christianity has built, I will point to the societies where moral standards are highest, where progress pushes back the frontier, where the law is able to keep peace, where the public schools and universities stand like lighthouses sending their gleams of hope for a worthwhile life into the darkest corners of the community. These are civilizations built on honor, justice, brotherhood, and peace. These foundation stones will not crumble under the weight of the years.

If you ask for a civilization that has sprung out of the Christian influence, read the story of China and Japan in the last few years, since they have opened their doors to the missionary.[4] They are struggling toward democracy, which recognizes the common people. They have uplifted their women to a more honorable position. They are turning from loveless marriages to ties of mutual love and esteem, and from such will come better citizens and more stable governments. What nation was ever influenced by atheism to regard the value of the common man?

What institutions have atheists built? Christianity built our colleges, hospitals, orphans homes, and humane societies, but what has atheism built? Let it bring out its record of accomplishments if it would claim a place in the world. If it would pull down a cause with such a constructive program, what has it to offer in its place?

What individual has atheism helped? Where is there one alcoholic who has been enabled to overcome his addiction by the powerful influence of skepticism or atheism? Name one convict who has been convinced of his wrongdoing and been led to a better path through these influences. What wrong has atheism righted? What feud has it settled? Such questions could be asked for hours, and no reply could be made. But if you ask the same questions relative to the influence of Christianity, the world could hardly contain the books and libraries of personal testimonies—of reprobates who have been made honorable, of liars who have learned to speak the truth, and of outcasts covered with shame who have been restored to wholeness by Jesus Christ.[5]

What spirit has it put into the people? Christianity's teachings are to love your enemies, to do good for evil, to pray for those who hate you, to give without expecting to receive again, looking to God for the reward. But what have been the teachings of atheism to its devotees? If someone hurts you, sue him; if another insults you, deliver one better back at him. Atheists' motto is "Look out for number one." And their one overriding priority is to exert their freedom to express the darkest and most degrading impulses that ever crossed a human brain.

THE ATHEIST'S OUTCOME

Just as atheism has no record of which to boast and no standard of morals to offer the world, even so it has *no hopes to give the oppressed.* It is a frequent thing that people who hear a sermon or a song or read the Bible are led to contemplate the eternal values their lives are lacking. They feel guilt and the need of forgiveness. What has the atheist to say to these people? He can only make a joke of their sin or try to convince them that their convictions are tricks and that listening to the preacher plays on weak minds.

Christianity does not treat these feelings as a joke. It looks on sin as a cold and stubborn fact and the most dangerous condition a person could be in. But Christianity recognizes a resolution. There is a Savior who can erase what seemed indelible and write out a new course. He can change circumstances and character. He can restore the broken life and heal the wounded heart beyond what we dared to believe possible. The witnesses to this fact are so numerous that they could join hands and form a chain around the earth, as they have done by their testimony.

What hope does atheism offer to the good? None. It tells them that their sacrifice, work, and faithful service will all go unrewarded. No one will take account of their selfless acts. Their lives are all for nothing. They have spent their wealth and will gain nothing; they have given themselves to useless labor for people who cannot repay them, and there is no God to notice. What they have poured out of themselves is a loss never to be regained.

How unreal this sounds to the person who has really put Christ to the test! Our labor and sacrifice are in the name and for the glory of Christ who has redeemed us, and we are assured that he notices (Matt. 25:40). But even if there were no reward in the life to come, the privilege of doing it for the One who has given us life is reward enough. We would do it for him even if we were plainly told that there would be no recognition in heaven.

What does atheism have to say to the one dying? It has followed him through life, snatching every hope out of his heart, making fun of every serious thought, and acting as shade to the light nearby. Now that he has reached the end of his life, what word has the skeptic for the dying man? The best word he has is that this is the last of him; tomorrow he will be put in the ground, the grass will soon cover the place, and the world will soon forget him. The brief little light that flickered through the years has now gone out forever. What hopeless despair! Better never to have lived at all. Better to have died in infancy and escaped all the pain, sorrow, disappointments, and heartaches of the unjust and capricious life.

But Christianity comes with a different word. It assures one that the grave is not the end; there is One who keeps his soul and at some future day will raise him to live forever. There is One who sees every righteous act and hears every longing of the faithful soul. When the mother gives up her baby and it is laid in the little grave, if she looks to atheism for comfort, it will break her heart. But if she looks to Christ, he will come with the silent embrace of understanding and assurance that the child yet lives.[6]

Suppose the attitudes of dying men should be compared. Contrast the last words or actions of those who have died without God and those who have died trusting God. What have they said and done? In 1679, Thomas Hobbes, the most noted infidel of that century, died, and among his last words were, "I am about to take my last voyage, a great leap in the dark."[7] Not very reassuring, is it?

Voltaire, the great French materialist, suffered such anxiety over what would become of his body after death that he went to extraordinary lengths to obtain a resting place consecrated by the church he had despised all of his life.[8] And likewise, Thomas Paine, approaching death at seventy-three, requested to be buried in a Quaker cemetery. The refusal upset him considerably.[9] Now if all religion is foolishness, why were these great thinkers so concerned with being interred in sacred ground? Who wants to spend his final hours agonizing over where his body shall rot?

But now listen to the last words of saved men. Immediately before Stephen was stoned to death, he said, "'Behold, I see the heavens opened, and the Son of man standing at the right hand of God. . . . Lord Jesus, receive my spirit'" (Acts 7:56, 59 RSV).

The testimony of Paul was equally joyful. He was slandered, beaten, and imprisoned for his hope. Finally, he was martyred, but the last word recorded from him was: "I am already on the point of being sacrificed; the time of my departure has come. I have fought the good fight, I have finished the race, I have kept the faith. Henceforth there is laid up for me the crown of righteousness, which the Lord, the righteous judge, will award to me on that Day, and not only to me but also to all who have loved his appearing" (2 Tim. 4:6–8 RSV).

William McKinley had built his character and life on the principles of the Christian religion. When he was shot by an anarchist, President McKinley's immediate reaction was to implore the crowd not to harm his assailant. In like manner, Woodrow Wilson, the greatest Christian statesman and national figure of his day, when the cold hand of death laid hold of him and he saw the end was near, told his physician, "The machinery is broken. I am ready."[10] The record of such testimonies could be multiplied indefinitely. Any laments or regrets that Christians express at death are not the frantic clawing of someone slipping over the edge of a cliff.

If the world is to decide the question of whether there is a God or not and decide it in the light of reason (which is the hobby of the atheist), let the finished product of Christianity and infidelity stand beside each other. Let the lives lived according to their teachings be evaluated for the benefit we who are left behind have received. We would risk the conclusions in the hands of the skeptics themselves.

NOTES

1. *Agnostic:* one who considers it impossible to know whether there is a God or not. *Skeptic:* one who doubts any religious doctrine, especially Christianity. *Infidel:* one who does not believe in the prevailing religion of his society. *Atheist:* one who believes there is no God. (*Webster's*)

2. Robert Green Ingersoll (1833–1899), lawyer and orator. To put this exchange in perspective: "With Beecher, he [Ingersoll] began a warm friendship that itself became the subject of a great deal of humor, particularly when they occupied the same [campaign] platform." David D. Anderson, *Robert Ingersoll* (New York: Twayne Publishers, Inc., 1972), 71.

3. See Thomas A. Bailey and Paul B. Ryan, *The Lusitania Disaster* (New York: The Free Press, 1975).

4. Dr. Melton's comments about China are relevant today. See Philip P. Pan, "China seizing churches in crackdown: Communist Party trying to contain religious revival," *Dallas Morning News,* 19 December 2000.

5. Dr. Melton does not devote so much as a sentence to the spurious claim that Christianity was responsible for such atrocities as the Spanish Inquisition and the excesses of the Crusades. In the final chapter he does discuss the fate of hypocrites who wear a mask of Christianity over un-Christian lives.

6. Scriptural support for the belief that children who die before the age of accountability return to the Father is strong. Consider Matthew 19:14: "'Let the children come to me, and do not hinder them; for to such belongs the kingdom of heaven'" (RSV); Matthew 18:10: "'See that you do not despise one of these little ones; for I tell you that in heaven their angels always behold the face of my Father who is in heaven'" (RSV); and the biblical principle that God takes the strongest measures to save us when we are the most helpless.

7. Verified in John Bartlett, ed., *Familiar Quotations* (Boston: Little, Brown, & Co., 1980).

8. Haydn Mason, *Voltaire: A Biography* (Baltimore: The Johns Hopkins University Press, 1981), 147–50.

9. Alfred Owen Aldridge, *Man of Reason: The Life of Thomas Paine* (Philadelphia: J. B. Lippincott Co., 1959), 315.

10. Tom Shachtman, *Edith and Woodrow* (New York: G. P. Putnam's Sons, 1981), 271.

12

A PARABLE
OF THE CLOCKS

*"Shall the shadow go forward ten degrees,
or go back ten degrees?"*
2 Kings 20:9

Hezekiah, one of the early kings of the Jews, was desperately
ill. Isaiah, the contemporary prophet of the land, was sent
with a message from God to tell Hezekiah to get his affairs in
order, for he was about to die. The prophet delivered his
message and went away. In grief Hezekiah turned his face to
the wall, wept, and prayed that God would remember his
obedience.

God heard his prayer and sent Isaiah back to tell him that
fifteen years would be added to his life. But the sick man
wanted to know that the promise came from God and not
just from the prophet, so he asked what proof Isaiah could

show him. Isaiah asked him if he wanted the shadow on the sundial to go forward ten degrees or back ten degrees. In our day we would say, "Do you want it to be forty minutes later or forty minutes earlier?" And as a token of God's promise to the sick king, the sun was called ten degrees backward.

It is not the sick king that I call attention to, nor to the good prophet, nor even to God who performed the miracle, but rather to the little insignificant sundial. There have been many kinds of instruments to mark the progress of time. We do not know when such things began to be used, but we find them far back in the earliest pages of history. The sundial, the hourglass, the clepsydra (which marks the time by water passing through a small tube), and the clock have each served its time and generation.

The clock itself has passed through many stages of development, and there are many styles and makes today, but all of them go back to the sundial for their origin. They claim kin with all the many contrivances throughout human history that have kept the nations of the world in step with each other and with the sun in its journey through the heavens. The sundial made way for the hourglass, the hourglass for the clepsydra, the clepsydra for the primitive clock, and the primitive timekeeper for the modern masterpiece of the present day, but these have all marked the progress of the same sun. As technology has advanced, each in turn has gone to the junk heap, but the sun has remained unchanged through all the shifting scenes.

The shadow on the sundial was nothing more than a confirmation of the new lease on Hezekiah's life, and the sun that cast the shadow did not add one minute to his years. These were agents in the hand of God to make his will known. Too often we give praise to the agent or instrument and forget that the real source of all blessing is God. The sun did not quicken its step toward the evening but backed up toward the fresh and jubilant morning, as if to make the day fuller, allow in more blessings, or freshen the wasting hours of life.

And thus the dial on which the shadows fell stood a mute but powerful witness to the mercy of God on this once-doomed king. Every time he passed that way he must have paused to give thanks for the added blessings—not to the sundial or to the sun, but to God. The time-marker was a continual witness to answered prayer and to the surety of God's promises for renewed life and opportunities. But it also stood as a reminder that the fifteen additional years were swiftly passing by and would soon be gone. Even so, the clock of the present day may be our friend or our foe. It may be a witness in our favor or against us; it may seem to mark time all too fast or slowly let the hours drag by. How often the silent timepiece has been placed in court to tell its secrets.

THE OLD REGULATOR

Some years ago I entered the store of a jeweler who had received a recent shipment of clocks. They were of many sizes and kinds, and all had been wound and started without any agreement as to time. Some of them indicated one hour and some another. No two told the same tale—while one was striking twelve, another was striking six, and maybe another three. My attention was immediately arrested by the confusion, and I began laughing.

The storekeeper inquired the cause of my amusement, and I told him that I had never seen so many timepieces in one room and remained so ignorant of the real time. If by accident some of the clocks told the correct time, others telling a different time made it so confusing that no one could be sure which was right.

But the merchant pointed to an old "regulator" hanging in the corner of the room, whose tick was slow and steady, and said, "There is the correct time. These clocks have not been regulated or set, but that old clock in the corner is checked up every hour by government time." At first, I went my way with little thought of the incident, but all day new lessons kept springing into my mind, and I was called again and again to compare my life with those clocks.

What is the regulator of life? The Bible. Leaders, organizations, institutions, and such things are like the little clocks: they are telling a false tale unless they are in harmony with the Old Regulator. This is the unchanging, unwavering spokesman for all eternity on the great fundamentals it contains. We may find ourselves greatly confused over the different interpretations and expressions of religious truth given out by the hundreds of denominations in the land, all differing and all claiming to be the divinely appointed teachers of God's truth. But if anyone finds himself thus confused and desires the last word of authority on the subject, let him turn aside from all the little clocks and look to the Regulator that never goes wrong. Go there for your doctrine, for your creed, and for your standard of living.

Clocks do not make time, they simply mark it and divide it. Neither do churches nor the Bible make truth. Things are not true and right because the church holds them or because they are in the Bible; these same things were true before there was a Bible or a church. They were later given recognition in the Bible and in the churches because they were right and just.

We often find ourselves embarrassed because we have been misled by unreliable timepieces. We have missed flights or been late for appointments because our watches stopped or our alarm clocks did not go off. And so it has been with many through the years who have listened to false teachers about the things of God. Instead of going directly to the Bible, the Old Regulator, they have gone to the little clocks and have received an erroneous report.

Too many people allow a minister, a friend, or a parent to do the thinking for them on all matters of religion. They are too willing to accept the decision of others and rest the case on conclusions others have drawn. Religion is a personal matter. Each individual must do his own thinking, reach his own conclusions, and learn firsthand what the will of God is concerning all great moral issues. If we are content to accept without question the decisions of others, we may find ourselves embarrassed at where they take us. Rather, let each one go to the Bible for himself or herself and learn in the school of God the great fundamental lessons upon which we must build our lives and hopes.

THE CLOCK SET WRONG

My illustration furnished another lesson I pass on to you. The fact that some of the clocks were wrong did not mean that they were worthless timekeepers. They had been wound *without being properly set.* They were wrong because they were started wrong.

How much depends on the start anywhere! Many have lost their usefulness in life because of the start they had. If they are converted late in life, they can never regain the missed opportunities of lost years. And growing up in a home with hardship and abuse requires years of healing and stabilizing before one can move forward. We all recognize the great achievement of someone who has overcome such early disadvantages to live a worthwhile life. This makes it a matter of great importance in every home and in every church to safeguard the early years of a young Christian. It will prove to be a fortification to him for the rest of his life.

TOO SLOW OR TOO FAST

Learn another lesson from the clocks. *Some of them run too slow;* they cannot keep up with the regulator. Turn them forward every morning and give them an even start, and by the next morning they are behind again. They must be set every day. Some Christians lose their usefulness and their joy because they run too slow.

I knew a good deacon who always lived in the past. He was constantly comparing present-day things with those of fifty years before. To him, religion was not what it had been previously. Preaching was different, too, and the change was not for the better. Nothing was as good as it used to be. This brother was not happy because he was not keeping up. There was much good around him, but he missed it because it did not have on the dress it wore fifty years ago. He was no doubt saved, but he was miserable because he was out of harmony with anything in the present age. He was running too slow.

But other clocks outrun the rest—*they run too fast.* And any Christian who runs too fast needs regulating worse than the one who runs too slow. We fear that too many among us today are running too fast. They have laid aside too much of the "old-time" religion and have become too caught up with fads.

Whenever someone professing to be a Christian lays aside the Bible as the inspired Book, he is running too fast. Or when he thinks he has discovered a shortcut to God other than the road of repentance and faith, this person needs to slow down; he is running away. Whoever denies the divinity of Christ, the divine authority of the Bible, the necessity of regeneration, the efficacy of prayer, the work of the Holy Spirit, and the other doctrines confirmed by the early church may be a member of a church, but it is our opinion that he is an infidel and not a Christian. He runs too fast to be a Christian. He is not in time with the Old Regulator.

NOT THE CASE BUT THE WORKS

The value of a clock is not determined by the beauty of its case. One of the most beautiful clocks I ever saw was a worthless, unreliable timekeeper. If measured by appearance, it would stand at the top of the list, but if measured by trustworthiness, it would be thrown in the trash. The likeness of people to clocks does not break down at this point of the analogy. You cannot measure others by their physical appearance or even by their intellectual advantages. *The person is measured by his spirit.* One's loyalty, trustworthiness, and altruistic spirit—these mean far more to the world than one's wealth, education, position, physical appearance, or reputation. The external life of a person is to the case of a clock what the spirit is to the works of the clock. And just as a good clock may be housed in a poor case, or a worthless clock be found in an excellent case, likewise, a person of striking physical appearance and advantages may have a mean spirit, and a body of insignificant appearance may be the house of a great soul.

I heard the story of a mountaineer who had seen a magnificent clock on exhibit in the town where he had gone to do his trading. It was of the old weight-type that was wound every day and would run until the weights hit the bottom of the clock, then would stop. He was so attracted by its beauty that he sold his produce and purchased it. After he had set it up in his little mountain cabin for his wife to admire, he had the neighbors from miles around come to see his prize.

It did well for some days, but one morning about daybreak something went wrong with the old clock. It began striking and did not quit until it ran down. The old man lay in his bed and counted far past the hour of day, past twelve, then twenty, thirty, fifty, and to seventy, before it ran down. When it stopped, he jumped out of bed and yelled to his wife, "Mirandy, get up quick! I never saw it so late in my life!"

The professions of some people are very loud, but their actions are limited. They talk a lot and do a little. They make many promises but seldom keep them.

JUDGED BY THE HANDS

The striking and the hands of a clock should be in perfect harmony. If the hands indicate three o'clock, it should strike three and not some other number. How necessary that the *professions* of Christians be *backed by consistent lives!* What the lips say, the silent life should say. What the public life says, the private life should say. And if there is lack of harmony, which is discredited, the striking or the hands? The striking. The hour indicated by the hands will be accepted before the one told by the stroke. In like manner, if there is lack of harmony between one's life and one's profession, which is discredited? The profession, not the life.

The story is told of a man who came into a jeweler's store with two old clock hands. He threw them on the showcase and asked the jeweler if he could do anything for his old clock. The jeweler asked where the clock was. The man replied, " 'Tain't nothin' wrong with the clock. The hands jest quit runnin'." He was informed that the trouble was deeper than the hands. If the clock were fixed, the hands would be right.

This is a very practical lesson. When a person's hands steal or his tongue lies or his feet lead him into the wrong places, the trouble is not with the hands, tongue, or feet; it is deeper than that. For the real trouble to be found, you will have to go to the heart. If you will adjust the spiritual condition of this person, then his hands, feet, eyes, tongue, and all other members will mostly behave themselves. The heart of all our troubles is the trouble with our heart. Behind every deed is a desire, and behind the desire is a principle. Behind the principle is an actuating spirit, and behind the spirit is the fountain of life out of which spring all things, good and bad.

Here is where Christianity surpasses all the religions of the world. The rest deal with the deeds, the external part of life; but Christianity deals with the heart, the fountain of life. Reformation will lead a sinner to leave off the worst deeds, correct his speech, and improve the general tone of his life, but Christianity purifies the heart so the principles of justice and righteousness will naturally express themselves in a better life.

Faithful When Unseen

Let the clocks speak again. *The unheard ticking at midnight is as important as that during the day.* Suppose an old clock on a winter's night should say, "It is foolish for me to be so careful to tick through this long, cold night. Everyone is asleep, and no one will hear when I strike or tick. I will quit until morning, then about the time for the family to get up, I will begin again and no one will know differently." Isn't this ridiculous reasoning? Every child in the house will know the difference. The clock's disloyalty and deception will be self-evident. They cannot be hid.

Yet some people are foolish enough to think they can do just this. They are away from home and are wholly unknown in this particular place. Talk from here will never reach home, so they dare to do what they would not do among acquaintances. They say, "No one will ever know." This is just like that silly clock. People *will* know. They may not know the specific sin nor the time and place it was committed, but they will know something has gone wrong. Your world will feel the loss of power; others will see the inefficiency and the lack of usefulness of other days. When you pray, they will know it. When you rise to speak and your words fall empty to the ground, they will know it. When you try to teach or lead as in other days, your audience will be impressed by your inability to do it with the results of former times. Daylight will reveal the midnight secrets. Silent betrayal will eventually speak out.

I was visiting in a home where my hostess pointed to a clock on the mantel and said, "Do you see that old clock? It has been in our family for more than fifty years and has never missed a stroke." Such a record is enviable. Through the long years of more than half a century, it had served the family with a faithfulness that merited the praise of two generations. It had been the silent witness of many events—births, deaths, marriages, dinners, receptions, private crises, and hundreds of forgotten incidents. Through them all, no one had to wonder what time it was. What a testimony to the value of long and faithful service!

Suppose the same could be said of us. What if Christians had such records of loyalty? It would have a tremendous effect on the world. It would mean far more than sermons to the lost. It would have a convincing power to outstrip the logic of the world. The dungeon door of evil would crumble before such lives. Such loyalty would silence the critics of Christ. It would close nine-tenths of the devil's businesses for lack of patronage. Let every church member keep holy things holy, and the unsaved would be ashamed not to. Christians who run as they were set earn the respect and open-mindedness of the rest of the world.

THE CLOCK THAT RAN ON ITS FACE

People are like clocks in another way. I had a little alarm clock that would not run unless it was lying on its face. *It had to be in a certain position, or it would not run at all.* This point of the illustration does not have to be strained at all for it to include a multitude. People will serve well and be happy if you have everything just right for them, but if something is moved in the least, they quit.

A most excellent family came for membership where I was pastor on one occasion, and we felt that we had made great gain that day by the family's coming. After the service the man informed me that he had served in a certain capacity in the church from which he came and would like to have a similar place with us. I told him the man in that office was well suited for the place, and we could not make a change there at that time, but we would give him another place until there was an opening in that position; then we would put him in.

This was more than he could stand. It seemed to him that we should be willing to make any change for his satisfaction. He came a few Sundays but soon quit entirely and was never of any service to our church. What a contrast with another man who came for membership about the same time. He said, "Anywhere you need me, use me." He was not always dissatisfied with his place but ready for any task anywhere and did his best without a murmur.

THE MOST IMPORTANT PART OF A CLOCK

Someone might ask, "What is the most important part of a clock?" I would answer that every part is the most important. A clock cannot be its best if there is a single broken cog in it. Not a spring can be broken, not a wheel out of line, not a screw missing, but that the entire timepiece feels the damage and is rendered less useful by it.

The importance of each individual member of the church may be illustrated by this point of the analogy. No church can be perfect unless *the individual members* are perfect. The church approaches the limit of its ability and possibility just in proportion to the number of members in place, functioning as they should. If one person in the church be out of synchronization, it jars the whole machinery. Or as long as there is one member who will not function, who cannot be depended on to keep time, the efficiency of that church is limited. Do not be the broken cog in the wheel. With all your power make the entire assembly feel the thrill of your harmonious movement.

THE CLOCK THAT MUST BE WARMED UP

I was once the proud possessor of a clock that kept good time in the summer, but was worthless in winter. It would run during the day when the room was warm, but after nightfall when the fires died down, it would freeze up and stop. *It had to be warmed up before it would run.* The application is not hard to see. That type of Christian is not as scarce as we wish it were. As long as the revival lasts, or as long as the church-going habit lasts, such a Christian is joyful and willing to do any duty assigned. He cannot see why everybody does not go to church and enjoy his religion. But this fever soon passes, and he is heard from no more until the next revival meeting comes.

As Loyal as the Clock

My family went away from home for a week during the summer. When we returned, the old clock was ticking away as if somebody's life hung on every stroke of the pendulum. Nobody had been there to hear it, nor to praise it, nor even to benefit from it, yet it performed its duty still. You say it is only a piece of machinery and knows no duty. This is true, but there are men and women in the world as loyal as that clock. They are assigned a task, and nobody stays to check up on their work, but they do it as conscientiously as if the minutest detail would be inspected. And there are many who live as honestly and purely in the dark as they would if they were being watched by the world. And there are many more who would account for every cent entrusted to them even if they knew they could take it all and never be caught. These people do not need to be watched to keep them going, to keep them straight, or to keep them from swindling their fellow man. They are more faithful than the clock that ticks the days away when no one is there to watch it.

Dirt will stop a clock. This is true of the little invisible particles in the room as well as of a larger quantity being thrown into the works. If neglected, the clock will lose time and then stop altogether because of the accumulated dirt and dust. The Christian life and influence are not only hindered by the outbreaking, shameful sins, but also the little thoughtless accumulations of evil—the uncontrolled temper, the "cuss words" that are so closely akin to vulgarity and profanity, the little advantage one takes of another. Many such things may come into one's life, and because they are not so shocking as tragic sins are, they are considered unimportant.

But as surely as airborne dust will hinder the timepiece, so will these little unguarded sins finally sap one's life of power and usefulness as a Christian. Self-examination before God, as in a revival, is as necessary for the spirit as regular cleaning and maintenance are for the clock. But as no clock ought to spend all the time in the shop, neither should any Christian have to be kept in a revival atmosphere all the time in order to work.

13

WHAT THEIR EYES DID NOT SEE

And sitting down they watched him there.
MATTHEW 27:36

The text describes the conduct of the crucifiers of Christ. When they had performed their official duty, and the condemned men were hanging on their ugly crosses in full view of the crowd, the soldiers sat down with a sigh of relief and fixed their eyes on the central figure, Jesus of Nazareth, who had been the subject of many remarks for the past three years. The thieves dying with him were nothing. But this man was the marvel of the age. He who had healed hopeless cripples and even raised the dead was himself condemned to die. The miracle worker could not save himself, so with curious eyes they looked on his torture and agony as a deserved fate and waited for the end to come.

THE MYSTERY OF THE DARKNESS

Some have endeavored to show what these curious onlookers saw that day, but it shall be my task to show what they missed seeing—to point out the things that transpired before their eyes, yet went unheeded. And the first mystery that passed before them was the darkness so graphically described by the sacred writers. True, the people saw the darkness, but that is all they saw. *God came slipping through that darkness,* and they failed to see him. To them it may have been seen as a very natural occurrence, merely an eclipse of the sun. And many of the enemies of Christ to this day try to explain away that phenomenon by saying that it was a solar eclipse. My answer to these critics is that it was not a natural thing at all, but the most unnatural thing that could happen at the time.

You will bear in mind that the crucifixion of Christ took place at the great feast of the Passover, which falls on the fourteenth of Nisan (March-April) on the Jewish calendar. This feast always took place at the full moon.[1] Now whoever thinks at all will know that the sun cannot be in eclipse when the moon is full. A solar eclipse is caused by the moon passing between the sun and the earth, thereby obscuring the sun for a brief time. But when the moon is full, it is at such an angle as to reflect the full brightness of the sun back to the earth!

But another reason why it could not have been a natural eclipse is the length of the darkness. Astronomers will tell you that a total eclipse of the sun cannot last over seven minutes anywhere on earth, but this darkness lasted three hours

(Matt. 27:45), making it impossible to explain on natural grounds. There can be but one explanation: God hid the face of the sun so wicked eyes could not gaze on the holy sacrifice. It was the last kind act of God to his Son when he was dying. Yes, these guards saw the darkness, but they failed to see God in the darkness.

THE EARTHQUAKE

God came in another form that day and passed before their eyes, but they failed to see him. *He visited them in the form of an earthquake.* But there have been many earthquakes, so what was different about that one? And some have maintained that the earthquake on this day was as all other such occurrences. Yet we see that if the reports of the phenomenon are reliable, it was in a class by itself. It burst open the graves of many of the righteous, woke them from their sleep of death, and sent them alive into the streets of Jerusalem to be seen and recognized by their friends.

This is unusual behavior for an earthquake. The history of such things has been to the contrary. These tremors are usually agents of death, but this one was a bearer of life. Others have filled the graves with lifeless bodies, but this one emptied the graves of their corpses. To the guards on the slopes of Calvary, it was nothing but a natural thing. To us, it was the shudder of God. Not only was the earth shrouded with darkness, but it reeled as a drunken man under a terrible blow. If this earthquake were a natural thing, it would have been harder to explain than to admit it was unnatural. But since it occurred at the time of the darkness and at the time Christ, the strangest man on earth, was being put to death, the question would naturally be raised, "How could so many natural things of such magnitude happen at the same time?"

THE RENDING OF THE VEIL

During the darkness, at the same moment the earthquake struck, the veil in the temple was torn completely in two, from top to bottom. This heavy curtain separated the outer holy place from the holy of holies. No one but the high priest went behind that curtain where the ark of the covenant stood. There he appeared once a year with the blood of the sacrifice to make atonement for the people (see Heb. 9). But when Christ was dying, that veil was rent by an unseen hand so that not a thread was left holding it together.

It may be claimed that the earthquake did it. But the temple was not damaged by the quake. The pillars that supported the roof were not moved. The building remained intact for another seventy years, during which time there is no record of rebuilding or repairs. Why should the curtain be torn apart when no other damage came to the holy place?

These men whose eyes were blinded by sin saw the rending of the veil, but they saw no hand nor power that rent it. God was in their temple, but they failed to see him. He came pushing aside their forms, ceremonies, priests, and ritualistic services and *opened access to the mercy seat to each worshiper.* God made it possible for the common people to approach him for themselves, without the intervention of priests or middlemen. They need no longer bring their sacrifices, for one sacrifice has been offered for all, even Jesus Christ, who was "the Lamb slain from the foundation of the world" (Rev. 13:8). Each believer may come for himself, pray for himself, and present his own cause to God.

The priests of Israel were sinful (as we all are), but here is a high priest without sin. The priests of the house of Levi died as everyone does, but here is a priest from heaven who will never die. The rending of that veil was the announcement of a new day for all the world. The Christian religion was to be a matter of personal relationship of the individual with God. There is not one step in all the Christian walk that can be taken by proxy. One cannot repent for another, nor can one have faith for another. Neither can one be saved for another, nor consecrate his life for another, nor live righteously for another, nor die for another. These are personal matters.

You have the same right and privilege to pray to God that a preacher or priest has, and God will hear you as quickly, if you come in the proper spirit, as he will these spiritual teachers. They may teach you about God, but you must trust him for yourself. They may instruct you in prayer, but you must do the praying. The rending of that veil, and the exposing of the mercy seat, demonstrated that there was now nothing between the common people and God—the chasm had been bridged (see John 1:51). The day of priests, rituals, and sacrifices as a means of approaching God had been done away with, and the throne of God became within reach of every soul.

CHRIST'S CRY OF ANGUISH

Just before Christ died, he gave a cry that was misunderstood by that group of watchers. He cried, "My God, my God, why hast thou forsaken me?" (Matt. 27:46). They thought he cried for physical pain and offered him a stupefying drug. But he refused it. The source of that distress was far deeper than physical pain. *God had withdrawn his presence from him,* and for the first time in his life, Christ felt the loneliness of soul that will come to the lost when they stand condemned before God. He died as the lost will die. And as surely as the lost will die without God, forsaken and alone, so Christ passed through the same dreadful experience. And just as certainly as the lost will be forsaken in death, so was Christ forsaken in his death. These men who sat down to watch him die heard the words he spoke, but how little they understood him!

When Paul wished to paint the darkest picture possible of the unsaved condition, he could think of no stronger words to use than "having no hope, and without God" (Eph. 2:12). And when Christ passed through the ordeal of his betrayal and death, he bore it without a word until he found himself cut off from God. This seemed more than he could stand and proved the greatest trial of all. It was such a blow that it wrung the only wail of his life from his lips, and it was the only experience in life for which he seemed unprepared. It was a literal hell to him. And it will be a literal hell to the lost soul to be cut off forever from the presence of God. The absence of God will be one of the pangs that will make hell indescribable.

THE RESURRECTION

The last misunderstood fact connected with the death of Christ that I have the time to enlarge upon is *his resurrection.* They who watched him die were also assigned the task of watching his tomb after he was dead. He was one dead man the Pharisees were afraid of. They said they were afraid of his body being stolen by his friends, but we believe they were afraid he might really make good his promise to rise again. So they sealed the stone of the tomb and set an armed guard to watch for trespassers. When that trespasser came, he caused such consternation among the guards that they all fainted dead away.

And when they woke up, they had a problem on their hands. They could not deny what had happened; they could not keep it secret, and they could not explain it.[2] Jesus was a bigger threat now than before. That empty grave mocked them every time they saw it. Every child on the street must have twitted them because they could not keep a dead man in his grave. The embarrassment became dreadful. But this unheard-of phenomenon meant very little to them apart from the physical side and the temporary complication. It was crowded with eternal truth, which they completely missed.

What great doctrines sprang out of the Resurrection? Several, but we shall enumerate four. *It gave us a new book, the New Testament.* Before the Resurrection, the world had just half a Bible, the Old Testament. It was a book of promises and prophecies but still just part of the story of God's redemptive efforts on our behalf. After the Resurrection of

Christ, historians began to record what happened, and the good news spread everywhere. And in time the most accurate of these writings were gathered into the New Testament.

It is the story of the risen Lord. If he had never come from the grave, these books would never have been written, for the world would not be interested in the story of a dead Christ. But the fact that he lives again charges the world with hope as lightning pierces the sky. That empty tomb is the source, fountain, and authority of a new message. It is the foundation of a new hope. It is the promise and guarantee of a new life. It is the inspiration of a new zeal. It is the appeal for a new consecration.

The second great doctrine that sprang out of the resurrection of the Lord was *a new holy day*. For ages, the Jews observed Saturday as the holy day. The followers of the risen Lord had no thought of changing the custom. They doubtless met according to tradition on the regular Jewish Sabbath. But on Sunday morning, a week after the Lord had come from the tomb, they must have met in a kind of celebration of the great event that had taken place a week before. This did not take the place of their worship on Saturday, neither did they decide to put aside that holy day. But another week passed, and by agreement they came together again on Sunday morning to worship him on the anniversary of his resurrection. This followed week after week until it became a custom by which they were known and by which they eventually bound themselves.

That rule has prevailed for almost two thousand years. The fact that we observe Sunday rather than Saturday is the testimony of our belief in the resurrection of Jesus Christ. These watchers by the tomb looked upon an empty grave, but they did not know what that vacant sepulcher would mean to the generations to come. Little did they think that the map of the world would be remade around it, and the divisions of time would be rearranged over its door. How little they saw compared to what they failed to see!

A third voice from the empty tomb is *a new institution, the church.* The Jews had been bound together by national ties, and their pride was in the unity and exclusiveness of their race. It was a thing to be gloried in that God was their God and not the Gentiles' God. They had no message and no hope to offer the other races of earth.

But following the resurrection of Christ, his friends and followers found themselves bound by new ties into a new brotherhood, with a new vision of life and a new obligation. They no longer looked for racial differences but threw their doors open to Gentiles as well as Jews, on the condition that those who came to accept this Christ as Lord believe in his resurrection from the dead and be willing to accept his teachings as the standard of life (see Gal. 3:28).

This little band of worshipers came up against bitter and stubborn opposition, but they continued to give the message of his resurrection to every person they met and to provide for its being told to unborn generations. This was a new institution with a new task and a new sense of responsibility and direction. How different it was from the Jewish national order based on forms and ceremonies rather than on a personal, spiritual contact of the individual with God. But when these armed guards looked into that bare vault from which the Lord had so recently come, they figured the excitement would soon die down and that the rolling years would blot out every trace of it.

But not so. After the stretch of centuries, skeptics are still busy trying to cover up that empty grave or explain its emptiness. But the more they explain, the more explaining they have to do, for the church with its millions of believers has circled the earth and has told the story of his resurrection in almost every land. An army of freedmen has discovered its truth.

This new, missionary, altruistic band of believers is one of the results of the raising to life of the slain Lord. And this institution would have never existed had Christ remained dead. If it is objected that the church was organized before the death of Christ rather than after his resurrection, let the answer be that it was invested with the authority and message of the risen Lord. Had he never been raised, the organization would have died before another convert was made.

The last voice of the open grave is *a new ordinance, baptism.* This is a New Testament ordinance, springing out of a New Testament condition and teaching a New Testament doctrine. Given in advance of the death of the Lord, it was a prophecy and pledge of his death, burial, and resurrection. And during the following years, the Christians took this means of publicly proclaiming their belief in his resurrection, by being submerged in water and raised up again.

This became the symbol of his discipleship. It was the pledge of a new life to be patterned after his and a prophecy of a new hope that one day all his believers would be raised up from the grave by his power. For centuries it has been a uniform custom that when one accepts Jesus as a Savior, he submits to the ordinance of baptism as a public announcement of his belief in the risen Lord. The form of this ordinance is as valuable as the authority of the church, the New Testament, or the Lord's day, for they all derive their origin and authority from the empty grave. One cannot be changed any easier than another, since they all sprang from the same sepulcher.

THE GRACE OF THE LORD JESUS

When the Roman officers sat down to watch him on the cross, what did they see? They saw a defenseless man die with hardly a word. No complaint, no criticism for anyone, no denial of the charges made against him, no justification of his claims, no rebuke of any kind. Such silence and such behavior were far from human. They publicly displayed a grace not known among men. Humans would have gone to the grave denying the false charges and with their last breath declaring their innocence. But he was silent, because he was a willing sacrifice.

In like manner, he proved the merit of his teachings by living up to his own standards. He turned the other cheek to those who struck him, which proved his teaching was not a mere theory but a practical rule of life. He also prayed for those who persecuted him, again establishing his authority to teach others to do likewise. He taught us how to treat our enemies, how to forgive, how to bear insults, how to behave in trouble and sorrow.

Poets have caught his spirit and have clothed it in words that have become immortal. Artists have expressed it on canvas in pictures of undying fame. Singers and musicians have moved their audiences to tears with the thrill of it. Those disinterested soldiers watched a man die that day who made such a profound impact on the world that his influence spreads and deepens every decade. How little did they know they were participating in a world event! How little did they think their actions would be read about by every succeeding generation and that their victim would be worshiped in every nation on earth!

THE SILENCE IN HEAVEN

But they failed to see another thing. The angels were witnesses of that same scene, and we are not wholly in the dark as to their behavior during that time. A little passage in Revelation 8:1 tells us that "there was silence in heaven about the space of half an hour." Certain Bible scholars have interpreted this to refer to the time of the Crucifixion. Whether this is the interpretation or not, it is a very reasonable thing, for it is natural from the human point of view.

The thought of the passage sends a thrill through every believer's heart. It is as if angels were singing their songs of praise, unconscious of what was taking place on earth. But the Father was watching every cruel step, and when the death struggle was on, he could stand it no longer. He turned to the happy throng of worshipers and hushed them into silence, saying, "It is no time to sing, but a time to be silent, for my Son is dying."

Or if the thought may be pictured in a slightly different way, God seemed to part the curtains of heaven to allow the angels to look on that scene, and when they had seen the pallid face of Christ on the cross, they hushed their merry-making and hung their heads in silence (see 1 Pet. 1:12).

This is the most human and natural thing possible. Some months ago I was called from my bed in the night to go to a home where a mother was dying. I found the room filled with relatives and friends who were walking on tiptoe and speaking in softest whispers. Then the end drew nearer, the last breath came—a struggle—and all was over. A moment of intense silence followed. Not a whisper, not a move of any kind. Every head was bowed, and that scene of Revelation was in the room of death.

This is no unusual thing. After Alexander Graham Bell, the inventor of the telephone, died, on the day he lay in state every Bell telephone in the United States was disconnected for one minute at twelve o'clock. The whole system was dead for one minute. In like manner, when E. H. Harriman, the great railway magnate, died, his entire system of roads suspended service for one minute. Every train stopped, whether it was in the city or in the desert. And every employee bowed his head in silence for a brief moment.

It seems only fitting that the angels should hush their songs and bow their heads when their Maker and Master hung—a lifeless body—on the cross.

These heartless Roman executioners shouted with the mob, but they did not weep with the angels. They howled like wolves for his blood, but they did not rejoice as the redeemed in the salvation it purchased. They saw a victim hang helpless and dying before them, but they failed to see a fountain opened for their cleansing (Zech. 13:1). They saw a prophet rejected, but they did not know he was the cornerstone of God's kingdom (1 Pet. 2:4–8). He looked to them like a worm dangling from a pole, but they did not know he was charged with a power that would send light into every dark corner of the world. What they saw was nothing compared to what they missed seeing.

NOTES

1. See Zola Levitt, *The Seven Feasts of Israel* (Dallas: Zola Levitt Ministries, 1979).

2. The guards' official explanation as recorded in Matthew 28:13 was that Jesus' disciples stole his body while they slept. This scenario falls apart under scrutiny. How could the guards know what happened while they slept?

14

SALVAGE FROM THE
WRECK OF LIFE

MARK 5:1–20

Some time ago the nation was in mourning because of a lost airplane. In a cross-continent flight the plane was lost in the mountains of the West. For days the region where it was last seen was searched, both on land and from the air, but no trace of it could be found. And the hopes of the families of the pilot and copilot slowly died as the days grew into weeks.

Finally, a cowboy found the ruins of a burned plane and the charred bones of unknown men. With tender hands these few bones were gathered together and sent back to their hometowns where they were buried with honors. This was all that could be salvaged from the sad wreck. And the story is a parallel of another wreck recorded in the fifth chapter of the Gospel of Mark, which we hope to study carefully.

Three miracles are recorded in the chapter. The first is restoration of a man wrecked by evil spirits; the second, the healing of a woman whose health was wrecked; and the third, the raising of a child wrecked in death. In each case Christ came saving the remnant—restoring reason to one, health to another, and life to the third.

In the first case he charged the man to go and tell about it, in the second case he instructed the woman to go and enjoy it, and in the third instance he forbade mention of it. In the healing of the demon-possessed man, he showed his power over the devils of hell and saved the unfortunate man from their grasp. When the desperate woman slipped through the crowd and touched his robe, it sent a thrill of joy through her because of his compassion and power to heal. And in the raising of the dead child, he proved himself the Master of even death, robbing the grave of its victim. So in the three instances he showed himself to be Savior of the mind and spirit, of the physical body, and of the life, with all that it embraces.

But lest this discourse should get too long, I must refrain from discussing all the points of interest in the chapter and confine my remarks to the first of the three miracles. The principal lessons might easily be grouped around the man and the Savior.

An Ostracized Soul

The text says that the man lived among the tombs. This was because the evil spirits that took possession of him had made it impossible for him to live with others or for others to live with him. Unfit for human relationships, he was therefore ostracized and doomed to live apart from his friends. This makes for a double problem, one for the sociologist as well as for the minister. *Sin not only disqualifies people for heaven, but for this life as well.*

I fear that in our anxiety about the effects of sin on the eternal destiny of souls, we are likely to overlook the effects of sin on the present life in this world. The man whose health is broken because of his sin has not only lost his soul, but has lost his present happiness and his present usefulness as well. The man who is behind prison bars because of his crime has lost not only his right to heaven, but his right to earth. He is unfit not only to live with angels, but also unfit to live with other people. So the problem of sin is not just a minister's problem, but a problem for the student of sociology, for the officer of the law, for the manager entrusted with a business, for the quiet workman in the rural community, and for people everywhere.

This thought is amply proved by the state; it need not be spoken from some pulpit. When the conduct of a person proves hurtful to society, the state lays hands on him and takes him to the courts where his crime is examined, and if the evidence is found to be sufficient, he is sent away to prison where he cannot associate with people who are trying to live good and honorable lives. The state has said that the sins of the man have disqualified him for association with others. This may be for a short period, for a longer time, or for the rest of his life, according to the enormity of his crime. And it is on this same basis that persons are excluded from heaven. Sin has disqualified them from the association of all who would serve God with pure hearts.

The temporal imprisonment for sin serves two purposes: It safeguards the public from not only the physical threat of such a life, but also from the influence that would pull others down. And why should not such an influence be quarantined like a contagious disease? When smallpox broke out in some filthy shanty, it was quickly put under rigid restrictions so it would not endanger the life of everyone in the community. Why should the moral reprobate be allowed to roam the streets at will, contaminating society with an influence that works far more harm than a physical disease?

Such an influence is more contagious than smallpox ever was. One slanderous tongue can destroy a person's life. One talebearer can scatter more poison than a swarm of mosquitoes or flies. One "adult" business will bring down a whole neighborhood. Hence, the man forced to live apart from his fellows is but an illustration of how sin always renders one unfit for association. The greater the amount of evil within him, the more dangerous he is, and the greater the necessity for his isolation from society.

THE ENEMY OF SELF

A second lesson may be learned from this demoniac, in that the text says, "And always, night and day, he was in the mountains, and in the tombs, crying, and cutting himself with stones" (v. 5). Cutting his own flesh, spilling his own blood, and inflicting injuries to his own body, he is an enemy to himself. And this is universally true of men and women under the influence of the evil spirit. The world is full of those who were once prosperous but today are penniless because they yielded to evil. *What strange things sin will make people do to themselves!*

Recently I talked with a man whose sun was sinking at the noonday of his life. He once had been highly esteemed, had a good income, and moved in the best circles, but temptation came, and he yielded. In almost a moment his whole life lay a wreck, and his future was as dark as midnight. His home was broken up, his salary gone, and he walked out penniless and helpless to begin life over with all the odds against him. If someone else had inflicted such an injury on him, all the anger of hell would have boiled in his soul, but he brought it on himself.

Such stories might be multiplied many times over. Those who follow sin are enemies to themselves. Go to the "red-light" districts and see that long line of victims who might have been the flower of the land, but for the sins they willingly accepted. Go to the prisons and look down another almost endless roll of names that might have been written among the great, but for the self-inflicted shame. Take your stand on the street corner and see the crowds pass by; look into the faces that bear the scars of weakness, of lack of character, and of crime. The hurt of the world is largely self-inflicted, for sin makes people shame themselves, injure themselves, rob themselves, and hurt themselves in all kinds of ways.

An Untamable Spirit

A third lesson is learned from the fact that he was a wild and untamable man. *He could not control himself,* and others were powerless before him. He could not be restrained by reason or force. Such is the case with the person who is possessed with any kind of evil spirit. No matter how miserable the alcoholic's life becomes, he feels powerless to change it. An evil temper is hard to control; any obsession is a stubborn thing by definition. In the calmer moments of life, it may seem that at last we have overcome the demon within us, but before we are aware, all is lost. The devils are unchained, the air is thick with hot words, the soul is aflame with anger, and all the good resolutions are shattered.

A wild horse may challenge the strength and skill of a man, but a wild man is a task for God. No one else can break his will, subdue his spirit, change his love, curb his passions, quiet his temper, or give him a new nature. If he is ever to be saved from the elements that unmake him and unfit him, it must be by the regenerating grace of Christ, whose sympathy will bring him to the side of the afflicted to drive out the devils with merely a word.

This poor demon-crushed man was powerless to heal himself. His helpless condition is typical of the state of all those under the influence of the devil. They cannot break the bands that bind them; neither can they lift themselves from their fallen state, nor give themselves a new nature. But their hope is in the coming of One who is able to do for them what they cannot do for themselves. The lost person is as powerless to save himself as this demoniac was to rid himself of his tormentors. Both must have a Savior whose power can overrule the evil one.

THE SAVIOR OF THE MAN

The lessons so far have been drawn from the man, but let us turn now to the Savior. *He crossed the sea that day to heal one man.* There is no record that he healed anyone else, preached a sermon, or did any other work, but he left immediately after this deed. Such an act was the thermometer of his love for a person, any person, one person anywhere. Many of his greatest sermons were preached to one soul. He did not save his best for the great crowds but hunted out the individual, whether it be man or woman, rich or poor, Jew or Gentile. It was to one man he preached that matchless sermon on being born again (John 3:1–21). It was to one woman he gave that marvelous discourse on real spiritual worship (John 4:7–38). It was a little handful of disciples who witnessed the Transfiguration (Matt. 17:1–9).

This singular act of crossing the sea to heal one man demonstrates Christ's love for the individual rather than humanity en masse. The individual is the unit in the kingdom of God, and people are saved one at a time rather than in groups. All the invitations of God are given to individuals, such as "if anyone hear my voice" and "whosoever will may come." All the "whosoevers" mentioned in the Bible mean any person in the world, each person for himself, without relation to any other.

Christ went himself as if to show that he would give the case his personal attention. He could have sent a disciple with power and authority to cast out the demons and heal the man, but instead he went in person. Religion is a personal matter. Christ deals with each case directly; he has no substitute, nor proxy. No preacher, no church, no ordinance, no parent, nor friend can save—only Christ. He does not delegate this power to anyone. Religion is a personal matter in that each one must come for himself or herself to Christ. The mother cannot come to Christ for her child, nor a man for his friend, but each for himself. Each must repent for himself, each must exercise his own faith, each must live his own life, and each must do his own praying. No mother can dedicate her child to the Lord in the true sense. She may do it in form and may do her best to carry out the spirit of it, but if the child is ever dedicated in the true sense, it must be when he takes it upon himself to do it.

CHRIST OR THE DEVIL?

The miracle stirred up not only the devils within the man, but also the neighbors in the community. They made a choice that day between Christ who was passing through and the devil who had been sitting on them. It was the same choice the people made the day Christ was condemned to die when they desired the release of Barabbas rather than Jesus (Matt. 27:15–26). It is the same choice that any person makes when he rejects Christ as his Lord to follow the devil by default. It is not a strange thing that the devils were excited and angry, for they knew he had come to drive them out. *But it is a strange matter that the people threw him out of their region,* since he had come to deliver them from their worst enemy, if they would let him. But it is typical of the perverting influence of Satan over people anywhere. Whoever follows him will be the enemy of Christ and anyone who speaks his name.

It happens today. Whoever carries on a business in conflict with the spirit and teachings of Christ will hate the church. Someone whose lifestyle is condemned by the teachings of Christ will hate those who live according to those teachings. Their example is so strong a reminder to the sinner of his guilt that he takes every opportunity to disparage and ridicule them. So the conduct of the people of Gadara in sending Christ away was natural for people used to accommodating evil spirits.

HOPE FOR THE HOPELESS

The action of Christ also gave hope to the world. This was a hopeless case—impossible for the skill of anyone else in the world. *All the cases Christ healed were of the impossible type.* How remarkable is it to heal a stubbed toe or a splinter in the hand? Christ healed the lepers, the blind man, the woman with a discharge of blood, the man with a withered hand, and many such cases physicians could not help.

The same thing is true in the moral realm. Saul, the murderer whose sins were covered with a veneer of righteousness, stood before Christ and saw himself as he was. The sight blinded but cleansed him, and he became the apostle who witnessed to kings (Acts 26:1–29). Zacchaeus, the tax collector, likewise became transparent to his own eyes as he looked at Christ. The revelation changed his attitudes and his priorities forever (Luke 19:1–10). The same assessment might be made of Nicodemus, the self-righteous man, and of the thief on the cross, who confessed to being bad altogether—both of them were fundamentally changed by their encounter with this man.

Redeeming the hard cases was the glory of Christ. A person's sins need not keep him from Christ, for Christ is amply able to take care of the worst of sins. The unwillingness to be saved is the only thing that keeps people away from him. This impossible, incurable, hopeless man arose out of the wreckage of his life to confirm that Jesus Christ is able to save to the uttermost all who come to him (Heb. 7:25). This claim has been put to the test by countless multitudes, from every race and language, every walk of life, and degree of sin. All who have come believing Christ have gone away whole.

Why should anyone despair? Are you a victim of uncontrollable urges? Have you tried every way you know to overcome them? Bring them to Christ. Are you beaten down in life and ready to give up? Have you decided it is useless to try any longer? Remember the demoniac whose life was broken under the weight of many devils he could not control. When Christ came into his life, the devils went out, and the man became quiet, peaceable, and in charge of himself again.

When the people asked Christ to leave, he did. It could not have been otherwise. He never enters a heart that does not want him. He does not forgive a sin until forgiveness is desired. He does not consecrate a life until consecration is sought, nor saves a soul until salvation is longed for, nor overcomes an evil temperament until victory is prayed for. Those who come to him with their wounds do not always know just what they need; all they need know is that he can provide it, and that is knowledge enough.

The least child has the power to dismiss Christ from his life, but the strongest devil cannot keep him away if the soul wants him. The "down-and-out" can be saved by receiving him, but the "up-and-in" will surely be lost by sending him away. He will make the first overture to the lost soul, but he will not force his way in. He will not override human wishes in matters of personal benefits. This explains why many are lost: they would not have him. He came, knocked, and called, but they sent him away.

Such deeds of restoration were the crowning joy of his life. He was never happier than when healing some unfortunate person, lifting some fallen one, or bestowing some blessing. So fascinating was such a life that when he was thus occupied he forgot to eat or sleep (John 4:34); he became intoxicated with the joy of it. He smashed customs and traditions that he might do it. He braved the wrath of the rulers that he might accomplish it. He even aroused the devils and fought his way through a legion of them that he might help one oppressed man.

The crying of distressed humanity drove sleep from his eyes, hunger from his body, and fear from his mind and sent him across the sea in the face of a storm that he might save a helpless victim. It was just such a call that brought him from heaven to earth, that sent him to the cross and the grave. He endured it all because of his love for us.

THE WITNESS OF THE SAVED LIFE

A final word has to do with this new witness for Christ. He wanted to go with his Savior and be with him the rest of his life. That was natural; it would have been strange if he had not so desired. But the request was not granted. Christ granted the request of the devils and allowed them to go into the swine. He also granted the request of his enemies when they asked him to leave. But he refused the request of his child. The man was sent back home to his family and friends to show them what the Lord had done. *Christ needed a witness in that place,* and who could serve better than the one who had been healed by a miraculous power? They could not question his word for he was a living testimony to its truth.

Such a witness is an unanswerable argument for Christianity. To deny the power of God in such a case will raise more questions than to admit it. This is the kind of testimony the devil dreads. Argument in the form of words and logic may be answered, but an undeniable example speaks for itself.

On one occasion when Christ healed a man born blind, the Pharisees could not get around it, no matter how hard they tried. The further they dug into the matter, the worse it grew for them. They called the man before them, and he told them just how it was done, giving Christ the credit. Now this would never do, since this man and his parents belonged to their synagogue.

So they called the parents, and they, to keep from being turned out of the synagogue, dodged the question by saying in effect, "All we know is that he is our son and that he was born blind. We don't know how it is that he can see now. Ask him." The parents had no further statement to make. But the matter could not drop here. So again the Pharisees turned on the man, but he showed them his open eyes as the proof of someone's great power (John 9).

This was a potent argument. If it had been a matter of mere words, those skilled debaters would have made quick work of it. But here was an unanswerable argument, and the whole city saw it. How could it be disposed of? Such a witness is every redeemed soul on earth who lives the Christ-life. It is not a verbal argument, but a living example that cannot be explained away nor laughed out of court. It meets the scoffer in the open and rebukes him for his unbelief without saying a word. Such a testimony is louder than any sermon and more eloquent than a choir of angels.

The healed demoniac was not sent to merely tell what had been done but to show it. The work of God's Spirit can be shown; it is not an intellectual supposition but a fact. It is not written solely in books but in human lives. The healed man had no higher desire than to spend his life at the feet of the One who had redeemed him, but Christ had a better idea. He put responsibilities on him, and made him a helper and coworker. He showed him that there were others in similar straits who needed his help.

The greatest joy of the newfound life is not just in singing and worshiping the Master, but in serving others in his name. This is the real spirit of Christianity: not saved that one may go to heaven, but saved that one may help others here. This is not a life of ease, but of constant warfare with the fiercest devils in hell. The worth of this life is not measured by the peace and happiness of one's soul, but by the peacemaking one has done for Christ. It is not a hope that rests on one experience only, but on many experiences constantly recurring through the days, each one drawing the heart and life closer to Christ (2 Cor. 10:3–5).

He obeyed the Lord. The records tell us he went throughout the whole land telling it. He roamed every hill, went into every village and through all the countryside, telling what a wonderful thing the Lord had done for him. What a rebuke this man is to many of us who claim to be saved but never tell another of the Lord who saved us! Our silence should shame us. Our conscience should hurt us. Our claims should arouse us. Our lack of interest should condemn us. Our prospects of meeting him again should stimulate us. Our professed love for humanity should drive us. Let us never forget that we are to be the channels of blessings through whom the Lord is to reach the rest of the world.

15

THE PERMANENCE OF CHRISTIANITY

He shall not fail nor be discouraged.
ISAIAH 42:4
"Upon this rock I will build my church;
and the gates of hell shall not prevail against it."
MATTHEW 16:18
"I give unto them eternal life; and they shall never perish."
JOHN 10:28

Here are three passages, one from the Old Testament and two from the New. They set down three stages of the same movement: one has to do with the builder, the other with the building, and the other with the tenant. Or expressed in other language, the Redeemer, the redeemed, and the brotherhood. In each passage the writer is declaring the real merit and permanence of the thing discussed compared with the passing away of the material, temporal things.

1 7 9

THE UNFAILING REDEEMER

Let Isaiah be the first spokesman. Living at the time when the Jews were about to be carried away into captivity, he was lamenting the failure of this race of chosen people. He had reminded them of the special blessings God had given them and how they had spurned him. Now, as a result of their rebellion and sins, they would be carried away. Then when the gloom of the situation settles so heavily on him that he is about to be crushed, suddenly he is inspired with a new thought: *there will come a Deliverer,* One who will not share the weaknesses of the rest, One who will not give way to sin, One who will be tried in every fire but will not fail. Evidently Isaiah was visited by the Spirit of God who pulled back the curtains of the future and revealed to him the coming of Christ as the hope of not only the Jew, but of all races.

The unfailing Christ, then, is set before us by the inspired writer as the hope of the world. And he is made more beautiful by the black and ugly background of all the failures of those who had lived and died without leaving one single son unstained by the ravages of sin. Let the eye sweep that long line from Adam to Christ and see that every one of them failed and limped off the field a cripple under the blows of sin. Now comes One, the prophet assures us, who will walk through the treacherous valley of life and emerge unspotted by defeat. Never has there been such a one before, and never will there be another. Adam had a good start to live a spotless life; he was created holy and perfect, but he found himself outmatched before he got out of the garden. Throughout life he bore the marks of imperfection and bequeathed them to his children after him.

The race deteriorated for many centuries, until Noah made a desperate effort to climb back to its original plane. But the seed of sin was in him and down he went with a crash as his sons carried the drunken father into his tent to hide his shame (Gen. 9:20–27). Abraham, Moses, Samson, David, and Solomon were all good men, but the story of their sins has been written along with their noble lives, until not one is left to bear the spotless banner of the kingdom of God. But Isaiah tells us that there will be One against whose life not one fault can be charged, and he will lead the failing race of mankind back to God.

Not only had all humanity failed by the days of Isaiah, but *all efforts to keep humanity holy had failed.* The first effort was individual: each person did what was right in his own eyes. But the eyes of mankind were wicked, and therefore they were led down destructive paths. Then came the effort of a select race to set an example for other races. But this race became as corrupt as the heathen races around them. This failure was followed by a king who would make the people do what was right, but he proved as corrupt as kings of other nations.

Prophets and priests were called to be mediators between the people and God, and with all their strength they tried to keep the masses in a right relationship to God, but in vain. The people's unruly desires carried them far off track. Physical force, embodied in Samson, shook itself like a lion until men fell before his superhuman strength like weeds before a sickle. But Samson and his strength were conquered by sin, and he lay helpless in the prison of his enemies because physical force cannot cope with sin. Militarism unsheathed its sword and cried, "Let me rule the world," but the great warrior Saul and his sons were killed on the battlefield.

Then the scene shifted. God showed the world that the best man among them could not save them: David, the man after God's own heart, was himself an adulterer and a murderer. Then wisdom tried its hand. Never was there one so wise and full of knowledge as Solomon. But sin laughed in the face of his wisdom and led him to his ruin as a dumb animal is led to the slaughterhouse. Thus, the disease of sin had spread to every member of Adam's race, until every page of its history told the story of failure.

But through the prophet the Lord promised One will come to prove himself stronger than evil, both by living free from sin himself and by delivering from the power of the devil all those who wish to be free. The prophecy has been fulfilled. *The promised One did come.* And when he came to the end of his sojourn here, wicked men themselves admitted, "'He saved others'" (Matt. 27:42). He was tested on every point and found to be faultless (Heb. 4:15). The powers of hell centered their attacks on him. First, he was rejected by kinsmen and acquaintances. He was disbelieved and misrepresented even by those he had helped. He was pronounced a heretic, an imposter, and a blasphemer. He was falsely aligned against Moses and the prophets and even against God. He was called the disturber of peace, the enemy of

Caesar, and even the ally of devils. He was held up to ridicule before the populace, the courts, and the angels of heaven.

No man who ever lived passed more literally through the fires of hell than did this One whom Isaiah declared would stand every test. He stood the moral test. Judas who betrayed him left his dying testimony to the innocence of Christ (Matt. 27:4). The judge in whose court he was tried publicly announced after all the charges had been heard that he found no fault in him (John 19:4). He was the purest man ever dragged into his court. The thief, dying for his crime, added his convictions to the others', that "'this man has done nothing wrong'" (Luke 23:41 RSV). And the centurion who supervised the Crucifixion was awestruck, saying in effect, "We have made a mistake! This is an innocent man—surely the holiest man ever hung on a cross" (Matt. 27:54, paraphrased).

If the thief with a keen eye for deception could find none in him, if the judge with a practiced discernment of guilt could find none in him, if the witnesses who were bent on his destruction admitted his good deeds, if the cold-blooded Roman officer who nailed him to the cross could call him a son of God, and if the intimate companion who turned traitor could exonerate him with his dying breath, it seems conclusive that Christ passed the moral test quite adequately.

THE UNFAILING REDEMPTION

Neither did he fail in his plan of human redemption. As stated before, there had been many efforts made to save mankind from the destruction sin brought, and all had failed. Conscience had failed, organization had failed, government had failed, the priesthood had failed, militarism had failed, human wisdom had failed, physical force had failed. Now comes Christ, relying on none of these things.

Facing the demands of a broken Law, he does not deny mankind's guilt, nor compromise justice. He simply gives himself to stand in the place of the condemned and pays the price in full, dying—the just for the unjust, the innocent for the guilty. This met every requirement of God's law, paying the penalty in full. Then the free offer of mercy and forgiveness was made to all who would turn away from their sins and accept the forgiveness. This scheme of redemption met every need of the world. The poor could obtain it as well as the rich, the unlearned as well as the educated, the sick as easily as the strong.

He did not fail as the Great Physician. Let the score of incurables who came to him and found healing be the witnesses—the blind whose eyes he opened, the deaf whose ears were unstopped, and even the dead whom he raised to life. Neither did he fail in death. The city passed by and watched him die by degrees on the cross, then his friends carried him to a borrowed tomb. And after friend and foe, Roman and religious authorities, had pronounced him dead, he burst the bars of the grave and came out. There are no limits to which the investigation of his adequacy might be carried. The prophet made no wild assumptions when he assured the troubled Jews that One would come who would not fail.

During the planning of the Brooklyn Bridge, the architect died from injuries received in a freak accident. As tragic and

untimely as his death was, there was no question about pro-
ceeding with the plans to construct the great bridge, for his
eldest son had been working by his side for years. He knew
his father's business and intent inside and out. Fourteen
years later, on May 24, 1883, the bridge was dedicated with
much fanfare and at great personal cost to both John A.
Roebling and his son Washington.[1] This is God's guarantee
of the unfailing Christ. The Son was proved capable of carrying out the Father's business.

Time passed, the prophet who uttered the words died,
and mankind continued to race down the steep slopes of the
moral plane toward a gulf of despair. When the prophet's
words were fulfilled in the coming of Christ, not a sinless
person was on earth to welcome him. And the nations and
governments that flourished in the days of Isaiah lay in ruins
around Palestine, with only the faintest traces of their former
glory to be found. Shadows of the great empires of the
Babylonians, the Medes, the Persians, the Edomites, the
Egyptians, and others lay to the north, the east, and the south
of the land of the Jews. The whole Eastern world was like a
great cemetery of fallen nations and kings.

Then Christ broke the deathly silence with the words
recorded in Matthew 16:18: "'Upon this rock I will build my
church; and the gates of hell shall not prevail against it.'" The
unfailing Christ promised an unfailing institution. All other
organizations and institutions had failed, and the history of
the nations was the witness to it. But over the ruins of these
fallen empires, Christ established one institution that would
not suffer a similar fate (see Dan. 2:27–45). One glimpse

back through the past would remind us that nothing had been able to withstand the corruption of the devil. He had dethroned the kings, disarmed the warriors, uncrowned the princes, and beat to the dust the armies of the world. In the face of that complete wreck, Christ set in place one kingdom that will not be thus overthrown. Here are one King whose scepter will not be broken and one army whose flags will never be furled until they have waved over the gates of every nation.

I do not share the fears of many who think that the church will come to naught. There were many in the days of the early Christians who had such fears. They saw Judas turn traitor, Peter become a profane liar, Stephen stoned to death, and the band of disciples scattered everywhere. For a long while the outlook was gloomy for the little church struggling against such odds. But it lived on and prospered.

Then in the Dark Ages, when knowledge evaporated and the dominant form of religion was exceedingly corrupt, it must have seemed that all was in vain and the true church would die. How could it live? But in God's good time the wells of knowledge and faith were opened again to water the vine of God's planting.

Then infidelity sprang up, and brilliant orators went everywhere dissecting the church, pointing out its flaws and ridiculing its worshipers, until many good people trembled for fear that it could not stand the strain. But the church went about its task, and the age of infidelity passed on.

Now in these latter days it is fashionable to be profane, discount the Bible, rewrite its histories, modernize its miracles, reject the divinity of its Savior, and in every way attempt to dress up the church in faddish clothes. Modernism has not made its attack from the outside but has come in the name of scholarship and with the look of piety. In many instances it has put on the clerical coat and delivered its bitter denunciations in the name of holy religion, of God, and of high heaven. Such attacks are far more damaging than open denial of God and Christianity. But like the rest it, too, will pass away,[2] and the church will go on with its mission of saving, serving, and blessing the world. For back of the church is the guarantee of God that the gates of hell will not prevail against it.

This does not mean that little local organizations will always continue. They may cease, and often they do close their doors forever. But this does not signal defeat for the kingdom of God. It may mean a shifting of that part of the army to other centers, or it many mean that these few have so shamefully deported themselves that God took away their blessings and gave them to others who would make better use of them. But such little defections do not retard the onward sweep of God's purpose any more than ripples on the water hinder the progress of the great ship plowing its way to the opposite shore.

This does not mean that nothing can hinder the kingdom of God. Many things have hindered it, and many more will hinder it. Often God waits for some little movement to spend itself or some little intellect to burn out like a meteor before he does what he meant to do. An overdose of modernism will make the church dreadfully sick, but God will administer an antidote and make it disgorge the poison. The church may be injured so that it limps along for a while, but the Great Physician will heal it. Or it may become dissipated until some child has to come and lead it back into the right path. It may even become so undernourished that it will reel for lack of strength, but it will not die. God has written his guarantee of perpetuity over its door, and it will live.

The pyramids of Egypt have stood as the sentinels of the Nile for over 4,500 years, but time is cutting away their surfaces until one day they will be laid as low as the desert on which they stand. Yet time itself cannot outlive the church that Christ built. The Sphinx was also the proud monument of the wind-swept dunes of Egypt from far back in the forgotten past. Abraham doubtless looked upon its face, and it was ancient when Moses was a child playing around its base. The history of that stark land has been fought out under the shadow of this silent god. But if time lasts long enough, it will fade as all earthly things do and be no more. But the church of Jesus Christ will exist as long as there are people on the earth to be saved and nurtured through it.

This is not a guarantee that denominationalism will remain. This is a great disappointment to some of us who measure the whole world by our creedal yardstick. When denominationalism is substituted for Christianity, it will fail and ought to fail. When denominationalism demands punctilious observance of ecclesiastical law and ceremony and disregards a broken and contrite heart, it ought to die while it is yet in infancy. When denominationalism sends its runners into the street to make proselytes to its faith and neglects to lead them to Jesus, it is doomed.

Our Scripture text has nothing to do with such movements but rather builds its bulwarks around the brotherhood that rests its claims, its hopes, and its destiny upon a crucified and risen Lord. When the church ceases to break hardened hearts with the consciousness of sin, it then forfeits its right to live. When it leaves off the gospel of redemption through the blood of a crucified Redeemer, it becomes the prey of a legion of devils whom it cannot control nor expel. The guarantee given the church does not extend to denominationalism.

An Eternal Church

The thought is carried further by the passage from John 10:27–28: "'My sheep hear my voice, and I know them, and they follow me; and I give them eternal life, and they shall never perish, and no one shall snatch them out of my hand'" (RSV). If Isaiah gave us the glimpse of an eternal Christ, then Christ gave us the promise of an eternal church *made up of eternal believers.* The permanence of the believer is made as certain as that of the Redeemer. One tie binds them both to the heart of God. We are brothers of his, "joint heirs," partakers of a common heritage (Rom. 8:17). We are the sheep of his pasture, and he is a Shepherd whose flocks will never fall victim to wolves.

One beautiful morning in August I saw three shepherds come from the Syrian hills with their little flocks. They met in the narrow valley, and the herds mingled while the shepherds exchanged their morning greetings. In a few moments one of the herdsmen left the other two, and as he went he gave a little yodel. What magic power that simple call had on his flock! The last one of his sheep left the mingled herd and followed the shepherd. He did not stop to count them, so sure was he that they were following him. This is Christ's meaning in the passage cited. This is also the meaning behind the Twenty-third Psalm. The call rings out above the roar of the storm and quiets the distressed children. Their names have not only been written in his ledger, but also have been engraved on the palms of his hands (Isa. 49:16). And he has declared "'that where I am you may be also'" (John 14:3 RSV).

Do not make the passage say too much. *It does not mean that all who make loud professions belong to him.* There are many spurious believers who are not under his guarantee. "'Not every one who says to me, "Lord, Lord," shall enter the kingdom of heaven, but *he who does the will of my Father*'" (Matt. 7:21 RSV, italics added). The multitudes will be sifted and separated according to their true relationship to God. Many whom the world thought righteous, or who thought themselves righteous, will be cast aside by him, and many whom the world forgot will be gathered up and crowned by him as the elect of earth. It is his sure promise that each redeemed child will ultimately be brought into the Father's house. Not one will be forgotten.

Another caution needs to be sounded: *Not all of the saved will succeed in life.* Many of us fail in this life. We fail in the vision and go through life as if blind, groping our way in the dark. While the uplands of life are all aglow with the glory of

God, we spend our days in the valley of shadows, miasmas, and pits. We may have failed in our influence; instead of sending our gleams across the sea, attracting to safe havens those who are battered in the storms of life, we have been as a weak, flickering light, and some may have perished within our easy reach.

We may fail in our task. Some do fail in their holy calling; they are so busy making money, they fail to make a life. Or they become so interested in gathering the treasures of earth that they forget to lay up treasures in heaven (Matt. 6:19–21). They may be so absorbed in making a home and finding new friends that they wholly lose sight of the heavenly home and the "friend who sticks closer than a brother" (Prov. 18:24 RSV). We may have our hands so full of perishable things that when the end of the journey is reached, we find we are empty-handed.

Some may fail in joy, in happiness, in service, in disposition, and in real worth. Ah, there are so many places and ways we may fail! But thanks to our unfailing Savior, we will not fail when the roll is called. Such a thought must not be used to justify reckless living, but rather move us to more earnestly give ourselves to the grace that saved us (Gal. 5:13–26).

We have heard of guides who, leading their tourists over great mountains, have inadvertently led them to their death. These guides returned distressed and forever discredited because of their failure. But here is one guide who will lead the last small child safely home. The shepherd may lose his sheep in the wilds of the hills, but this Shepherd will keep all who listen for his call. The physician may stand in helplessness and watch the patient die, but this Great Physician will confer unbreakable health. The teacher may do his best to instruct the pupil, and on the day of examination see him fail, but here is a teacher whose lessons carry eternal staying power. An attorney may see his client sent to prison for the rest of his life, but the heavenly advocate can "spring" the guiltiest client. The farmer may plant his seed and watch his crops be wiped out, but the great husbandman from heaven will have no such loss.

The destiny of God's children does not rest in our own hands but has been committed to the hand of our Savior. He gave us the desire to be saved when every disposition of our life was to rebel. He breathed into our conscience the first sting of remorse for sin, put the first prayer on our lips, and the first tears in our eyes. He saved us when we had nothing to offer: no merit, no goodness, and no hope. Therefore our salvation rests on nothing in us but only on his sufficiency. He guided our straying feet with a hand so gentle that we did not know he led at all, up to the hills toward the city of God. And we are sure that when we stand at his bar of justice, he will not fail us in the end.

NOTES

1. David McCullough, *The Great Bridge* (New York: Simon and Schuster, 1972), 61, 99–101, 215–17, 530.

2. Modernism was not new, even in Dr. Melton's day. The apostle Paul wrote the Letter to the Colossians to counteract the similar Gnostic heresies infecting the church (see especially Col. 2).

ABOUT THE AUTHOR

William Walter Melton was born on a farm in Navarro County, Texas, on January 19, 1879, the second of twelve children. In addition, twelve orphaned children were raised along with the family. Melton was a cowboy and ranch foreman until the age of twenty-one, when his father persuaded him to try college for a year. He enrolled in Decatur Baptist College for what was essentially his first formal education, and graduated six years later. (DBC moved to Dallas in 1965 and became a university in 1984.) He was ordained to the ministry at the age of twenty-three; the following year he began his first pastorate at Bellevue, Texas. At age twenty-six, he married Orah Shipp, and together they had six children. He received a Th.D. from Southwestern Baptist Theological Seminary in 1912, then in 1919 received a B.A. degree from Baylor University.

After serving at churches in Duncan, Oklahoma, and Everman, Texas, Dr. Melton accepted the call to pastor Seventh and James Baptist Church in Waco, Texas, where he served from 1912 to 1941. It was during this pastorate that he wrote *Sifted but Saved,* the second of at least thirteen books. He left that ministry to assume duties as the secretary of the executive board of the Baptist General Convention of Texas.

Then in 1945, Dr. Melton became pastor of Columbus Avenue Baptist Church in Waco. He was elected chairman of the board of trustees of Baylor University in 1946. When he retired from active ministerial service in 1957, he asked the Columbus Avenue Church to give itself a gift of $20,000 for an elevator. (The church already had a shaft, but it was empty.)

As an administrator, Dr. Melton was considered far-sighted and practical. As a counselor, he was kind and wise. And as a preacher, he spoke with spiritual depth, humor, and brevity. ("I can tell them more in fifteen minutes than they are going to obey," he once explained.) During his ministry he compiled over four thousand sermon outlines. And, at the end of his most compelling sermons, he would often close with, "That's my simple little message for today."

Dr. Melton died at his home in Waco on October 6, 1967, at the age of 88.

Thanks to Ellen K. Brown of the Texas Collection at Baylor University for providing this information.

BIBLIOGRAPHY

Aldridge, Alfred Owen. *Man of Reason: The Life of Thomas Paine*. Philadelphia: J. B. Lippincott Co., 1959.

Anderson, Courtney. *To the Golden Shore: The Life of Adoniram Judson*. Valley Forge: Judson Press, 1987.

Anderson, David D. *Robert Ingersoll*. New York: Twayne Publishers, Inc., 1972.

Bailey, Thomas A. and Ryan, Paul B. *The Lusitania Disaster*. New York: The Free Press, 1975.

Bartlett, John, editor. *Familiar Quotations*. Boston: Little, Brown, & Co., 1980.

Dugan, James. *The Great Iron Ship*. New York: Harper & Brothers, 1953.

Dunstan, Roger. *Gambling in California* (website: http://www.library.ca.gov/CRB/97/03/crb97003.html#toc), January 1997.

Gray, Thomas. *Elegy Written in a Country Churchyard*. Boston: The Atheneum Press, reprinted 1909.